In loving
memory of

Molly Marie McEvoy

1988-1996

Heart/Double Lung
Recipient

Women Going For It!

TAKING RISKS AFTER 50

Women Going For It!

TAKING RISKS AFTER 50

DIANA COLEMAN

Diana Coleman

WOMEN
GOING
FOR IT
PRESS

Rockland, Maine

Published 2018
Women Going For It Press, Rockland, Maine
WomenGoingForIt.com
Printed in the United States of America
ISBN: 978-1-7320952-0-5 (print)
ISBN: 978-1-7320952-1-2 (e-book)
Library of Congress Control Number: 2018903537

Dedicated, with love and admiration,

to

Carole Mazzarino, my kind and sweet sister,
who always seeks new challenges;

to

Dr. Vickie Driver, my "bestest" friend,
who persists with monumental achievements;

and to

all other women over 50 who are "Going For It!"

CONTENTS

INTRODUCTION

At 14 or 15, I auditioned for a singing role and got a callback ... but I didn't go back. Even at that age, I was afraid of being rejected. Forty years passed and I never forgot I didn't go back.

—Gladys, from the Dempsey Theater stage, Harlem, New York City

Then, she joyfully and passionately belts out "The Impossible Dream." At age 55, Gladys ("Survivors") found the courage to go to a callback for a singing role.

Women are strong, resourceful, and resilient. We *have the power* to do what is meaningful to us in the time we have left. We *can take risks* we are passionate about that will lead to increased confidence and greater fulfillment.

But have you or others said, "I wish I had the nerve to take a risk like she did" or, "I'm too old to do that"?

This book challenges you to rethink what you're capable of.

Change your life after 50? The heart of this book is stories of women doing just that—taking risks to realize their gut-deep desires. Many books address career change or launching a business later in life. I wanted to explore *all* kinds of risks.

Risks are usually equated with danger. We are counseled to avoid them. What drives older women to take risks? Can bold choices be empowering? How does our perception of risk differ among women? Change throughout our lifetimes? These are some of the questions that propelled me forward to write this book.

Over four decades, as a career counselor, nonprofit administrator, fundraiser, teacher, and board member, the compelling dynamism of women globally has been at the core of my mission-driven work. I have an enduring belief in female fortitude and risk-taking power.

Taking risks has positively affected my life.

Moving to midcoast Maine at 58 knowing no one after living thirty years in San Francisco, and traveling to remote areas in Kenya and helping to find a safe boarding school for a couple of runaway girls, were risks. One of the hardest risks for me was quitting my job at 60 to be a caregiver for my partner, Sara, and hoping I would be effective in helping her maintain her independence. At 56, Sara struggled against an aggressive cancer that would take her life. Even in her frail state, she proudly risked challenging her oncologist by refusing to stop chemotherapy, and gained another year.

In talking with hundreds of women and girls globally about their lives and aspirations, I hear older women express increasing awareness that time is fleeting. Some feel invisible despite being vibrant. Many are eager to take risks and test themselves.

My fascination with "older" women's perspectives led me on a quest to find women taking a variety of risks in their second half of life. I asked them these questions:

- What is a risk for you?
- Why did you take this risk?
- How did you overcome your fears and obstacles?
- What do you still want to do with the time you have left?
- What advice do you have for others?

While driving cross-country for seven weeks to meet with women whose stories I was documenting, I stopped at a restaurant and overheard a conversation between two women discussing a 74-year-old woman who had recently been widowed. One woman said, "I told her to go to a museum and have lunch, but she doesn't know how. She was never allowed to have friends or see anyone but her husband's family. If I had her money, I'd go on trips. She's too afraid. She says she's going to see if she can go to Starbucks for a cup of coffee. If she sits at a table by herself, she thinks people will feel sorry for her."

Hearing about this woman afraid to go to Starbucks reinforced that risk-taking comes in many forms—and fears, in all shapes and sizes.

Risks are personal. Each of us has a different idea of what a risk is.

The women in this book confessed they had self-doubts. And each woman found the courage to do the things she wanted to do. Some didn't see their experiences as risky. Others had to overcome their fears. Haunted by memories of mental and physical abuse, Rosemarie ("Survivors") published her memoir at 81. Carole never wanted children and changed her life at 55 when she embraced the adult child she had given up at birth ("Family Love"). Although skydiving is an ultimate risk for many women, it wasn't for 72-year-old Felicity ("Adventurers").

Heartwarming and real, the book's twenty-six stories celebrate women's resilience and stamina. Feisty, funny, tough, and determined, these women tell about their *new* experiences in their 50s, 60s, 70s, and 80s. They have persevered and triumphed over obstacles—finances, health, abuse, lack of education, and family obligations. From Maine to California, Costa Rica to Kenya, women share their backgrounds and thoughts about risk, and offer advice.

The stereotype that women are more risk-averse than men, perpetuated by the media for years, is being refuted by risk researchers globally. Women who take risks can illuminate the way for all of us. Risk-taking stories can encourage and motivate women to "Go for it!"

What's a risk for you? Is fear holding you back? Fear of failure or of others' opinions?

In Part 2, "Going For It!," you'll find 10 Keys to Taking Fulfilling Risks and thought-provoking exercises to help you determine what matters to you, identify your perceived obstacles and ways to overcome them, and move forward in taking the risks you are comfortable with.

You have heard people talk about what they hoped to do and didn't. And people who pursued what they wanted to do and are happier for it. Now is the time to challenge yourself. You *can* try something new. The thought may be exciting and scary. Risks and new experiences can be satisfying and thrilling!

Regardless of your age or gender, I hope you find these women's stories enlightening and entertaining. May they ignite your passions and interests, inspire you to take beneficial risks, and help you do what matters to you in your second half of life.

Please don't go to your deathbed regretting that you didn't do something because you didn't think you could.

What are *you* going to do with the time *you* have left?

Although every effort was made to obtain clear photos of the women profiled in these pages, the pictures vary in quality. Still, I thought you might enjoy seeing them as you get to know each woman.

Sadly, two of the inspiring women who shared their stories died during the production of this book—Carole Link Fleming in October 2017, and Mimi O'Hagan in May 2018. These wonderful women are fondly remembered and very much missed.

Part 1

RISK-TAKING STORIES FROM WOMEN AFTER 50

CHAPTER 1 — ADVENTURERS

BETSY COOLEY

Special Education Teacher to Retiring to Costa Rica at 60

BIRTH YEAR: 1952

Betsy, a shy girl from Connecticut, grew up spending much of her childhood playing outdoors. Interested in teaching learning-disabled children, she student-taught and got a master's degree in special education. She worked with special-needs children in the United States, Venezuela, and France, interspersed with travel. At 60, Betsy and her husband, Bill, retired, sold everything they owned, and moved to Costa Rica with two suitcases and one cat apiece.

Earlier Years

The middle child between a brother and sister, Betsy, who often hid behind her mother's skirts, loved the outdoors. On her family's large Litchfield, Connecticut, property with ponds, gentle slopes, and woods, she swam, fished, ice-skated, and went sledding and tobogganing. During the summers, she went to a YMCA overnight camp. Family vacations consisted of camping trips in New England and Canada. Later, she taught swimming, archery, and riflery as a camp counselor; was on a softball team in high school; and, though shy, was a cheerleader.

Her dad, an electrical engineer, imported and exported goods; her mother was a homemaker and later, a librarian. Betsy was enticed to travel after hearing about her dad's and uncles' business trips and after her cousins and sister went abroad as students. She used to stare at a large map of the United States in her father's home office, wanting to visit all fifty states. Enjoying the photographs of places in *Life* and *Look* magazines, she sent away for travel brochures.

Betsy's first time outside North America was working as a chambermaid in Cornwall, England, and tagging on a visit to France, during one summer of college. After graduating from Russell Sage, a women's college in Troy, New York, Betsy spent a semester student-teaching in an elementary school. Empathetic with the plight of "underdog" children, and uncomfortable standing in front of a classroom, she realized that working with learning-disabled children in small groups and one-on-one appealed to her.

Though not a city person, she went to Columbia University's Teachers College for a master's degree in special education and lived in an apartment with closet-sized rooms. When her father drove her to New York City to begin her one-year graduate program, Betsy thought, *Please don't leave me here.* "It was scary for me," she said later. "There was trash on the streets. It was gray, with lots of buildings."

After surviving Manhattan, she taught at a preschool inclusive of special-needs children in Washington, DC, and then taught children with learning disabilities in Connecticut.

Betsy tested her outdoor survival skills during vacations over the years by going on Outward Bound trips: a sailing trip to Hurricane Island, in Maine, to learn nautical techniques; and a three-week backpacking trip in northern California that included managing on her own for two days in the wilderness.

Interested in teaching overseas, Betsy secured a position through International School Services, taught in Venezuela, and loved it. Using her fourth-grade-through-college Spanish, she made friends with native speakers. "The uncertainty was scary for me then. I got to know my fellow teachers, who became my family, and shared an apartment with another teacher." Meeting a navy pilot from Costa Rica who owned a Beechcraft airplane and loved traveling, she went with him from Venezuela to Costa Rica to go white-water rafting. The river was high and swift during the rainy season, and their raft flipped, sending the passengers downstream in a fast current. One of the teachers suffered a large gash on her head and was bandaged up by the Red Cross personnel called in to help. They had to stay overnight in a shack used to store corn and were escorted out on horseback. "I haven't been white-water rafting again," Betsy said. "I have a healthy respect for water." She didn't see much of Costa Rica then, driving from San Jose to the river and back, but enjoyed the lush green scenery—the hills, mountains, and banana and coffee plantations.

From Venezuela, she became a guidance counselor and consultant on learning disabilities at the American School of Paris in Saint-Cloud, France.

With her parents aging, Betsy returned to the States, taught learning-disabled children in Vermont, and met her future husband. Deciding to leave Vermont, where the summers were too short, she and Bill, a professional photographer, moved to his home state of Virginia. In Roanoke, she resumed teaching, and she and Bill designed and built a 2,800-square-foot house on nine acres with a flower garden and lily pond.

After twenty-five years of working with learning-disabled children, Betsy taught in regular second and third grades and coached new teachers. Tests and data analysis became the top priorities in teaching. "We had to teach to the test," Betsy said. "There was a lot of pressure to have the students perform well, as the schools were evaluated by test results. It took the fun out of teaching. It was no longer worth it to teach."

Originally, Betsy and Bill had planned to retire when Betsy was 65. They talked about selling everything, buying an RV, and traveling around the country. After "crunching numbers," they determined they could retire when she was 60. Betsy suggested moving away from the United States and living in Central America. Over several summers and at Christmas, they visited Costa Rica, Ecuador through the Andes, and Panama. They debated between Costa Rica and Ecuador. Jack and Lucy, their dearly beloved elderly cats, made the decision. Since there was a direct, four-hour flight from Charlotte, North Carolina, to San Jose, Costa Rica, versus a longer, indirect flight to Ecuador, Costa Rica it was.

Retiring to Costa Rica

Putting their home on the market, Betsy and Bill sold everything they owned, including a tractor and Betsy's much-loved red-and-black Mini Cooper Clubman. "I struggled with selling our things, thinking the buyers of our possessions wouldn't appreciate them as much as I had, but I knew I had to let go of stuff," Betsy said. In June 2013, Betsy, age 60, and Bill boarded a plane to begin a new life in Costa Rica.

Before leaving the United States, they secured a reasonable, one-year furnished house rental in Herradura de Rivas, in southern Costa Rica, from a guy who was traveling around the world. They bought their landlord's 2002 Toyota 4Runner, which had 68,000 miles on it. There weren't as many ex-pats in this village, which they preferred. Sitting on eleven acres with streams and lush vegetation near Mount Chirripo, Costa Rica's largest mountain, the attractive wooden house with a tin roof had a magnificent backdrop of hills and valleys.

Discovering they were sharing their quarters with twenty bats shortly after moving in, Betsy and Bill valiantly pushed them outside one at a time. A local guy closed off the space where the bats entered.

Poco a poco, or "little by little," "don't worry about it," is the Ticos' (Costa Ricans') philosophy. They enjoy *pura vida*, "the pure life," meaning "it's going great," a phrase borrowed from Mexico and used in greetings and farewells. "The native people have been friendly and welcoming, inviting us into their homes, to ceremonies, get-togethers, and town council meetings," Betsy said. "A neighbor woman who became our housecleaner helped me speak Costa Rican Spanish, and I helped local children and teens learn English." Pleased to be invited to the local Women's Club, Betsy attended her first meeting, and although she had trouble understanding what the women were saying, they were friendly. "Everyone was very patient with my minimal Spanish." Her understanding of Spanish has improved; she is more comfortable speaking the language and took a weekly conversation class taught by a non-English-speaking woman.

Betsy likes exploring the country with its many microclimates and different types of vegetation, plants, birds, and animals. She has seen the beaches on the Caribbean Sea, the turquoise water of the Pacific Ocean, towns and cities, and cacao and banana plantations. She has practiced yoga at a mountain retreat, kayaked through mangroves, and fished for trout at a restaurant's stocked pond. "Being my avid fisherman father's daughter, I rose to the challenge when given the option to catch the fish my five companions and I would eat for dinner," she said. A native woman put a worm on her line tied around a wooden block. After Betsy caught one fish, the woman poked its eyes out and used them as bait for the next catch. Betsy caught six fish for their dinner. "It wasn't real fishing," she said, "but it gave me a few moments of closeness with my father."

She hiked around Cloudbridge Nature Reserve, which is being reforested to restore it to its natural state, the way it was before it was cleared for farming. Careful while balancing along the high mountainsides, she and Bill volunteered planting saplings. *Cafetals*, or coffee plantations, and cattle farms surrounded them. Climbing steep trails with switchbacks took their breath away, whereas the locals effortlessly passed them on rugged trails, hauling heavy bags of coffee beans. On the roads, decorated ox carts passed by, loaded with coffee beans to dump off for the local co-op agency to pick up.

They are thrilled to see parakeets (which are much larger than in the United States); emerald toucanets; squirrel cuckoos; tanagers; flycatchers; colorful large toucans; many species of monkeys; iguanas; lizards; pizotes (or coati, from the raccoon family); tayras (a type of weasel); and vibrant pink, purple, orange, and red flowers—orchids, anthuriums, and ginger. Warned about poisonous snakes—fer de lance, rattlesnakes, pit vipers, and coral snakes—they have encountered several—fortunately not too closely.

Wanting to be part of the community, Betsy and Bill helped their neighbors by giving them rides (they purchased a 1974 Land Rover with a broken odometer for local travel) and volunteered to prepare food for festivals and village gatherings. Betsy found that Ticos of all ages and sizes are strong—chopping wood, grinding corn for flour, pounding garlic cloves (called teeth), and hauling supplies. Working on a tamale assembly line in preparation for the Costa Rica Adventure Race (530 miles, ten days of running, biking, kayaking, and rafting), with worldwide teams passing through their village, Betsy chopped massive quantities of onions. Her eyes teared badly. Placing a glass of water by her, a local guy said it would help. She didn't know whether she was supposed to drink it or put the onions in the water, but was told she didn't need to do anything. It worked. The glass of water prevented her eyes from watering because it absorbed the gas emitted from the onions. "Another University of Life lesson," Betsy's neighbor observed. Raw meat from a butchered cow had been spread out on a table wiped down with a not-so-clean rag, and banana leaves were placed on top. "Most of the 'bad stuff' is probably eliminated when the tamales are boiled," Betsy said.

Shopping at the *ferias* (farmers' markets), Betsy found rice, beans, papaya, oranges, pineapples, bananas, watermelon, garlic, kale, and sugarcane plentiful. *Casado* is a popular and inexpensive dish of rice, beans, salad, and fried plantains, with meat, chicken, or fish, served at lunch at most restaurants. At home, Betsy and Bill eat lots of greens, fresh fruit, chicken, and fish. Not fond of the typical fresh rubbery cheese, they found a Tico family trained to make harder cheeses from their organic milk and some fellow immigrants who make creamy goat cheese.

After their one-year rental expired, Betsy and Bill found another rental—a wooden home with a tin roof a mile high at the base of Mount Chirripo, in San Gerardo de General, a twenty-minute walk to the village with a population of 350. This home had exquisite views of the hills and valleys. "It was beautiful," Betsy said. "In college, I loved the beach more than the mountains. Living in the mountains is rejuvenating and more in line with refreshing nature. It's deeper in my soul."

Mold was an issue in their cloud forest home, so they used dehumidifying cups that collected moisture. Poor-quality dirt roads with major potholes are dusty in the December–April dry season and muddy in the rainy season, May to November. Tarring their local mountain road was challenging because no cars were permitted on the road from 7:00 a.m. to 2:00 p.m. "When the long road to our village was being improved, heavy machinery cut our water lines. When our Internet crashed, it was discovered that a cow had flipped the connection switch! Repairs may take longer but are done by good-humored, helpful people who automatically assist. Their attitude is that they are neighbors; of course they will help and not expect payment. Native people in this area have limited incomes and are resourceful—brooms are made with a bristly, stiff-leaved plant tied to a stick. Everything is utilized; nothing goes to waste."

Although they enjoyed their lovely home and area, there were an increasing number of break-ins in the vicinity. Concerned about security, they moved to another attractive rental home northeast of San Jose in the hills near Braulio Carillo National Park. Volunteering twice a week at the local Toucan Rescue Ranch, Betsy and Bill enjoy handling food prep, cleaning cages, and interacting with the toucans, parrots, macaws, sloths, monkeys, owls, and a river otter. "It's tiring but fun!" Betsy said.

Initially they had ninety-day visas, which they renewed several times by leaving the country—opting to go first to Panama, then Nicaragua. They went through Costa Rica's passport office at the border, dealt with conflicting information about how long they needed to stay in the other country (three hours to three days), passed through the other country's immigration office with the required documents to get the proper stamps, and returned.

Later, they got a two-year residency visa, eliminating border runs. Eventually, they hope to get a longer-term visa. Securing a two-year *pensionado* residency required purchasing the desirable and reasonable National Health Insurance (CAJA) and getting a *cedula*, or local identification card, that has perks, including less costly admissions to attractions, avoiding the higher tourist rates. Obtaining their CAJA and cedula cards was taxing, as each required one to have the other, but they persevered.

Year-round temperatures range from 68 to 88 degrees Fahrenheit, with the thermometer rarely dipping below 60. Drizzle during the rainy season is called *pelo de gato*, or "hair of the cat."

"Health care is excellent," Betsy said. "I had to have two basal cell carcinomas removed from the top of my head. Despite being scared about the possibility of the cancer spreading, worrying about my hair being shaved, and having to wear an uncomfortable bandana tied around my head and chin, the procedure went well. The doctor helped me get a hotel and gave me his cell number to call if I had problems or questions.

"There are significant differences in health care between Costa Rica and the States. The doctors don't have nurses, and get the waiting patients themselves. Patient forms are completed by the doctor, who asks the questions and fills in the answers. Patients do not disrobe for general exams. Doctors listen to your heart and lungs through your shirt. Payment for a consult and any procedures includes any and all follow-up visits. After surgery to remove the two basal cell carcinomas, there were numerous return visits at no extra charge."

Later, during an annual physical, Betsy's new gynecologist gave her a transvaginal ultrasound, which she had never had with a routine exam. That test may have prolonged or saved Betsy's life, because it was discovered that her uterus was filled with blood, leading to a hysterectomy and removal of a large fibroid. Having cancer in her family, Betsy feared she had cancer too. She was given a clean bill of health. "It was another high-quality medical experience, and my total bill of $5,000, which included a one-night hospital stay, was a fraction of what I would have paid in the States."

Betsy is learning about the country's customs. She attended a fifteen-year-old girl's *quinceanera*, an elaborate wedding-like celebration of her rite of passage to womanhood. When visiting a cacao farm by the Caribbean coast, a young indigenous Bribri woman explained the chocolate-making process and talked about some Bribri women who still practice traditional birthing customs. "Pregnant women go off into the forest and stay in a little fort they build," Betsy said. "No one is to enter to help her with the birth. If she needs anything, they pass it to her in a halved bamboo stalk. She cuts the umbilical cord herself with a machete she purifies in a fire. A shaman visits her after the birth, which could be a couple of days or weeks later. The shaman purifies her body from the pregnancy and birth. Then she is able to rejoin her family and community."

When the husband of their housekeeper friend died from lung cancer at 53, his widow created a home altar for him. For nine days, people came to visit, say the rosary, and have coffee and bread. On the ninth day of this *novena* (from *nueve*, or nine), church services were held all day. The nine days of prayers help the deceased make it through the pearly gates and aid others in working through their grief.

Betsy once fantasized about being a world-class figure skater. Now she would like to go tandem skydiving, but not bungee jumping.

She doesn't imagine ever living in the States again. "I've seen most every state and have done that," she said. "I'm interested in living in other parts of the world." She and her husband looked at the possibility of living part of the year in Ecuador, but there are visa complications, with required lengths of stays. Using Costa Rica as their base, they have enjoyed trips to Patagonia, Ireland, Japan, and New Zealand. They may experience living in different areas of Costa Rica as well. If they decide to move from Costa Rica, they may live in Ireland and Northern

Ireland, and their length of stay will depend upon tourist visa limits. They have many country options.

Thoughts and Advice About Risk

"I'm so glad we did it," Betsy said about moving to Costa Rica. "It was scary to make this move. It was my idea, and I was more scared about it than my husband. It's hard to leave people and what you know."

Getting rid of everything she owned (she scanned reams of photos onto Flickr and tossed prints) and keeping only some clothes and jewelry has been okay—she doesn't miss anything except for her cute Mini Cooper. With her parents deceased (Betsy was 40 when her mother died from cancer at 70, and 46 when her father died from heart complications at 78), it was hard to say goodbye to her remaining elderly aunt and uncle, knowing she probably wouldn't see them again.

"Don't go blindly," Betsy recommends to others who may think about moving to another country. "Spend time in the countries you're thinking about moving to. Don't buy a house for at least a year after moving. Give things a year to try out." Betsy and Bill have no desire to buy another home. "We enjoy renting for the flexibility and not having to worry about maintenance."

Wanting to speak the language and feeling insecure about using her limited Spanish, Betsy said, "I had to put myself out there, forcing myself to speak to my Costa Rican neighbors to be a contributing member of the community. I had to make arrangements for cleaning the house and yard, cat-sitting, and unexpected repairs."

Preferring the lifestyle and culture of other countries, Betsy, a quiet, reserved woman, said, "It has taken courage and inner strength to travel and move to places. It has come from my gut." She enjoys immersing herself in other cultures and countries and is interested in how people live and do things differently. "It's been liberating," Betsy said about getting rid of everything, moving to another country, and enjoying the retired life. "After sixty years of being obsessed with gotta do, gotta do, now we don't have 'to-do' time. I feel retired. It's rather refreshing!"

Betsy by a walking tree at Los Cusingos Bird Sanctuary, Pérez Zeledón, Costa Rica

Photo by Bill Green

CAROL LARSON

Official Roller Derby Skater at 68–70+

BIRTH YEAR: 1946

Known as "Itsa Mazin" on the flat track, petite grandmother Carol is one of the world's oldest official women derby players. Skating since age 6, she broke her arm twice and retired from the sport at age 12—until 35, when she resumed skating infrequently. After breaking her arm at 55, she recovered and skated until her early 60s. Determined to try Roller Derby after her 66th birthday, her dream was nearly shattered during the final ten minutes of boot camp testing.

Earlier Years

Growing up on a dairy farm outside a small town north of Seattle, Carol was the middle child between two brothers. When her dad began raising strawberries, she and her brothers helped in the fields—picking up rocks and sticks while their dad drove the tractor. There were a hundred acres of strawberries, and he employed five hundred pickers, including many students. He had teachers working as bus drivers and field monitors during the summer's three-week season. Her quiet, intuitive mother had a strong personality and did the business bookkeeping.

Carol liked swimming and running 10K races. "I never played team sports, though, as I didn't have good hand-eye coordination. In softball, I couldn't see the ball coming and swung wildly—I do better without equipment." She liked roller skating as a child until she broke her arm a second time in sixth grade. That's when she hung up her skates.

After high school, she attended college, soon dropped out, went to business school in Seattle, and worked as a data-entry operator. Moving to Redondo Beach, California, she met and married her husband and had a daughter. Later, she divorced, was a single mom, worked in computer-aided design, and resumed skating. When she bought skates, she was surprised that the wheels moved over sand along the strand. The beach skaters never wore protective gear, only light clothing.

She met and married a guy named Max and moved to San Diego, and then relocated to western Washington, where she held a series of part-time temporary jobs and helped her commercial fisherman husband during the summers. Skating at a rink, she broke her right arm again. "My injury slowed me down, but I still loved skating," she said. "I was a rink rat, and the feeling of skating is powerful for me. I think of Audrey Hepburn in a gown, beautiful and poised, gracefully coming down the stairs in *My Fair Lady*. Skating is the closest I'll ever come to feeling like that scene. It's all on me—I feel confident and beautiful when skating."

After her arm recovered, she met a woman during the open sessions of rink skating who had taken up Rollerblading in her 70s. Together, they skated at different rinks and once took a train to Portland, Oregon, to skate at The Oaks, "a cool old rink with an organ player, just like in my youth," Carol said.

Retiring to eastern Washington, she and her husband lived "off the grid" in the middle of nowhere for six years. Her adventurous and inventive husband installed solar panels to generate electricity. They owned four horses and a mule, and Carol took up horseback riding at age 60. Their large quarter horses were massive and intimidating to petite Carol, who is barely five foot two. Trail riding on hills with rocks was daunting for her, and she had a teenage girl help her to gain confidence. "I thought skating was easier," Carol said. "You're closer to the ground when you fall while skating. I also worry there is a lot of horse equipment I'm not familiar with, like straps and saddles that require constant adjusting. Equipment failure often causes accidents. With skating, I only need to check my wheels and toe stops, and I can do that."

With no local skating rinks, she skated only when traveling—ice skating in Canada and roller skating while visiting friends on the West Coast. When she and her husband moved to Anacortes, she resumed skating at a nearby rink.

At 65, watching the skaters from the stands warm up at a Roller Derby game at Seattle's Key Arena, Carol thought, *Roller Derby looks like fun! I want to do this!* "I needed a challenge—I was too comfortable skating in rinks to music. I thought I could do this and was thrilled with the idea. It was instant love. I'm going to do it even if I just have to be the mascot."

Getting Into Roller Derby

It took six months to find a league close to her home, and Carol drove thirty minutes each way to practice Roller Derby on a rough concrete floor in a lumberyard building. "It was hard skating on cement, though many Roller Derby teams do—this was pitted cement, which made it tougher."

After twisting her knee, she had several months to reflect while recovering. "I was not happy with the cement floor and doubted my fit with this team. I decided I would try another team and found the Whidbey Island Roller Girls. When I went to their practice, I knew it was the right fit for me."

At age 66, she began a ten-week Roller Derby boot camp in Oak Harbor. She wore a helmet, wrist guards, elbow pads, mouth guard, and four-wheel skates, and added a butt pad for extra protection. Although timid at the beginning of boot camp, she felt confident by the end.

"You have to be outgoing," she said. "I don't yell enough. I was always in trouble in school with my yelling. My voice carries, and I was called out of class. Now I get to retrain my voice and yell more. I spent years working on my anger. In Roller Derby, it's controlled assertiveness. It's mental. If you believe in yourself, you can do it."

Picking a cool name for yourself is part of Roller Derby. "My brother thought I should be Old and Bold. Actually, that was pretty good, but I didn't want a name that highlighted my age. The first name I threw out to critics was FabuLush. Well, that just was too much for some. People wanted to quit being my friend because it was all I could talk about. I cycled through hundreds of choices, as a lot of the good ones were already taken. As I'm driving home, I spot a sign: Itsa—I liked Itsa, and Mazin just follows. Finally, I have a name."

Because she and her husband often go south in the winter, their vacation interrupted her boot camp, so she enrolled in another boot camp later that year. During the final ten minutes of testing, she fell and broke her arm for the fourth time. "I knew right away it was broken. *This sucks!* I thought while sitting and absorbing this new injury and trying to deal with it. My husband was called, and that concerned me. Though my husband was always supportive of me playing Roller Derby and never tried to stop me from doing it, he always said, 'Don't come home broken' when I left for practice.

"I cried and was disappointed after returning home from getting X-rays at the hospital. I lay in bed and thought, *What's happening?* and told myself I had come back from a broken arm before. I exercised—walking and planks up to four minutes to keep up my core strength and stay fit. It's easy to go into depression and negative space—I turned it around again. I was thankful it was my left arm this time. I'm right-handed and had already broken my right arm three times. It took six months to recover."

Carol was scared to do Roller Derby at first, which she admits was hard to get over. "With drills, I'm not too scared. You ache, and Roller

Derby wears your body out. Some days I'm sore from playing. I still don't hit hard enough. I'm dealing with it to improve. I'm not attracted to the fight mode. I tell myself I can do this. I think about Diana Nyad's swim from Cuba to Florida. She said, 'Find a way.' When I have my down moments, I think of her and know that no other human accomplished what she did."

When she had doubts about continuing with Roller Derby, Carol met with a trainer to review the goals she needed to attain to complete her Minimum Skills Requirements according to the rules of the Women's Flat Track Derby Association. Her team was supportive and encouraging with their critiques. Confessing to almost giving up because of all the rules and paperwork, Carol said it was a serious commitment.

After turning 68, she passed her Minimum Skills Requirements while attending a third boot camp. "Standing still on one foot for thirty seconds was almost as daunting as the twenty-seven laps around the track in five minutes (known as the 27/5)," she said. "I'm competing with girls who could be my granddaughters. The veterans are usually 25–27 years old and are top-notch skaters. When I was in school, sports for girls weren't promoted.

"My father always encouraged me and gave me lots of confidence. Both my parents did, but especially my father so I could always speak up to men—that's the way I was raised."

Located near Whidbey Island Naval Air Station, Carol's team has a strong military influence. There are women who served and are serving in the navy, are navy wives, or who are deployed overseas with the military. There are also teachers, graphic designers, and Safeway and Subway employees. The other team that plays at the lumberyard had a pastor, dentist, and casino dealer. Team members are a diverse racial and ethnic mix.

"We have skaters with multiple piercings and tattoos, and even though I don't, I never feel judged by my teammates—we look at what we each contribute individually," Carol said. "The women that I practice with are so incredible to me. I feel so fortunate to be a part of this team. I cannot even begin to express the admiration that I have for the women. The more I learn about each woman, the more I am amazed and feeling special to be included. It makes me smile. I go to bed with derby spinning in my head and I love it!" The Whidbey Island Roller Girls' website advertises, "We welcome women of all shapes, sizes and skill levels. 'No Excuses' is the motto we live and play by."

Carol was up to 162 pounds at one point, and Roller Derby helped her lose weight. In her first scrimmage at age 68, Carol played for about five minutes. "I felt so proud of myself," she said. Soon after, she passed the 27/5 and debuted in a bout as an official player on the team's roster three months later. On the track eight times as a blocker, she fell once and another time landed on her knee, but she bounced up quickly.

"It was the most fun! I smiled the whole time! I was so happy! I was in heaven!"

Improving her speed since passing the 27/5, Carol did 28.75 laps in five minutes and is shooting for 30/5. Although she acknowledges that she may never be a jammer (the player who scores), one of her goals is to try an apex jump, though it frightens her. It's a difficult maneuver requiring a skater to cut inside the track by jumping over it without falling.

"*That's crazy ... that's impossible!* my brain says as I listen to what I'm being told we'll be doing during practice. For example, we skate in line, weaving in and out of each skater, and then have to weave in and out of skaters in line going backward; or we skate in a pack close together and the skater whose number is called needs to fall and make themselves into a ball to avoid getting hit; or we skate in a pack and then turn around backward and fall. Falling in a pack of moving skaters is freaky, as you're supposed to trust your teammates to skate around you. By the end of the session, we've done it.

"That's what keeps me in Roller Derby—feeling powerful about myself," Carol continued. "I think there are lots of abused women in derby for that reason. You learn to depend on yourself. It's a team sport, but the hard thing for me to overcome is to be close to other people. I was used to doing physical activities on my own, like swimming and running."

In season, Carol skates three to four times a week with one or two skate sessions and two derby practices. Exercises are done during practices and cool-downs. Outside of skating, she walks fast up and down hills. "Walking sounds wimpy, but I don't like gyms. My legs are strong, and I practice breathing with my walking." Doing her own form of aerobic exercise, Carol squats while gardening. She believes in hydrating, drinking about a half gallon of water a day, and notices the difference in her stamina.

Conscious of eating well, she eats lightly the day before and day of practice. Since her retirement, she often joins friends for lunch. After having a beer one time, she had no energy at practice that night, so she cut out wine and beer on practice days. Oatmeal for breakfast, a small salad or cheese and crackers for lunch, and a peanut butter and jelly sandwich three hours before practice is typical. Liking chocolate milk, she adds it to her oatmeal, and she puts lemon juice in her water for electrolytes. Some women prescribe pickle juice or Pedialyte to help muscle cramps and jittery legs—everyone's different.

"I'm not into making myself miserable," Carol said about not wanting to take diet and exercise to extremes. However, she stressed, "If you're not in good shape—feeling secure and strong—you're a risk to your teammates."

Their season starts in January and there are no bouts the last two months of the year. Practice is all year (three weeks in November and two weeks in December) on a flat track in an old barn. At monthly scrimmages they divide their team in half and play against each other—friends and family are invited for free, and the refs get to learn their jobs.

To be in compliance their league is required to do community volunteer work. Carol and her teammates participate in numerous fundraising events—children's Halloween parties, car washes, brewery tastings, and Roller Derby demonstrations during the Oyster Run, an annual motorcycle rally with twenty thousand motorcycles. It's a well-known event in the area, and roads are closed off in a full loop, people are advised to stay home if they're not part of it, and the players are excited and get into the thrill of it.

When Carol takes a Roller Derby break during part of the winter, she and her husband escape cold Washington to spend time in their cottage in Bishop, California, in the east-central part of the state, below Yosemite, near Nevada. It's high desert at four thousand feet, surrounded by sagebrush and mountains. Four-wheel driving in their jeep at seven thousand feet, they hike into the gold mines.

"I probably would stay home if it wasn't for my husband wanting to do these activities," Carol said. Her husband doesn't skate—he's afraid of falling—but he supports Carol with Roller Derby, because she loves it. "Some skaters get flak for playing; others say, 'My husband lets me play.' It makes me crazy that women feel they need their husband's permission."

Carol maintains there's a level playing field between herself as an older skater and the younger women skaters. "I no longer have a child at home," she said. "I have more time, so it's easier for me to focus, and I can buy the best equipment. Younger women skaters have hectic lives with work, children, and keeping a house running." She doesn't think she's that unusual. She admires roller figure-skating competitors, including women in their 70s. Carol, a four-wheel "quad" skater, is proud of her daughter, who Rollerblades.

Residing in the community she grew up in, Carol attends school reunions with classmates and participates in many events. She enjoys being a grandmother and likes seeing what interests her grandchildren. Speaking rapidly, she is enthusiastic and laughs easily.

When she is less physically active and needs something to entertain herself, Carol would like to scoop ice cream and make sundaes in an ice cream shop.

Painting inspires her and appeals to her. She's never painted and would like to try it someday.

Thoughts and Advice About Risk

"Going out on a sailboat!" is how Carol defines risk. While sailing with her husband one time, the mast broke and came down in chunks. Cables fell into the water. They were able to get back on their own with engine power, but it was traumatic for her. She has sailed since, but that experience has taken the joy and fun out of it.

Carol mentioned that people have different fears and risk-taking perspectives. By way of contrast, a friend of hers was out with her husband fishing when their boat sank and they had to be rescued. Having weathered that experience, they bought another boat. It didn't faze her friend to get back out on the water.

Despite the sport's danger, a broken arm during testing, and a wrenched knee, Carol doesn't consider Roller Derby a risk. "You're geared up with a mouth guard and helmet. You fall at least four or five times every practice. I broke my arm because I resisted the fall. I didn't go with the flow and slide like they teach us." Told, "Fall like you're sliding into second base," Carol said, "'I don't know about that, as I always struck out in softball.'

"If you can push through whatever fear you have, it is worth the end result. It is totally worth the effort in getting over being scared."

Surprised when her woman friends say they're afraid to go out to dinner or to the movies by themselves, Carol says it's not an issue for her because she was raised differently. She asks them, "Why do you think you can't do it?"

Going up on a glider has been in the back of her mind. She may try it, though she would never jump out of a plane.

As a young girl, she walked over Washington's famous two-lane Deception Pass Bridge connecting Whidbey Island to Fidalgo Island in the Puget Sound region, as part of a camp activity. "I wouldn't want to cross it on foot now—it's too scary. It was easier when I was younger, as I was with a group and other kids weren't scared—there were hiking trails on either side, and we were taught lessons like 'Don't throw rocks over the edge.'" Carol drives over the bridge on the way to practice and sometimes wonders whether it's safe.

A determined, proud, spunky woman with a great sense of humor, Carol admits she doesn't like being fussed over for Roller Derby skating in her 70s. "Age shouldn't matter," she said. "I'm not special and shouldn't get kudos for something beyond my control." She'd like to be known for achieving Roller Derby skills without focusing on her age.

Carol would like to learn "jam skating," a modern jazz-style roller skating combining dance, gymnastics, and skating.

During Roller Derby practice and each season, a roster of official players is selected based on evaluations. Carol knows at some point she won't be picked to play on the Roller Derby team. She promises herself not to be disappointed when that happens. "I'm willing to be the team mascot in that case." She also joined the Geritol Mafia, a Roller Derby team for all players over 40, who do not practice together, but play together. Carol says, "I am lucky to be healthy enough to still be able to enjoy my passion. My derby window is small, like a hand mirror. I'll have to give up derby someday, but not skating!

"Part of the reason I continue Roller Derby is you do not know what tomorrow will bring." Her cousin died within two months of developing a brain tumor.

"Roller Derby is a way of honoring the healthy body I have, and I want to use it as much as possible. The empowering feeling is the draw. It's an adrenaline high. You get addicted to it. Skating is my meditation and my sport. It's been especially helpful when I'm dealing with life's problems. It's a relief from everyday life requiring me to focus on skating.

"It makes you feel so great inside."

Carol in action with the Whidbey Island Roller Girls

Photo by Jeff Jackson

EOLA BALL

Spiritual Leader and Solo Traveler Who Fell in Love in Nepal at 67

BIRTH YEAR: 1944

A nature-loving and spiritual, four-foot, ten-inch woman from Maine, Eola became a social worker, was a United Service Organizations director, and later married and had a daughter. In her 50s, she became a shaman follower and launched a healing center. At 67, she traveled alone to India and Nepal. Trekking through the Himalayas, she felt a spiritual connection and fell in love with the mountains and her young male Nepali guide.

Earlier Years

Named after two grandmothers, Eola Ann went by Ann as a child since Eola was too hard to pronounce. She liked the name Eola, however, and started using it in college. The youngest of six children, Eola was born in Damariscotta, Maine, and moved to the shipbuilding town of Bath when she started school. Her seamstress mother made clothes—from tailored men's suits to Civil War uniforms for reenactment battles to dance costumes—and worked from home. Eola's parents divorced when she was two, and her mother raised the six children.

Summers were spent at her grandfather's camp on an island in a lake, where they picked berries, swam, and took out rowboats. If you could swim the half mile over and back from the island, you were permitted to take a rowboat out on the lake by yourself, which Eola did at age 5.

Loving school, except math, she liked and was good at sports. She was fast on the basketball court and also enjoyed softball, volleyball, badminton, bowling, the hiking club, and the riflery club. Interested in being a physical therapist, Eola worked as a nurse's aide during high school and college, but the closest physical therapy schools in Boston were expensive, so she went to Gorham State College and pursued an English and education degree. When she was a college senior, she dated a guy who proposed and gave her a diamond ring. Because they dated that year, she felt she should marry him. Dazed while walking up the aisle at age 22, she realized that marrying this man was not what she wanted, but she honored her commitment.

Eola was a social worker in Maine and Connecticut, got divorced, and traveled solo to Europe. Particularly memorable was meeting three women on the west coast of Scotland who invited her to stay at their "wee cottage" on a bluff. Built in the 1500s, the cottage had walls three feet thick. There they enjoyed sherry and listened to Viennese waltzes while overlooking the Hebrides.

Later, Eola worked for the Department of Human Services, grew tired of the bureaucracy, and got a job providing entertainment and leading outdoor activities for the United Service Organizations (USO) near Reykjavik in Iceland. After her job ended, she took her Volvo and a tent on a solo nine-month road trip across the United States, camping and putting 32,000 miles on her car, before working for the USO again—this time in Stuttgart, Germany. In this macho male, military environment, a general called the women "girls." "There are no girls here, only women," Eola replied. She began graduate work in counseling psychology, did dream research, and, during vacations, biked through much of Europe. She later went to Indiana, pursued interpersonal relations and meditation through rainbow colors with light healing, and completed her master's degree at Ball State.

Returning to Maine, she met Edsel, joined him while he was traveling in Europe, became pregnant, and opted not to marry until after having daughter Kea. They fixed up an old Cape Cod–style house in

Damariscotta, later built a passive solar home in Newcastle, and had a greenhouse business.

In her mid-50s, Eola decided to reinvent herself. "I started running at 53 on the high school track and got really buff. I had a spiritual awakening at warp speed." Always interested in extrasensory perception and the afterlife, she attended shamanic trainings at New York's Omega Institute and met shaman practitioner John Perkins, whom she later assisted in his work.

Traveling to Ecuador with a shamanic follower, Eola went into the Amazon rain forest. In Otavalo, she worked with shaman families and participated in the nude in ancient healing practices using *trago* (sugarcane alcohol) and eggs. "Each person rubbed an unlit candle over their bodies. The shaman lit each candle, read the flame, and told participants about themselves. He put trago in his mouth and emitted a fine spray over the group of nude bodies. At the end of the healing, he blew trago through a flame, creating a large fireball."

Eola met indigenous people who have little contact with the outside world. The Shuar and the Quichua use Ayahuasca, a plant spirit medicine. Called the "vine of life and death," it often induces visions, can produce physiological changes, and is boiled with herbs for up to eight hours. Drinking a small amount causes dreams and visions and often vomiting and diarrhea. Eola says, "I had deep experiences. The amazing thing is the jungle wakes up. I could hear everything acutely—sounds were amplified, intense and loud. I heard bugs crawling on the earth—it was fascinating and comforting. I took Ayahuasca three times, and each time, the reaction and visions were *very* different. It is taken at night with no lights, as your eyes are very sensitive. The shaman chants and shakes rattles, and each person has a personal healing. The shaman listens to your experience and interprets it with you. The next day there is no hangover."

At 56, Eola started One Heart Energy Center out of her Maine home, leading shamanic, new-moon drum circles, group workshops, and individual healing sessions. During guided drum journeys, Eola says, "I do whatever intuitively comes to me and through me. Everyone responds differently. People share and dance their wild selves, and I teach that you're your own healer. We end with a *Shungo* circle. *Shungo*, a Quichuan word from the Andes of Ecuador, means 'from my heart to your heart.' I open some doors and guide you on your journey."

She joined the Crimson Circle, a movement based on the principle "Relax into Enlightenment," started practicing Tai Chi, and drew her dreams and visions. She built a sweat lodge on her property and led groups of people who sat for hours as water was poured over hot rocks, creating steam to purify the mind, body, spirit, and heart. While engaged in spiritual work, Eola also worked for a philanthropic family, headed an organization funding women's projects, and taught business courses for a women's career program.

At 67, Eola took a Crimson Circle trip to Egypt, then traveled on her own around India. From there, she took buses and a rickshaw, and walked the last several miles across the border into Nepal.

Falling in Love in Nepal

After a long bus ride, Eola arrived in Pokhara early in the morning. Standing on her hotel room's balcony and seeing the white-capped Himalayas for the first time, she burst into tears.

She was thinking of going on a three-day trek. The hotel staff urged her to go longer and recommended a guide. Wanting to meet the guide before spending nine days with him, she was introduced to Bijaya, a hotel manager and trekking guide—a shy 25-year-old man with a nice smile. The plan was to fly to Jomsom, the gateway for one of the most popular Himalayan trekking routes in the Annapurna Mountain Range, and trek back nine days to Pokhara. Weather delayed flights, so they toured around the city on Bijaya's motorbike. When the bad weather continued, they decided to trek to Jomsom and fly back.

It was spring but cold and icy in the mountains in March. They walked together through villages for nine days. "That's when I fell in love with the mountains and a mountain man," said Eola.

It was a steady uphill on steep stone stairs and wooded trails. They crossed many streams. Bijaya carried Eola's small backpack, and she used two walking sticks for balance, preferring short ones to hold her better if she slipped. Eola walked slowly and steadily, seldom stopping. They walked six to eight hours a day. "We went through a spectacular rhododendron forest with trees two to three feet thick and huge, five-inch red, white, and pink blossoms." They wore winter jackets and headlamps when getting up at 4:00 a.m. to hike one and a half hours up to see the sunrise. The moon also guided them. At night, they stayed in teahouses or people's homes.

Eola and Bijaya talked about all kinds of things. Bijaya asked her about breastfeeding. Nepali mothers breastfeed, and Bijaya was breastfed until age 5. "We felt a strong personal connection to each other unlike anything I have felt before," Eola said. They shared a room with two beds when only one room was available, and Bijaya asked if he could sleep with her. She said no. Several nights later, she thought, *Why not have a little fun?* "The sex was gentle and wonderful."

In Kagbeni, past Jomsom, they saw a string of caves high up across the valley. Eola was drawn to them and wanted to go there, but there wasn't time. In Muktinath, there were Hindu and Buddhist temples near each other. When she asked Bijaya about his religious background, he said, "I'm Buddhist but we're all one." Hindus and Buddhists get along in Nepal and use all of the sacred temples, not just those of their religion. The Hindu temple was a thirty-minute climb up, with the spectacular mountains as the backdrop.

"*I am in love with these mountains, and I am so in love with this man.* I visioned the two of them coming together. I cried happy tears," Eola said.

Back in Kathmandu, each of them said they wanted to be together. Eola needed to go back home, and promised to return within six months.

She had spent a glorious three weeks with Bijaya and was in love.

Returning home to Maine, Eola divorced her husband of thirty years. "For a long time, we had not operated as a married couple," she explained. While packing, she was shocked to find a note she had written to herself ten years prior and forgotten: "Come into my cave. You are the mountains. You are the Himalayas."

"During two spiritual weekends in Maine—at a new-moon ceremony and a sound healing—Bijaya came in through other people," Eola said. She heard about Max, the ancient crystal skull from Guatemala, thought to be ten thousand years old and used by Mayan priests for healing and rituals. A legend proclaims that thirteen life-size crystal skulls will be rediscovered and reunited for their collective wisdom one day. Some people believe that Max helps people. The skull is shown around the United States. In New Hampshire, Eola sat with Max. She asked a turquoise skull for sale, "Do you want to go to the caves in Kagbeni, Nepal?" When it responded "Yes," she had people blow their energies into the skull.

Three months later, Eola returned to Nepal and Bijaya with her turquoise skull. In thinking about what to name the skull, simultaneously Bijaya and Eola said "Maya," which means "love" in Nepali. Climbing up steep shale, they reached the Kagbeni caves. They looked in many caves with relics—white chalky cones left to preserve dead people's spirits, and *khatas*, traditional Tibetan ceremonial scarves in white, yellow, or red—until coming across a cave with only a large round stone. This was the cave destined for the turquoise skull. In this cave they received incredible energies from the earth and the mountains that came through the cave and Maya.

Bijaya was excited to introduce Eola to his family. They rode thirteen hours by motorbike on dirt roads, forded a river and small streams, and arrived in a remote, lush, green, hilly countryside in the Sindhuli district. Bijaya's parents are self-sufficient farmers growing rice, barley, wheat, corn, and cucumbers. "His family was wonderful, generous, and welcoming," Eola said. Bijaya is the youngest of five children. Eola was a few years older than Bijaya's parents.

The house was dung, wood, mud, and straw with three bedrooms—for his parents, Bijaya's brother and sister-in-law, and their sons. During festivals, new dung was rubbed smooth onto the house and floors. Goats, chickens, and buffalos stayed in an open area under one section of the house. Eola slept in the children's room while Bijaya slept on the upstairs porch. She met many family members living close by. His 96-year-old grandmother lived two hours' walk uphill near other relatives. His great-uncle is the main shaman in the village; his father and his uncle assist him. The family cooked with wood, sat on the floor, and ate rice and vegetables using one hand. Goats and buffalo were killed and divvied up for the neighbors during festivals. The people also ate chicken and small fish from the river. Eola brought gifts of jewelry for the women, US flag T-shirts for the children, books, and games, including badminton and Twister, which they thought was hilarious. Although Bijaya didn't explain to his family during their first visit together that he and Eola were a couple, she figured they knew and accepted her.

In Pokhara, they had an apartment for $200 a month. Wanting to be together, and driven by the fact that Eola would no longer need to leave Nepal every five months because of a visitor visa, they began the process of securing a marriage certificate, though Bijaya said, "We're already married in our hearts."

Encountering a frustrating bureaucracy, they were stymied by an ineffective lawyer and later an angry judge, who said to Bajaya, "What do you think you're doing?" Months later, after paying off another lawyer and many visits to offices for required stamps, they got a marriage license and Eola was granted the visa she needed. They found a ring for her and had one made for Bijaya—each was a pale blue aquamarine stone from the mountains.

A year after meeting, Eola, 68, and Bijaya, 26, were married in Kathmandu. They threw a party that night and celebrated with friends at a restaurant. For their honeymoon, they went on a nine-day trek to Annapurna Base Camp—the "trek of ten thousand kisses."

Eola returned to the States for the summer when her daughter, Kea, had a baby. Kea had guessed her mother was in love with Bijaya when they phoned each other while Eola was first trekking in Nepal. Eola was pleased her daughter was supportive.

In Nepal, Bijaya and Eola launched a trekking company, Dawn of the Heart Expedition. People came from around the world to take treks, including to Mount Everest and Annapurna. They loved entertaining and had many couch-surfing visitors to their apartment. Bijaya, a fabulous cook, usually made lunch and dinner, and they shared the housework and shopping. They ate dal (lentil soup with spices), fried vegetables, rice, and sometimes pieces of chicken and buffalo.

After marrying, they returned different times to visit Bijaya's family, and Eola continued to be welcomed by his relatives.

More than three years after meeting, Eola and Bijaya's marriage developed problems. "Because there were a few instances of him lying to me, I felt I had lost my trust in him," Eola said. "I had planned a trip to the States and decided to end the relationship at that time." At age 70, she returned to the United States and bought a home in midcoast Maine.

Loving to travel, she would like to visit Ireland, Eastern Europe, and Mongolia, and walk the Camino Portugues, the religious route from Lisbon to Santiago de Compostela (though she wouldn't be doing it for religious reasons), trek in Patagonia, and go to Everest Base Camp.

From her 1910 Maine home, Eola leads new-moon drum circles and other ceremonies and will see whether her healing practice morphs into something different.

"We are enlightened beings and have come into this lifetime to experience being enlightened and remaining in the body," Eola said. "Everyone on the planet will eventually go through this process. It's about breathing and allowing—it's a process of learning how to be in the world fully and joyfully. And there's the *And* ... the And of knowing that there are many dimensions that we can play in at any given moment."

Thoughts and Advice About Risk

"My risk bar is set high," Eola said. "A risk is doing something really dangerous, like climbing a high mountain like Everest." One thing this feisty, petite, jolly, world-exploring woman may *not* do is skydive. "Jumping out of a plane would make me nervous, as free falling would scare me, though I tried paragliding and that was really fun!"

"Go for it!" is Eola's advice to others who are thinking about traveling on their own.

"Many fear traveling by themselves or think they can't afford it," she said. "Travel doesn't have anything to do with money. You just need to make a decision to do it. Traveling to Europe and generally Asia is easy—especially with the amenities available and English spoken most places. In the early seventies, I couldn't speak another language. If you don't speak the language where you are, relax. Someone will show up who you can talk to. You can communicate with body language. Be creative.

"As a child, I always felt I was going to make a difference and help people but was not sure how it would be manifested," Eola said. "I think of my experiences as ordinary. This is my life. These are just things I do. Even when I was married, I did things and traveled on my own. I have always thought I'm watched over."

She admits to being nervous occasionally while traveling. "The only time I was really frightened was when I was 67 in India by myself at the Pakistan border. A large crowd gathered every day for a military marching and music hoopla. There was a wide street with men on one side, women on the other. People started pushing and shouting, surging toward a narrow doorway. I was scared of being trampled. Women were pushed into a barbed-wire fence. As I got close to the doorway, I popped through it, and a short distance later, landed on both feet in the open area."

Different cultures have different views about women traveling by themselves. "In India, I was a curiosity—people were interested in what I was doing and wanted to take photos of me with them. In Nepal, people were in my face sometimes, though they were friendly and warm. Ask people if you need help. Magical things happen when traveling.

"I don't see going to Nepal, falling in love, getting married, and starting a business with a younger Nepali man as a risk. Our ages didn't make much of a difference. I thought it would bother Bijaya more than me. He totally loved me and wasn't afraid to kiss me in front of others in our home and sometimes in public, even though there are no public displays of affection! We have so many shoulds, buts, what-ifs. We just have to say 'And.' Have fun, enjoy yourself, and enjoy the other person."

Eola hopes to return to Nepal. She misses Nepal, the mountains, and Bijaya. "The enlightened me knows our souls are in tune and that we are always together. I am that I am, Enlightened Eola."

Bijaya and Eola with the Himalayas

Photo by Unknown

FELICITY BOWDITCH

Teacher and Lifetime Traveler to Skydiving for Charity at 72

BIRTH YEAR: 1939

Born and raised in Pennsylvania, Felicity had an English mother and an American father. A shy girl, she took family trips to England and Holland, spending summers in Maine. After marrying, she had three children, co-taught prekindergarten in Massachusetts, and traveled extensively. Felicity moved to Maine in her 60s and volunteered at a local children's museum. Seeking sports adventures, she went white-water rafting, gliding and later, zip lining, and parasailing at 70. Always wanting to fly through the air, she skydived for the first time at age 72.

Earlier Years

Felicity grew up in Philadelphia with a younger brother. Her mother was a homemaker; her dad was in banking. She never wanted to be the center of attention and describes herself as an average student, terrible in math, and a good reader who enjoyed escaping with books. Suffering from knee joint pain and weak ankles, she sometimes fell flat on her face. At 15, she had surgery to remove a cyst and cartilage from her knee, which improved her mobility until a knee replacement years later.

Her lifelong interest in photography began with a Brownie camera and her dad's encouragement. Toting her camera everywhere throughout her life, she amassed many slides from her travels, later switching to digital format.

She spent enjoyable summers at her family's property in Camden, on

Maine's coast, where she met her future husband as a young teen. She recalls swimming at Lake Megunticook, drinking tea in the afternoons, stopping at the local bakery to get Vienna rolls, and seeing the northern lights (aurora borealis). "They were incredible sheets of bright, colorful lights," Felicity said.

Starting when she was 9, she and her family took trips to England to visit her maternal grandmother, whom she adored. The first time there, Felicity climbed to the top of a tree in her grandmother's yard. It was very high up. Anticipating a fall, her family figured an ambulance might need to be called, but her father talked her down. "That was a scary experience for me," Felicity said.

When she was 13, her father chartered a cabin cruiser for a family trip through Holland's canals. "Pulling our boat up alongside streets, we spent time exploring the country and eating piles of boiled potatoes in restaurants," said Felicity.

She went to Miss Porter's, a girls' boarding school in Connecticut, where she was active in the camera club, and later enrolled at a junior college in Massachusetts.

At age 20 while visiting England, Felicity paid $1,250 for a new, robin's-egg-blue VW Beetle with a sunroof for a four-month trip with a girlfriend. Before leaving England, her dad made her take off the tires several times so she would know how to change a flat. There was no gas gauge—unscrewing a dial let more gas in when you ran out, enough to make it to a gas station.

They explored England and Scotland; crossed by ferry into Holland; drove to Norway, staying with friends in a huge home where a prince visited; skied in Austria; and went into East Germany just after the Berlin Wall was erected. As they walked through Checkpoint Charlie, the infamous Berlin Wall crossing point between East and West Berlin, guards confiscated their passports. Despite being told "No photos allowed," Felicity took photos, including one of Brandenburg Gate, the landmark national symbol at the start of the road from Berlin to the town of Brandenburg. Their passports were returned. No one caught her taking photos. They went on to Italy, sent the car home, and headed to Greece.

While in her early 20s in England, a boyfriend talked her into taking a glider ride. "It was an open cockpit, and I leaned out into the air," Felicity said. "There was no noise. The scenery from above was beautiful. It was wonderful!"

Married at 24, Felicity later moved with her husband to the Midwest, gave birth to identical twin boys, resettled in Boston, and had a daughter. She co-taught prekindergarten in a private elementary school, which didn't require a degree. Relocating outside Philadelphia, Felicity volunteered at an environmental center. "It was huge fun," she said. "I took walks through the woods with inner-city kids who had never been to woods before."

When she and her husband moved to Maine while she was in her early 60s, Felicity volunteered in a public kindergarten and helped with a children's program taking "Go and Do" science displays—on topics such as the wind—to schools as fun, educational activities. Later, as the volunteer vice president, she and other board members put together the beginnings of the Coastal Children's Museum in Rockland.

Since her family trips as a girl and her four-month trek when single in her 20s, Felicity has traveled extensively. She's enjoyed adventurous and educational trips, including a cruise to Central America, where she visited an orphanage; rafting on Maine's Kennebec River rapids; visiting the Galapagos Islands, seeing wildlife in its natural state; going to China to observe teaching methods in an elementary school art class, where each child assembled identical pieces; and a trip on her own to Kenya, where she joined a group for a safari. She has shown her travel slides to appreciative audiences—from young schoolchildren to older people in nursing homes.

Observing animals in their natural habitats, she loved Antarctica, traveling aboard an icebreaker boat. There were daily trips ashore with rigorous walks up and down hills. "You had to hang on to the grasses," Felicity said. "The scenery was gorgeous, with magnificent icebergs. The fur seals and many species of penguins were amazing. We were told not to go any closer to penguins than fifteen feet. Penguins are curious, however, and they came right up to us and checked out our shoelaces."

At 70, on a Southern Caribbean cruise, Felicity went zip lining by herself for the first time over an island's lush, tropical rain-forest canopy. Strapped into a harness suspended from a cable, she stepped off the platform. "The first two legs of the thirteen-station course were hair-raising. It was less scary after the first couple of landings." Of signing up for parasailing, she said, "I wasn't scared to try it. When I got up and hung around in the air for a while, it wasn't much fun. It was nerve-racking. There was a heavy wind, so the boat stayed still. I didn't like the feeling, and the harness didn't seem secure. I asked to come down after a while. It wasn't pleasant."

Skydiving for the First Time

Since she was a teenager, Felicity thought it would be fun to float around in the sky. At 72, after hearing a friend describe her incredible experience skydiving, she was determined to do it. She researched the place—Skydive New England in Lebanon, Maine, near the New Hampshire border. She and her colleagues decided Felicity's skydive could raise funds for the Coastal Children's Museum. Raffle tickets were sold at $5 apiece for three prizes (brunch for two at the Samoset Resort, a birthday party at the museum, and $100 cash). Felicity's "flying adventure" was promoted to generate publicity and increase raffle ticket sales.

"Most of my friends and family, including my husband, wanted no part of it and were nervous for me. I had a knee replacement twenty-three years ago and was scheduled for another knee replacement in two months. I figured skydiving wouldn't cause any further harm, though I didn't tell my surgeon. When my 6-year-old granddaughter was told that Granny was going to jump out of an airplane, she asked, 'Isn't that dangerous?' I was excited and never scared, including the day of and moments before the jump. The museum president came with me to watch."

On jump day, there was a half-hour orientation consisting primarily of filling out and initialing numerous forms to limit the company's liability. Climbing into the sky were six other jumpers and instructors besides Felicity and her instructor. Because her knee had limited mobility, the hardest part was crouching down low in the plane's narrow doorway. "My position in the plane made me first to go. My instructor flew out backward with me attached. I saw the curvature of the earth. You free-fall until the parachute opens. It didn't feel like we were going that fast. You're so high up, it doesn't look as if you're coming down quickly. I thought it would feel like we were crashing down through the air. I didn't have that sensation. It was rather like floating. Things on the ground below got bigger a little at a time.

"I was fourteen thousand feet up in the air, going 126 miles per hour. My hair stood straight up and my face was distorted, with my cheeks puffed up against my eyes. I wore a jumpsuit and goggles—nothing on my head. I never had to touch anything—the instructor pulled the cord and orchestrated our landing. Before hitting ground, he told me to put my legs out. There was a strap on the jumpsuit to hold on to to keep my legs out in front of me. He touched his heels on the ground and scooted forward. We stopped with him sitting and me sitting in his lap."

Felicity had asked to do a flip in the air while diving. On the ground, she asked her instructor if they had done a flip. "Yes, I was told, right as we backed out of the plane, but I had my eyes closed then. I missed our flip!

"It was fun and I would do it again. The only thing I'd do differently is take Dramamine, as I had slight discomfort when flying through the air, but it wasn't that big a deal and was still fun." More than $1,000 was raised, and the names of the raffle ticket winners were drawn at the jump site.

Two months later Felicity had her knee replaced, spending three days at Portland's Maine Medical Center. She brought along the photo of her instructor on top of her in midair. "This is what I really had fun doing," she told the medical staff.

Enjoying adventure travel, Felicity looks forward to more trips—to Churchill, Canada, "the polar bear capital of the world," to see polar bears on the tundra from a train-like movable hotel. Other favored destinations are Greenland, Iceland, Northern Norway, the Amazon, and South Africa. She'll take photographs as she always does—perhaps macro-shots of an elephant's eyes or a tundra landscape.

Felicity welcomes taking her six grandchildren to the Galapagos Islands—"to understand the importance of Darwin and his discoveries, to go where humans haven't harmed the animals, and the animals are not afraid of people. It's a fascinating and intriguing experience to share with them and my husband."

A longtime board member of the Coastal Children's Museum, Felicity has been a devoted volunteer there. Loving nature and the outdoors, she has enjoyed hovering over the touch tank with excited children holding starfish and crabs, explaining how little creatures turn themselves over and the fact that starfish have eyes on the ends of their arms.

As in childhood, Felicity is a shy adult. She doesn't care for big groups and is often content reading and enjoying her home. On trips with groups, she said, "I'm still there with myself and like to do my own thing. I am a loner who loves to travel."

During April each year, after enduring Maine's frigid, snowy weather, Felicity and her husband go to Florida, where they have a good time being with their grandchildren and family.

Thoughts and Advice About Risk

"A risk is something out of the ordinary—a discovery, for example, adventure travel." Felicity says she is a risk taker. "Ever since I was young,

I've taken risks—like climbing to the top of my grandmother's tree. I didn't see skydiving at 72 as a risk because it's common now; known to be safe; and I was jumping in tandem with the instructor, who was a young, good-looking guy with a thousand hours of skydiving experience. However, when I was a mother with young children, I wouldn't risk my life then and it wasn't a popular sport.

"I think of risks I've taken as nonthreatening. I tend to do things that others have done many times. However, I wouldn't walk down dark alleys in bad parts of cities."

Felicity's advice to others interested in skydiving or another physical challenge is "Go for it! If you're really scared, don't do it, because you won't have fun. If you would kind of like to, but aren't sure, you should try it. Adventures should be fun. You can't be scared to enjoy them."

Felicity at 126 mph, 14,000 feet, with tandem instructor Dan Lane, Skydive New England

Photo by Meaghan Meehan

CHAPTER 2 — ALTRUISTS

ELKE IBRAHIM

Musician at 50; Community Organizer in Her 50s Through 70+

BIRTH YEAR: 1940

Born in Germany (now Russia), Elke Ibrahim grew up extremely poor. She and her five siblings were split up as children when her parents divorced. Displaced by war when young, Elke later became a nurse. Marrying a man from Somaliland, she had four children and later settled in Nova Scotia. Her husband returned to Somaliland. At 50, she took up the clarinet and joined a concert band. At 58, she overcame her shyness and became a community organizer.

Earlier Years

Elke Gramatzki's father had two children with his first wife, who died young. After he remarried, Elke was his third child, born during World War II in Königsberg, East Prussia, Eastern Germany. Destroyed in the war, the town later was renamed Kaliningrad and became part of Russia. Her family members were forced to flee to what was then West Germany as refugees and were taken in by a farmer. Ten families lived in a huge farmhouse. Elke's family of seven lived in two rooms there for several years. All the women took turns cooking; washday was every Monday. Because they were living in close quarters, contagious diseases, such as hepatitis and polio, spread among the families. Elke's brother was hospitalized for two years with a deformed back as a result of contracting polio.

Her father, a scientist and academician, leased several acres near

Kellenhusen, a small Baltic Sea town, where he built a house with bricks he hauled from nearby bombed-out houses. They called it *Vogelsang*, or "birdsong" in German. Along with a garden, they had a cow, geese, chickens, and rabbits, and were self-sufficient in a remote region surrounded by woods and fields. "My father became a greengrocer and, with a wagon and a blind horse, traveled from village to village in the late 1940s, selling vegetables from our garden," Elke said. "That's how we survived. We were very poor and had no material goods, but we had each other. We enjoyed the outdoors, and my childhood was lovely."

Parcels of food and clothing were sent by relatives in America, and the girls wore shoes they received; the boys went barefoot. With one more sister born, Elke had five siblings. Post-war schools were overcrowded with refugee children—many teachers had been killed in the war. Her first school was held in the lobby of an old hotel.

When Elke was 12, her parents divorced. "It was hard, as I was asked which parent I wanted to live with as my family was being split up," Elke said. "I chose my father, and along with an older sister and brother, we moved to Hamburg, Germany." Her mother, Elke's younger sister, and two brothers later moved to a coal mining city in Germany. "Our lives were separated. It was traumatic, but we eventually overcame all that. I saw my brothers and sister periodically and only saw my mother once when I was 13 and not again until twenty-five years later." Her father remarried, and at age 13, Elke had a new baby brother. At school, she was best at languages and played the recorder for a year. "My father played classical music LPs in the evenings at home. All was calm and beautiful."

After high school, Elke went to Edinburgh, Scotland, as an au pair to a nice family with two little girls. The family were acquaintances of her father's.

"Thinking I should meet people my own age, the family took me to the local International House, where students socialized," Elke said. There, at age 17, Elke met Ali from Somaliland (an autonomous region in northern Somalia), who was studying at the Edinburgh Medical School. When the relationship turned serious, her family encouraged her to become a nurse if she was going to marry and move with her physician husband to Africa. She returned to Hamburg, went to nursing school, and continued their long-distance relationship.

At 20, Elke married Ali in Hamburg with a few witnesses. Because one had to be at least 21 to marry in Germany, her father had to approve the marriage of his underage daughter. They moved to Hargeisa, Somaliland's northern part, where Elke gave birth to their first son on a very hot night with only a nurse assisting, because her husband—the first medical doctor in Somaliland—was in Russia for a seminar. Her husband's younger brother and sister, who were of high school age and spoke English, came to live with Elke while he traveled.

"Life was good," Elke said. "We had all the comforts of a Western house. Sirad, my shrouded-in-black mother-in-law, thought that as a white woman, I was too thin and pale and milk would do me good. So a cow and servant for milking was brought, and I began to make butter. From then on, there was plenty of delicious cold milk to drink—since the usual camel milk did not agree with me."

When her husband was called to work in the capital city of Mogadishu, they relocated there. With her nurse training, Elke helped out occasionally in a pharmacy, giving antibiotic shots to the Somali women who were shy with male doctors. There was rampant political corruption, the environment was tense, medical supplies were stolen, and a civil war was brewing. The northern part of Somalia was under a British protectorate; the southern part, Italian. Fighting broke out when the country sought independence. "It was impossible to attain democracy with a tribal system. The political situation became unbearable for my husband," Elke said.

After living two years in Somaliland, Elke and Ali moved to Bonn, Germany, where their second son was born. Later, when Canada needed nurses and physicians, they relocated to Ottawa, where Elke worked as a "graduate nurse," a rank under a registered nurse, since her German nursing papers were not fully accepted in Canada. With two small children and very little money, they had a third child, a daughter.

The family moved to different parts of Canada and lived for five years on the remote island of Norway House, which had no stores, no TV, no roads, and no cars. Their food came twice a year: by barge in the summer on Lake Winnipeg or by tractor train on the frozen lake in the winter. Elke took her sons to school in a motorboat—the rivers and lakes were the highways. There was no junior high school, and when their eldest son was turning 12, they moved to New Brunswick and later to Glace Bay, Nova Scotia. Ali's three nephews from Somaliland, orphaned as teens, came to live with them, and the couple helped them get university educations.

After living thirty-six years in Canada, Elke's husband returned to Somaliland when their youngest son was in the university. Ali wanted to return to his country, where he built a lab and clinic, and Elke did not want to leave Glace Bay. "There were no animosities," Elke said. Ali remarried, and he and Elke remained good friends.

A Performing Musician and Community Activist

When she was 50, Elke saw a notice in the newspaper about a woman starting a community band in Glace Bay. Music had been an important part of Elke's life growing up with her father in Hamburg. With her children grown, she was excited about this venture and went to the meeting. No one there had had musical training. Loving the sound of the clarinet, she chose a B-flat clarinet to learn on and took a few lessons. "We sounded pretty good after a couple of years," Elke said. She became part of the Glace Bay Community Band, playing with them for three years until the group folded. At age 55, she started playing with the Second Wind Community Band of Cape Breton.

In the meantime, her hands became arthritic and she couldn't continue playing the B-flat clarinet. Her youngest brother, Thomas, the only family member remaining in Hamburg—a freelance professional musician—suggested she try the bass clarinet. It's larger and taller than a standard clarinet, and the player uses keys to cover the holes rather than her fingers. After she heard Thomas play with the North German Orchestra at the United Nations and Carnegie Hall in New York, they visited instrument shops in New York City. "Thomas tested several clarinets in sound booths and chose a tall bass clarinet for me," Elke said. "I've been playing it since age 63. Playing music is uplifting. It's a stress-buster and makes you happy." She's joined by like-minded people in the community band, made up of a cross section of the area's populace, including high school students, physicians, plumbers, teachers, housewives, and veterans. "I'm the oldest," she said proudly. The band performs two to three concerts annually, raising funds for community needs.

When she was 58, Elke read in her local paper that Glace Bay's town hall was slated for demolition. It was a beautiful old brick building in bad shape. "I wanted to help, and that was my New Year's resolution." When she told a friend she wanted to get involved and save the building, her friend said, "I wouldn't touch it!" Elke nonetheless contacted the press and local television station and requested that a woman radio reporter be a spokeswoman for the cause. They had no name for the effort—they were just a group of concerned citizens. Elke led the way and organized a meeting. Because she was so shy, she enrolled in a public speaking course. "I wanted to get over my shyness. It was crazy! I couldn't even say my name in front of three people!" One hundred supporters showed up at the first meeting. "We didn't want the building to become a parking lot. It was a rainy, sleeting, snowy day, and we went into the building through broken doors, with no heat and leaking foundation walls, and met in the upstairs council chambers."

The Friends of Old Town Hall was formed. After learning it would take $50,000 to tear the building down, the Friends suggested getting the $50,000 as seed money to save the building. "While unable to obtain these municipal funds, we worked for four years to raise the seed money for the Glace Bay Heritage Museum with the Glace Bay Heritage Museum Society and the Glace Bay Historical Society. We produced a recipe and history book in Cape Breton with entries from people with connections to the building—selling over four thousand copies. We applied for government funds, and the woman minister of heritage took a personal interest in the building's restoration, which helped," said Elke. Federal funding of $500,000 was allocated for the first phase, along with other government funds and private donations, and renovations continued. A new roof was added to the five-story building, windows were replaced, the Heritage Museum was created, and a gift shop was added. Exhibits were developed, including one on the history and heritage of Jewish people in Glace Bay. The area was known for its coal mining industries and still maintains its vibrant fisheries. A mining exhibit displays tools and equipment with facts about how badly the coal miners were treated, and a fishery exhibit depicts a mural of Glace Bay Harbour in the 1940s when the swordfish industry thrived.

Elke's brother Ernst "Goller" Gramatzki, a taxidermist and artist whose work is displayed throughout the United States, made sculptures of a pit horse used underground in the mines, donated supplies, and created permanent exhibits. Since Goller's death, his legacy has been documented as one of the museum's Heritage Heroes.

The heritage building, housing the Glace Bay Heritage Museum, Bookstore, and Old Town Hall gift shop, was reopened to the public in a grand centennial celebration in 2003 at the Old Town Hall site. At one time, the building held the mayor's office, council chamber, courtroom and judges' chambers, jail, and the police and fire department with stables and haylofts for the engine horses in the back. Guglielmo Marconi, the inventor of wireless communication, is memorialized in the mayor's office. The building evokes many great stories brought alive through exhibits and tours led by volunteers.

Elke has been committed to this elegant town centerpiece through the

Glace Bay Heritage Museum Society. She has enjoyed ushering visitors around the building and regaling them with stories from the past. One of her favorite stories is about the town's first magistrate, A. B. MacGillivray, who had no legal training but was appointed to the position because of his common sense. When a local was defending himself and said, "As God is my judge, I am not guilty," MacGillivray responded, "He's not, I am, and you are."

"It's a pleasure to volunteer there," Elke said. She sees herself as a "jack-of-all-trades"—conducting tours, raising funds, and writing grants. "I don't like fundraising, though it's critical. It's also important to have a good rapport with the press and the community."

Compelled to take action, Elke also became involved in an environmental cause when green space was threatened. Arrangements were being made behind closed doors to erect a huge thirty-foot-high monolithic concrete monument in Cape Breton Highland National Park. It was to commemorate fallen soldiers who never came home. The plans also included making three hundred parking spaces within the park. It concerned Green Cove on the eastern shore, in the pink granite area of the park—an interesting place where geologists from universities bring students to study the unique rock formations.

"It was crazy to ruin nature this way," Elke said. "My heart told me I needed to fight this. It was my duty to help and make it right. It would be a great tragedy for nature. Many people in the north responded, and I got many local people involved. There was an enormous outcry, and the cause was taken up nationally and internationally. The old government had no appetite for anything beautiful in life—they only supported war efforts." Fighting the monument required writing many letters and driving to numerous meetings two hours from her home—often through snowstorms.

"Fortunately, the then-new government with its dynamic, smart woman minister of the environment rallied behind the cause and pointed out that there was a mandate for parks to 'preserve nature for future generations.' The monument proposal was rejected. We worked very hard for more than two years. We won the fight!"

She continues to perform with the concert band and was delighted when a concert's proceeds provided a music program for the local hospice. "For people extremely ill and near the end of their days, music increases their quality of life."

When Elke was in her 40s, she finally reunited with her North American siblings for the first time when her brother hosted a family reunion in Wisconsin. "It was so wonderful to see my brothers and sister after so many years. From that point on, we started a reunion tradition every four years in different places."

Elke celebrated her 75th birthday for more than two weeks with twenty-five family members who came from Germany, Vermont, California, and across eastern Canada to spend time with her and each other in Nova Scotia—hiking, going to the beach, enjoying a dinner at the Heritage Museum. Her three sons, her daughter, and grandchildren were there. "It was the first time some of our relatives met each other. It was an exciting and very special time."

She was pleased to take her visiting granddaughter to a special celebration and memorial service for coal miners in the town, attended by hundreds of people gathered around the Heritage Museum. The Men of the Deeps, the coal miners' chorus who have been singing for more than fifty years, performed. Summers are busy with activities and family and friends visiting, so she stays at home. Off-season, she travels to Vermont and visits her children; she also hopes to go to Germany.

Elke enjoys gardening on her home's three acres. "It's beautiful and looks like a park and overlooks the ocean and trees. One acre is fenced off for my dog—a terrier and black Lab mix."

Thoughts and Advice About Risk

"Mostly I do something because my heart tells me to do it," Elke said. "I do with my heart more than my brain. It was a risk going to meetings—

to fight against building a monument in a national park. When your heart says something isn't right, try to do the right thing. For example, taking in my orphaned nephews and helping them get an education was doing the right thing.

"A risk must have a social meaning for me—the betterment of world and society. However, I would not risk going into politics. I have very strong ethical values and would not be willing to compromise.

"Whether taking up the clarinet and playing in a concert band in my 50s, 60s, and 70s was a risk, I don't know. I didn't know much about making music, architecture, fundraising, or fighting rich businessmen with government connections—but I learned as I went along.

"My advice to other women is 'You must have the ability to commit—not one week this, one week that. You must choose your line of interest. I don't play golf, bridge, or go to Florida every year—I'm not that kind of person. Follow your heart and stick it out. Music wasn't easy—many times I sucked. During bad weather I didn't feel like going to practice, but I was committed as part of the orchestra—and needed to be there. Playing uplifted me and made me happy—I find it rewarding.'"

An exuberant, cheerful, and grateful woman, Elke says, "I am proud of how my children turned out and the African boys who lived with us who consider me their mother. We were able to put them on the right path.

"I'm very happy and content and am pleased I am accepted in my community. It's a good life."

Elke playing the bass clarinet

Photo by Tessalyn MacNeil

EMILY TRASK-EATON, DO*

Medical School Graduate at 56; Attending Physician at 59

BIRTH YEAR: 1946

Coming from a long line of seafaring Mainers, Emily Trask-Eaton was raised on Mount Desert Island. A musically gifted, athletic, strong-willed, outdoorsy girl, she was a daredevil and loved spontaneous fun. She sang and played the piano, organ, and drums as a young girl, later earning college and graduate degrees in music. An interest in crafts led to an entrepreneurial retail career. Balancing art with her childhood science and medicine interests, she took a long and circuitous route to becoming a physician, entering medical school at 51.

Earlier Years

A fearless child, Emily, known as Emmy Lou after her grandmother Emily and her aunt Louise, grew up in a beautiful Maine home built in the 1880s in the fishing village of Bernard. The fourth child of five and the second daughter, Emmy spent an idyllic childhood, much of it outdoors, enjoying summers in her mother's Moore family home on Gott's Island off Mount Desert Island.

While he was in high school, Emmy's father, Orville Trask, gave students rides to school in his car. One of the students, Esther Moore, an island girl boarding on the mainland, didn't like him. After graduating,

---

**A doctor of osteopathic medicine is a licensed physician practicing in all areas of medicine, with additional training in osteopathic manipulative therapy.*

Orville moved to Chicago and married, but he divorced and returned to Maine. Esther had a change of heart about him and they married. Following generations of Trask fishermen, he became a lobsterman, fishing two hundred traps. "My dad loved fishing and being out on the water," Emmy said. "He knew the bottom of the ocean like the back of his hand.

"Probably because our family needed more money, my father got a teaching certificate and was a junior high school substitute teacher when I was a student there." He died of a heart attack at 52 when she was a high school freshman. "His death was hard for our family," said Emmy. "My family was poor, though we didn't know it. Everyone in our community was at the same economic level; there was no disparity. We all knew the community cared about us, and everyone looked out for the kids." Careful with their limited funds, her family recycled everything.

Emmy's mother, Esther, and her family grew up in a double-peaked white house on top of the hill, visible as you approach Gott's Island. As a child, her mother played with the Micmac tribe's children who came to the island to gather sweet grass to weave baskets. Gott's Island was a thriving fishing community year-round, but the population now consists almost exclusively of seasonal residents. The death of Emmy's grandfather Philip led to her grandmother Lavinia "Viney" Moore leaving the island to live with her children. That marked the beginning of the year-round community's decline, because the general store and post office in the back of their home closed when he died.

Ruth Moore, Emmy's aunt, became a significant literary figure, publishing numerous novels, books of poetry, and short stories. Her book *Spoonhandle* was on the *New York Times* best-seller list and made into the movie *Deep Waters*. Aunt Ruth, or "Uppy," as she was known to the family, lived with her longtime author companion, Eleanor Mayo.

Emmy's mother had a degree in English and taught school before marrying. "My soft-spoken, intelligent mother never imposed herself on anyone and often read by the kerosene stove," Emmy said.

Athletic, Emmy climbed to the tops of trees and did whatever the boys did but tried to do it better. "Each of the kids in my family had our own boat—mine was a little scow." Emmy rode her bike everywhere and played sandlot baseball with the neighborhood kids.

At age 11, she began working during the summers to pay for school clothes. She babysat the children of women working in the fish-packing factory. "One day, because I didn't hear the factory whistle blow indicating I needed to babysit the children, I didn't respond and was fired." Later, she waitressed.

Her grandmother paid for Emmy's piano lessons as a young girl. She began drumming in junior high school and later played in the high school band. She enjoyed gym class and cheerleading and was a good runner. In church, she played the organ and sang in the choir.

Sundays were often picnic days with other families on different islands. Her family went out on her dad's thirty-eight-foot boat. "We had no fear on the boat," Emmy said.

At 16, Emmy went with her aunt Ruth and Eleanor to New York City, where Ruth met with her editors at William Morrow and Company. "We had an amazing lunch at the publishing firm, seated around a giant circular table in a private room with a ten-foot-high fruit arrangement. They were playing up to my aunt, who was, by this time, a respected, renowned author."

Her family often went to Ruth and Eleanor's home for Sunday dinner, where Emmy and her siblings sang and played instruments—Emmy played piano. "It was a lot of fun. I put many of Uppy's poems to music and we performed them. Ruth and Eleanor were wonderful mentors to me and my siblings."

Emmy enrolled at Bard College in Annandale-on-Hudson, New York, and helped pay for her education by working on campus and, between terms, as a psychiatric nurse's aide at a Philadelphia mental hospital. Initially signing up for math and science classes because of her interest in medicine, she switched to psychology and then to music.

"I shifted from the left brain science side to the right brain music side," Emmy said.

After receiving a bachelor of arts degree in music, she married fellow Bard student Jim Eaton. They moved to Champaign-Urbana, Illinois, where Emmy got a master's degree in music from the University of Illinois. She gave private piano and voice lessons, volunteered directing the town's information center, helped organize a community day care, ran candidates' campaigns for school board, and worked part-time in the university library.

They returned to Maine with their two young daughters, eventually moving to Waldoboro in the midcoast, and bought an old Federal-style house. Interested in crafts, Emmy established a retail operation called House on the Hill in their home, selling goods from Maine craftspeople. Sewing, knitting, and making the children's clothing, she grew tired of the repetition. She relocated the crafts store and later bought the local 5 & 10 store. For a while, she kept both stores operating, and then she closed House on the Hill.

Pursuing Medical School

Years later, Emmy asked herself, *Now what? What haven't I done?* "There have been moments in my life when the sun popped through the clouds. The answer was clear." Always interested in being a doctor, she learned about becoming a doctor of osteopathy (DO). "At age 47, I talked to an admissions counselor at the University of New England [UNE] and asked, 'Am I too old?' He asked, 'How old will you be in seven years? If you go to medical school, how old will you be in seven years?' His encouragement was what I needed." Years before, when she was a high school senior, her doctor asked what she wanted to do after graduating. When she responded that she wanted to be a doctor, he said, "You can't do that! You're a girl!" "I wasn't aware at the time how much of a deterrent this was to pursuing medical school, but looking back, it was. I [had] really admired that man.

"I had last taken biology in high school and had no science in college, so my pre-med classes at age 48 were a real shock." Emmy took basic science courses at the University of Maine at Augusta, and became a local emergency medical technician with her husband. She was admitted to the University of New England and the University of Vermont (UVM).

Emmy entered medical school at UVM at age 51. Initially, she and her husband kept the store going, but they sold it when it became too difficult to manage.

Medical school proved daunting. "It was a huge volume of material to absorb in a short time," Emmy said. She didn't do well in her courses and was asked to leave after one year. Feeling discouraged, she was offered a sales job with a pharmaceutical firm, but she didn't want to pursue that: she still wanted to be a doctor. Having been accepted at the University of New England the prior year, and with her husband's encouragement, she called the college in June and asked if she could apply again. They told her they would honor her previous admission but that no seats were available for the fall. "On the first Tuesday in September, the dean of the medical school called me and said, 'A seat has come up. I have to know by the end of the day and you must be here Thursday at 8:00 a.m.' On Wednesday, I rented a tiny house in Biddeford on the beach. It was important where I lived. I needed to be on the water and have scenic beauty to get me through." On Thursday, she was in her seat as requested, knowing what she was facing as she began her second first year.

There were two more years of on-campus lectures and studying. "I doubt I would have made it without my study partners," she said. Her third-year rotations were split between Lancaster Hospital, in the heart of Pennsylvania's Amish country, where she stayed in student housing; and in Lewiston and Bangor, Maine. Her final year, she worked in several private offices. "It wasn't easy being separated, but Jim was on board. We have always supported each other in pursuing our goals."

Emmy received a DO degree from the University of New England in 2002 at 56.

Typically, graduates and family medicine physicians intern for one year, followed by a two-year residency. Emmy started at Maine-Dartmouth Family Practice in Augusta but didn't measure up to some of the attendings' expectations. She was asked to extend her internship an additional six months. "If you're told you're not good enough so many times, you start to believe it, and I wondered if I should continue," Emmy said. "The third-year residents generously gave their time and tutored me through that period. And I don't give up easily." Finally, she was promoted to full resident.

Wooed by Michigan State, she transferred to a teaching family practice in Bay City. She was treated well; her trainers had respect for her unique skills and life experience, and patiently brought her up to speed. A friend said data showed she was the "oldest new resident in the country" at that time. Emmy had a wonderful experience, despite seeing a cardiologist there as a patient. "One day at lunch, my cardiology mentor took the time to listen to my story of chest pain with no abnormal test results. He said, 'You need a cardiac catheterization.' I wound up with my first cardiac stent. I told him, 'Maybe you didn't save my life, but you saved my quality of life.'"

An Attending Physician at 59

Two months before her 60th birthday, Emily Trask-Eaton, DO, began practicing as a family physician at Miles Family Practice (now Lincoln Health) in Waldoboro, her hometown community. She opted not to take on patients who were friends. "I wanted to have boundaries between friendships and professional relationships and didn't want to have to tell a friend, as a patient, that they had cancer or to know their deepest secrets."

With numerous changes in the health care field, physicians face many challenges. "There is an increased volume of paperwork—lots of insurance and prior-authorization forms to complete for patients—and there are big issues with uninsured people—inability to pay and unable to get care, so when they finally come in, they are even sicker and cost more to treat—though that was improved for some by the Affordable Care Act," Emmy said. "A physician must meet benchmarks to prove their successful management of patients' medical problems. Pay is partly dependent on outcomes and will become more so over time." For example, if, after Dr. Trask-Eaton talked with her patients about the importance and benefits of getting a flu shot or other health maintenance issues, they chose not to follow her advice, her work of counseling didn't count. It was the result, or outcome, of the work for which she was paid, not the actual work itself. "Regardless of how much time a physician spends talking about the benefits of flu shots, or management of their diabetes, and so on, many patients decide not to get one and the physician loses a portion of pay.

"I like talking with people and enjoyed being in the room with my patients. That is why I went into medicine. I used my knowledge of psychology, my life skills background, and my medical knowledge as well as my mothering skills. The Waldoboro 5 & 10 store was the heart of the community, and I did more than just sell products. I counseled people about running their homes and their lives. I enjoy problem solving. You use the broadest base of knowledge in family practice.

"Being a physician is prestigious (though less so than in the past) but very hard work. It's important to do something worthwhile with people, and that was my ultimate reason for doing what I did. I was always interested in being a doctor. In elementary school, the principal visited our classroom and went around the room asking us what we wanted to do. I said I wanted to go into medicine. He commended me and said, 'Look what Emmy wants to do—she wants to help people.' We didn't discuss what position I would be—for example, doctor or nurse. I expect we would have disagreed."

Active in politics throughout her life, Emmy ran for state representative from Waldoboro several times—and was not elected. "I'm still interested in politics but have to limit my exposure, as it is so stressful."

Emmy enjoys gardening and quilting—she likes piecing, cutting, and blending colors and patterns. "I would have been a textile artist had I known that was an option," she said.

"I would like to travel and visit Saint Pierre-et-Miquelon, the only remnant of New France in the Atlantic Ocean, off the coast of Newfoundland." After fifty years of not being able to go to Cuba, she finally visited the country she had heard so much about as a teenager. She would like to see the Galapagos Islands, Alaska, Iceland, and Greenland. "Travel is always stimulating and teaches you more about yourself than anything else, but my idea of a real vacation is to go to Bernard, sit on the porch, and watch the boats and birds.

"I'm proud of my family—my parents, my siblings, and my daughters Alison and Katherine. I greatly admired my aunt Ruth and her many writings, and am pleased her books were brought back into circulation by Maine publisher Gary Lawless. My upbringing formed the roots of my liberalism.

"Today, there are more options for women—such as in sports. There are team sports and individual sports—like running and going to the gym. I loved the feeling of running as a child, but I have a bad knee now, so I walk. I lift weights and work out every morning on an elliptical." Emmy likes trying new things, gets bored with repetition, and admits that once she figures things out, she moves on as she did as a child.

Thoughts and Advice About Risk

"I think of risk as an adventure—it's not fearful, it's a challenge. I'm probably not a true risk taker. The risky things I did as a child were done in ignorance and the arrogance of youth. I wouldn't travel to certain areas of the world now, for example. It feels dangerous, and I can find plenty of things to do and experience in Maine and the United States.

"I suppose I risked failing when I went to medical school and at other times in my life, but it's okay to fail. The costs incurred with medical school, however, are a challenge and probably one of the biggest risks I've taken. I'm still paying off my loans even in retirement.

"I would definitely do the things I did—like buying the 5 & 10 store with minimal business experience and running the successful House on the Hill. Luckily I was a quick learner." Despite her athletic background, Emmy says, "I'm not interested in physical risks like skydiving, which may be exhilarating, but I don't need to do that."

For other women interested in pursuing a medical degree later in life, Emmy says, "Be prepared to be beaten up! You have to have your armor on as an older female. You are not seen as being as competent as a male doctor. You may be seen as taking space from a young person. But there's a balance. There have been many wonderful people that cheered me on. Friends gave me a party and money before I went to UNE. That's how I paid for my textbooks. Many attendings provided time and support at difficult moments. It's also critical to talk with the admissions director."

Emmy retired as a full-time physician at age 69, ten years after starting her career. She then took a part-time, temporary "locum tenens" position. Reflecting on her experience, she says, "I think my strength as a doctor is listening carefully and explaining the complicated medical system and medical problems to people in a simple way. I am visual and often draw pictures of what I am trying to describe to patients. A doctor is not a friend, but an adviser and interpreter or teacher who brings order to the chaos of medicine. However, it is impossible not to form strong relationships with some patients. If you listen to your patients carefully, they will always tell you what is wrong. It is humbling to see how people deal with adversity, either emotional or physical, and how they simply carry on with their lives in spite of the misfortune of a bad diagnosis, whether random, genetic, or self-inflicted.

"I would not change my decision to do what I did for anything."

Emily Trask-Eaton, DO

Photo by Daphne Lehava Stern

KIM McFARLANE

Donated Her Kidney to a Stranger at 52

BIRTH YEAR: 1962

Kim was a shy, introverted child and young adult growing up in Florida with a brother. She was a dirt-bike-riding tomboy who married at 17 and had a son. The family lived along the East Coast, and when her son was in high school, her navy husband left. She later remarried, and retired after a career in banking. While line dancing, she met a woman kidney donor who inspired her. Just before her 53rd birthday, Kim donated her kidney to a stranger.

Earlier Years

Born and raised in Central Florida with a younger brother, Kim spent most of her free time playing outside all day, hanging around the pond in their yard and going to the beach. Living on a dirt road, she enjoyed riding the dirt bike her dad bought her. "I was a bit of a daredevil when young," Kim said.

After her parents divorced, Kim lived with her mom and saw her dad frequently. She found a garter snake in the yard and kept it for six months before letting it go. Three pet armadillos named Amos, Andy, and Kingfisher hung out in a pen. When the armadillos were small, they came along on a family road trip to visit her grandmother in Virginia.

In high school, she worked as a grocery store cashier to earn gas money for her car. At 17, she married a man who was in the navy, and they moved along the Eastern Seaboard to different places where he was stationed. Kim had a son and attended college classes in Charleston, South Carolina, but wasn't motivated to continue. She worked for a time as a teacher's assistant at a nursery school. Later, living in Saratoga, New York, she fell into banking with the help of a friend who worked for a credit union. Seeing Kim as a "people person," her friend suggested she apply for a teller position. She got into the lending field after a management shake-up and some underwriting experience and courses, and became a loan officer, which she enjoyed.

At 37, just before her husband left her when her son was in high school, Kim got her first tattoo. It was her zodiac sign, Pisces—two fish. The tattoo artist said two types of people get tattoos: those who get one during their life, and those who return for many more. He predicted Kim would return.

Kim's more than thirty tattoos are primarily from photographs of favorite places she's been—a conch shell from Key West; around her right arm from her shoulder to below her elbow, a Caribbean coral reef; and three life-size iguanas seen in Aruba that extend from her hip to below her knee. "Some people have their spider veins removed; I just covered mine up," Kim said.

She remarried at 39 to Blair, a member of the credit union where she was a teller. Always wanting to ride a motorcycle, Kim got her license at age 45 and rode smaller bikes, promising herself she would get a Harley at age 50. Five years later, she got a 1600 cc Harley-Davidson Electra Glide touring bike. Her husband, who had never ridden a motorcycle, rode on hers for three years before getting his own.

Interested in helping veterans, Kim and Blair became volunteer Patriot Guard Riders. In New York, Kim was one of the few women captains. She had heard about the Patriot Guard Riders from a friend and mistakenly assumed you had to be a veteran to join. Her family has extensive military service experience—her grandfather was in the navy; her dad, in the marines; her ex-husband was in the navy; her brother is a retired marine; and her son is an air force veteran. At the invitation of families at veterans' funerals, they ride in procession—the organization's primary mission. Riders also participate in special ceremonies and greet veterans at airports who are returning from duty. For an honor flight, Patriot Guard Riders led a procession of three hundred motorcycles converging at the airport to send off veterans to Washington, DC, to be honored for their service.

Kim enjoys participating in veterans' events and has become close to vets she has met through years of volunteering. In New York, where they formerly lived, Kim and her husband adopted a 93-year-old vet, taking him out for motorcycle rides on her husband's three-wheeler. She and Blair also liked treating vets to meals at their local diner. "I always wanted to be one of the guys. Now I am one," Kim said.

She and her husband have been on numerous motorcycle trips for pleasure. They drove four thousand miles from Cohoes, New York, to Oklahoma, passing through eighteen states, and went to Virginia Beach with a stop in York, Pennsylvania, to tour the Harley-Davidson motorcycle factory and the Hershey factory. They visited the Outer Banks as well as Chincoteague and Assateague. With other motorcyclists, they toured Vermont up to the Lake Champlain Islands in Canada.

Inspired by a National Public Radio story about altruism, featuring a woman who donated her kidney to a stranger, Kim thought, *I could do this*. She tried getting information but didn't find much and let the idea pass. Four years later while line dancing, a woman dancer said she had donated a kidney to her husband when she was 63. She told Kim about the Northeast Kidney Foundation. Checking online, Kim also found the Kidney Connection website and its stories about people living in New York who needed a kidney, and the Living Kidney Donors Network, which "educates people in need of a kidney transplant about living donations."

Donating Her Kidney to a Stranger

One of the people looking for a kidney donor was Thomas, a 35-year-old man living in her hometown. He had the same blood type as Kim. His wife, Hillary, had posted his story. He'd been born with a genetic disorder, and his kidney was working at only 15 percent capacity. He had been waiting for a kidney for nearly two years. Kim sent Hillary an email on August 25, 2014, and Hillary replied almost immediately.

To find out if she was a match for Thomas, Kim went to the Center for Donation and Transplant at Albany Medical Center. From her first blood test in September 2014, Kim was a match for Thomas, meeting five of the six markers. The "protein" marker was not a match since she wasn't part of his family. She took further tests, including a CAT scan, electrocardiogram, and numerous blood tests.

Kim assumed the transplant center was keeping Thomas and Hillary posted on her testing progress. She was surprised at the end of October when she received a message from Hillary saying they appreciated Kim's willingness to be tested, but since they hadn't heard anything from her, they assumed she was no longer interested in donating her kidney to Thomas.

"On the contrary," Kim replied immediately, "all is looking good and I am committed to being Thomas's donor." She had not realized that patient privacy laws prevented the center from sharing her information. From that point on, Kim kept Thomas and Hillary posted on her testing, which moved along well.

After enduring multiple tests, Kim had a three-and-a-half-hour psychiatric evaluation. "I knew I was healthy, and I didn't have any concerns about my mental health, but the thought of a long psychiatric evaluation made me nervous," she confessed.

The transplant center does not encourage potential kidney donors to meet their recipients before surgery, because a donor might not like the intended recipient and change their mind. However, the center staff said it was okay if they wished to meet each other. Kim, Blair, and their 32-year-old son agreed to meet Thomas and Hillary at a local coffee shop. They hit it off immediately and talked for four hours.

Thomas explained that he started losing kidney function in his 20s and was feeling sicker in his 30s. Kim also learned that Hillary had recently received a diagnosis of chronic myeloid leukemia, a type of cancer. Their 6-year-old daughter had neurofibromatosis, which causes tumors to grow in the nervous system. Coincidentally, they discovered she attended the school where Blair was a substitute teacher.

Five months after Kim started the testing, her case was reviewed by the transplant center's ethics committee, which focuses on "Do no harm." Thomas would be receiving beneficial surgery, but Kim had no need for surgery, and it could be harmful to her. With approval from the ethics committee, Kim met with an independent kidney specialist who reviewed her tests for her prognosis for living with one kidney. "I was told about all the possible things that could happen—like developing hernias or scar tissue around the bowels." She also met with a male nurse, an independent donor advocate. His job was to look out for Kim's interests up to the surgery. He advised her that she could cancel for any reason with no questions asked. "I'm the kind of person who follows through on commitments," she said. "Everyone was so nice, caring, informative, and provided me with lots of resources during the entire process."

Kim always felt her kidney would go to Thomas after she saw his profile and underwent the tests to determine if she was a match. Hillary was particularly apprehensive, because they had thought once before that they had a donor for her husband and it hadn't worked out. Kim reassured Thomas and Hillary. "I am committed. It will be all right. I never had a negative thought about it."

Kim and Thomas were scheduled for a final pre-op test together. The doctor needed to check Thomas's potassium level. It couldn't be above 5 for the surgery. Thomas had consistently had a potassium level over 5, so they waited anxiously for the test results. Kim felt strongly that this time, his level would be fine.

Thomas's level was 4.8. They got the go-ahead for surgery.

The surgery was in February 2015. During pre-op preparations, a member of the transplant center medical team told Kim that she was helping not only Thomas, but also someone else. Thomas would be removed from the waiting list for a cadaver kidney, and another person would benefit from that.

At the transplant center at Albany Med, no children or flowers are allowed. The center is in a separate wing of the hospital to help protect a recipient's immune system, which is completely wiped out in the procedure. "It's like rebooting a computer," Kim says. "The body has to learn how to accept its donated kidney."

Kim was told her surgery would take four to five hours. It took a little over three. "Everything went even better than a textbook case," Kim said. She left the hospital four days later. Thomas's surgery lasted three hours. He said he felt better pretty much right away. He recovered well post-surgery and left a few days after Kim. He and Hillary were excited about resuming normal activities, such as going out to a movie.

It was three weeks before Kim was out of pain. "It was not a big deal, but they cut into me in four places." There were three 1½-inch laparoscopic incisions, and her kidney had been removed by hand through a larger incision. Kim had had a few medical procedures before her kidney surgery—a C-section delivery with her son in 1983 and a hysterectomy in 2010. The kidney surgeon had gone through her C-section and hysterectomy scar for the kidney transplant. "My husband wondered if the surgeon should put a zipper along the scar," Kim said.

"There is temporary pain for a good reason. I want people to know it's not so bad.

"My care was awesome and perfect. I was diligent about following doctor's orders. This is bigger than anything else I've done. I didn't want to screw it up. I was told to wait two weeks before driving and dancing. My three dogs wondered why I didn't take them out for our usual walks right away after returning home." The only other restriction was not lifting anything over 5 pounds for three months. Standard follow-up procedures include checkups after two weeks, six months, one year, and two years post-surgery.

Kim says she received signs at different times that donating her kidney was the right thing to do. "There were people in my path that kept me knowing I was doing the right thing. I never told people I was going to be tested about donating a kidney. I just said, 'I'm donating my kidney.'"

Because she and her husband are vegetarians, Thanksgiving is not a big deal for them. They volunteered to deliver meals on the holiday to benefit an organization helping domestic violence victims. On Thanksgiving 2014, as she and Blair sat waiting with other volunteers to deliver meals around Albany, a guy near her overheard her say she was donating a kidney. He turned around and thanked her. He had been a kidney recipient years earlier.

"When I'm asked, 'How could you donate your kidney to a stranger?' I say, 'Because I can.'"

Before her surgery, Kim and Blair decided to move south because they preferred warmer weather over cooler upstate New York. They sold their home just two weeks before the surgery. Later, they rented a town house in Florida and then bought a home in Sarasota on the southwest coast, six miles from the beautiful white sands of Siesta Key Beach.

In Florida, Kim continues to ride. She downsized to a red Road King, 250 pounds lighter than her Electra Glide. She and Blair join other Patriot Guard Riders weekly to ride to Sarasota's National Cemetery for indigent veterans' burials. The Riders also escort the annual Wreaths Across America trucks to the local cemetery. "It's amazing to see the headstones with wreaths, including those of the indigent veterans, which makes me feel good," Kim said.

She has taken up golf and joined a line dance group that visits nursing homes. They dance for an hour and bring cowboy hats for the residents who enjoy the entertainment, clapping along with the music. At least once a week, Kim and Blair go out kayaking and see dolphins, manatees, and occasionally, alligators. Loving to travel, they plan to take more trips.

Kim added a "Donate a Life" logo tattoo to her leg with the letters *bkcthj* for the names of her and Thomas's families—Blair, Kim, Chris (her son), Thomas, Hillary, and Julia (their daughter). "I love sharing our story," Kim said. "I made the decision to become a living donor because I heard one woman's story. If someone else hears my story and decides to become a donor … awesome!"

As a kidney donor advocate, Kim participates in Advocacy Day for Organ Donors, making people aware of the need for live kidney donations. It is estimated that only 1 percent of live kidney donations are to strangers.

Kim claims she's not that patient, but the things that used to bug her are not as bothersome now, and she lets some things slide.

She stays in touch with Hillary and Thomas, who has been doing well. "We are quite close. We've become family," Kim said. Thomas's wife, Hillary, said, "Kim gave a very important piece of herself to my husband. This kidney will forever change our lives. There are no words that you can say that will ever capture how important a gift that is. Kim is our miracle. She is the true definition of a hero."

Kim is modest about her gift of life. A warm, cheerful woman, she said, "It's been a really neat experience. What started as a donation to a stranger turned into gaining a new family. People may think I'm a nice person for doing this. I have to uphold that. Not that I was a hellion, but people might believe I'm better than I am!"

Thoughts and Advice About Risk

"I was a scaredy-cat when young," Kim said. "I would never take risks—go dancing or ride on a motorcycle. To an extent, I am a risk taker. I ride a motorcycle, but I protect myself. I took the safety course, and I wear a helmet, heavy leather jacket, and heavy-duty boots. I take precautions.

"I wouldn't go parachuting. My son did it and cracked his vertebrae in his back, so I wouldn't do it. I formerly considered bungee jumping, but not now, as I think about the recuperation time it would take if something happened.

"I'm more of a spur-of-the-moment person. I don't plan ahead. If I'm on a trip and an opportunity arises, I will do it."

While Kim was vacationing in Jamaica, a guide at a river went six feet under the water, swam through a crevice under a rock, and came out the other side. "I won't be the first one to try something," Kim said. "The guide did it and I wanted to as well, so I did. Another woman in our group said no way would she do it. I said to her, 'When will you have a chance to do this again? You can do it!' I convinced her. We jumped off together and I held her hand. We swam under the rock, and after coming up, she was ecstatic and said, 'I can't believe I did that!'"

Snorkeling in Key West, Kim saw a shark, so she hung around and took awesome photos. A barracuda appeared and she followed it—"It was beautiful." Her husband was in a panic when she described the scene. "The shark wasn't interested in me," she maintained.

"A risk is something that would impact me and other people. That's why I took my husband and son into consideration with my decision to donate a kidney. I asked my husband, 'What are your thoughts?' knowing this decision would impact him. My husband was beyond supportive."

The transplant center's head physician told her that his job was to scare her. He reviewed everything that could happen. "He didn't scare me, but he educated me. My husband was nervous the day of my surgery. I had a good support team. I had full faith in the doctors and was confident in their abilities. I wasn't nervous," she said.

For others contemplating donating their kidney, Kim recommends reading as much as possible about it. "Definitely educate yourself. I read everything I could find about the process. There is a lot of information online about it, including Rock1kidney.org and the Northeast Kidney Foundation."

Since donating her kidney, Kim carries a medical alert tag ("one kidney—on right") and a "Medical ID" page on her smartphone in case she's ever in an accident and can't talk.

"Kidney donors need to be a little more aware of their surroundings. I'm more aware of risks, having only one kidney. My doctor says I shouldn't ride my motorcycle in case of an accident. I won't do anything uncomfortable now—it's not worth the risk. I'm not self-destructive and am still fine riding my motorcycle.

"I feel good and my lifestyle hasn't changed.

"If you have a once-in-a-lifetime chance to try something, go for it!" she advises. "Life is short—you only live once!"

Second day post-op, Blair, Kim, kidney recipient Thomas, and his wife, Hillary

Photo by Unknown

LYNN DINES

Pharmaceutical Executive to Peace Corps Volunteer in Morocco from 52 to 54

BIRTH YEAR: 1956

Hailing from Washington as a child and moving to the San Francisco Bay area as a young girl, Lynn experienced fun years growing up with friends and a small, close-knit family. After graduating from the University of California, Los Angeles, she enjoyed a pharmaceutical industry career. She traveled internationally and vacationed off the grid. Lynn took early retirement at 51. At 52, she joined the Peace Corps, volunteering in a rural Moroccan village. At 58, she married for the first time.

Earlier Years

The youngest of three girls, Lynn was born and spent her early childhood in Seattle. Her family and friends summered in Montana, where the kids slept in an old trapper's cabin with an outhouse. All meals were cooked outside on a woodstove, and they swam in the lake, took long walks through the woods, played endless games of cards, and read. In Seattle, Lynn walked to school and played Kick the Can and other games with the neighborhood kids. Holidays and celebrations always included the relatives in her inseparable family. At 10, she moved to Moraga, California, where her father worked for Aetna Insurance and her mother worked at home. As a teenager, Lynn babysat and worked her first sales job.

Her parents were good role models in helping others—her dad

was active with Kiwanis International and volunteer chair of the board of Goodwill International, traveling to the Philippines and China on behalf of the organization. "My dad provided a legacy of volunteerism for me and my sisters," Lynn said. "My mother volunteered through my dad's affiliations, and I observed their commitment."

Interested in the study of medicine, but not wanting to practice as a doctor, Lynn went to the University of California, Los Angeles. She held jobs on campus and volunteered with her sorority's community projects.

With an undergraduate degree in psychobiology, Lynn looked for a career that would be a good fit with her interest in medicine and business. After researching positions with pharmaceutical firms, she went into sales with Eli Lilly and Company, headquartered in Indianapolis. She climbed the corporate ladder and became a sales and marketing executive, traveling to different regions and working from Indiana and California. "The pharmaceutical industry gets bad raps, but they do amazing and ethical work. I was invested in the firm. The people I worked with are good friends to this day," Lynn said.

During vacations, she traveled off the beaten path in South Africa, Botswana, Kenya, Peru, Turkey, Bali, Bhutan, China, and Europe. On safari with friends in Tanzania, she visited a women's cooperative in a village where the husband of a woman named Mama Anna, as his family spokesman, talked about receiving a cow from Heifer International. This livestock gift brought them productivity to invest and allowed them to use their land more efficiently for crops. Lynn was impressed with the effectiveness of Heifer's model. Mama Anna had transformed her community beginning with one cow, leading to Lynn's support for Heifer.

Because she was able to and could afford it, Lynn took early retirement at age 51 after twenty-nine years with Eli Lilly. Her parents died the year after she retired, and she explored options about what to do next. "I became a more active volunteer and wanted to stay busy.

"There was no seminal moment that sparked my interest in joining the Peace Corps," Lynn said when she checked out the organization's opportunities, attended meetings, and read lots of blogs from volunteers in the field. After completing the extensive application process—paperwork, interviews, and medical exam—Lynn was accepted as a Peace Corps volunteer. She opted to have the Peace Corps choose the place and position most appropriate for her skills, experience, and background.

Peace Corps Volunteer

In the Peace Corps, Lynn began her twenty-seven months' service, including three months' pre-assignment training, to prepare for working in Morocco. At age 52, she headed to Philadelphia for "staging" to learn about regulations and meet other volunteers. Lynn was assigned as an adviser within the Small Business Development sector. In Morocco for in-country pre-service training, she went to Rabat for several days, followed by intensive language training in Azrou in the Atlas Mountains.

While living with volunteers in a hostel, Lynn was to learn Darija, the official, unwritten Moroccan Arabic language. Organized into small groups for community-based training, they were given a language and culture facilitator/teacher.

Lynn traveled to her learning site town of Ain Leuh (southwest of Azrou) and lived with a host family—the father, a mason; the mother, president of the Weaving Cooperative; and their two children. Quickly introduced to the area, Lynn met lots of family and women's collective and community members. Celebrations with music and dancing, tea and sweets, were everywhere. Ramadan and fasting started after Lynn arrived. Darija lessons began—conversations in Arabic.

Assigned to the Berber village of Ribat El Kheir with thirteen thousand people, an hour's drive from Fes, the largest town in the area, Lynn was to work with the Adwal ("connectedness") Women's Weaving Cooperative. Morocco is a leader in crafts production—the government promotes the large handicraft market. The country is home to a rich weaving history, and there are a variety of carpet styles—from deep-pile hand-knotted *zrbya* to the more intricately patterned weave *hanbl.* Nomadic Berbers have woven products for personal use and created patterns from their environment. This cooperative produced some of the best carpets in the country and had been formed several years before Lynn's arrival. Lynn was to teach the women skills to manage the organization's finances, market their products for profit, build capacity and sustainability, and implement succession planning.

Posted for two years in Ribat El Kheir, Lynn initially lived with another host family—the parents were teachers with four daughters. The Peace Corps requires two months in homestays before volunteers get their own place to live. After living with her host family, Lynn rented an apartment. She had to purchase everything—small refrigerator, butane water heater, butane stovetop, furniture. Apartments are usually bare—no closets, shelves, or drawers. The souk (market) provided inexpensive stuff with which she could fill her place.

Lynn wrote in her blog, "You had to stop in many *hanuts* (stalls)—with just a counter inside a doorway. You tell the shopkeeper what you're looking for and they get it. One may have buckets, but no brooms, one may have dishes but no silverware ... Most shops have food and staples only. You poke your head in, and everything stops and everyone stares, maybe whispering *mesqina* ('poor thing') to one another while sneaking glances at you. I found that the greeting *Salam Alaikum* ('Peace to you') usually got a friendly response and a smile. Struggling to communicate, I wasn't always understood, but if I ... asked them to repeat what they said, they were patient with me. The world really is a mirror, and you get what you give" (1.6.2009).

Lynn's Achilles' heel was learning Darija. Although some people thought that older volunteers would struggle to learn a new language, Lynn said, "Perpetuating the belief could be a self-fulfilling prophecy." Learning and speaking another language also challenged young volunteers. Most volunteers were in their 20s. Language proficiency tests were administered periodically. To swear in, volunteers were expected to be at the "novice high" level. (Novice, intermediate, and advanced are the levels, with low, medium, and high within those categories.) Lynn scored at the "intermediate medium" level despite her concern about absorbing and using the language.

"You speak like a child when you're learning the language," Lynn said. She supplemented the provided tutor help with additional tutor hours she paid for to ensure she could communicate well. She had to teach and facilitate business workshops in Darija. The Cooperative women didn't speak English—they spoke the Berber Tamazight dialect or Darija and could not read and write. The illiteracy rate for women in rural Morocco is 82 percent. "Literacy is not ignorance," Lynn said. "People often equate the two erroneously. Women in the Co-op sat behind their vertical looms, hands flying, weaving intricate designs from their heads passed on through generations, while talking and singing. They walked miles from their homes to the Co-op. The women kept the machinery working. When the looms broke down, they figured out how to fix it. It wasn't the prettiest fix, but they made it work."

Children learn to read and write classical Arabic. French is the language of business. Girls' ability to stay in school is predicated on available bathrooms. Many rural schools do not have bathrooms. If girls need to use a bathroom while in school, they go home and usually don't return. Most rural schools are now getting girls' bathrooms built to encourage girls to be educated.

"It was demanding to teach the women weavers how to use a computer to create spreadsheets to budget and track expenses and revenue, and use design software to develop marketing materials—like business cards and brochures. They were not too interested in learning how to use the computer—they wanted me to do it, which was challenging." She was later able to secure grant funding to send two members to computer training.

The women Co-op members were primarily young and unmarried and not dependent upon the income. Fatima, an outstanding woman, and literate in French, traded off being the president with another woman, Zahra. They were well respected and learned how to weave, and recruited other women to join the Co-op. The government selected the Cooperative as a training site for paid weaving apprentices, which became an important source of income. Fatima was ambitious and became an elected official after the king passed a ruling requiring that 10 percent of the employees of government organizations be women. "Morocco grows strong women," Lynn said. "I was constantly impressed with the Co-op women's ingenuity and initiative outside and inside the home. The women carry a big burden for the house but didn't complain. They just get things done."

The vertical weaving looms were portable so the women could also use them in their homes. There were flat and shag weaves. Horizontal looms were used to weave fabrics to supplement the more labor-intensive and expensive vertical-loom carpets. Knitting machines were used to make leggings.

Lynn led a process for the women to develop a logo to brand their products. They selected the design and traditional colors—brown and green. She encouraged a strong sense of ownership among them and taught pricing strategy to determine how much their carpets cost to make, how to research their competition's prices, and how to set a price to earn a profit. They discussed the importance of understanding what customers want and what sells, that is, the gorgeous Berber designs. "At one point, the women chose lime green and bright pink acrylic yarn, thinking that's what tourists would want to buy, but the lack of sales provided a good lesson in knowing what customers want and expect," Lynn said.

She helped the women identify and connect to resources to aid their business. "The Peace Corps has an advantage in being on the ground, in the communities, and really knows the people." She stressed the importance of succession planning. "Building sustainability" is the Peace Corps's philosophy and goal—that is, "not doing for the native people, but to help initially and then step away as they take ownership." Lynn helped set up craft fairs so the artisans could manage the fairs themselves. "It was important that the women get to choose how they wished to have the Co-op operate." Lynn's personal slogan was "It's not what you do while you're there. It's what they do when you're gone."

Throughout Morocco, Lynn developed and led trainings in different business skills in Darija—teaching women and networking with people who could help promote the women's weavings. Lynn worked with businesspeople to create packages to promote tourism—offering visitors a day trip to the village of Ribat El Kheir to see the women at the Co-op use natural dyes and weave on the looms, participate in a "hands-on" couscous-making workshop, and view a traditional horse-driven olive press.

When Lynn realized that the women lacked adequate health care, she was able to schedule a health program with women doctors to provide mammograms for breast cancer screening and Pap smear exams to screen for cervical cancer, with follow-up for women who tested positive.

Morocco has many different terrains and weather contrasts: very hot, dry summers in the Middle Atlas Mountains; rains that bring green fields with olive trees and wildflowers; and cold and snowy winters. The dampness caused mold inside buildings.

In the heat, the electricity often goes out and there's no water. The busy wedding season occurs during the heat of the summer—a three-day affair with dinner often at two in the morning. "Everyone in town is invited and obligated to attend the party," Lynn said.

Lynn enjoyed the food, especially fresh vegetables from the souk. She liked the *harira*, traditional tomato, garbanzo bean, and pasta soup eaten with hard-boiled eggs. She learned how to make couscous from scratch with flour and water. Other delicious and plentiful foods and beverages included mint tea with lots of sugar, fava beans, cucumbers, mandarin oranges, dates, yogurt, fresh bread, olives and olive oil, chicken, lamb, and grilled goat.

Despite the good food, Lynn kept Pepto-Bismol tablets handy, especially during the summer heat when your "system was *shwiya*" ("so-so")—which also afflicted the locals. "If you suffer from the 'runs,' Imodium helps 'keep it in' you and is good to take if you're faced with a twelve-hour bus trip. Pepto-Bismol helps your system normalize faster by 'letting everything out,' so it's recommended only if you have access to a bathroom!"

Traveling required patience—taxis wait to fill with people before they move, which can take an hour or longer. "Moroccan women don't want to sit next to a man, making for interesting logistics," Lynn said. There are vans seating sixteen, but they're often overloaded with twenty-five or more people, products, and animals.

During vacations, Lynn visited a Moroccan friend she knew from California—a woman from Tangier, a much more prosperous area and a marked contrast to the village life where Lynn was. There is a huge economic disparity in Morocco, with wealthy people living primarily in the major cities and many very poor people in rural areas. On another vacation, she saw gorillas in Uganda after a strenuous hike. She returned twice to the States—once for a memorial service for a dear aunt and once at Christmas.

Adhering to Peace Corps protocol and local customs, Lynn had to inform the local chief of her whereabouts. She had a few encounters with the local chief. Once he yelled at her about a document she needed that she didn't know about at the time and sorted out later. "You learn the Gumby Game in Morocco. Go with the flow. Don't sweat the small stuff. *Swiya b swiya* ('little by little')." The chief used to check up on her and show up at the Co-op when she was on business in other towns. However, Lynn avoided the common harassment that younger women were subjected to—such as being called a "gazelle," and being closely followed and touched. Life in Morocco also requires "getting used to a lot happening at the last minute, not much planning. Things may be canceled or rescheduled."

An estimated 5 percent of Peace Corps volunteers are age 50 and over. "Being older had its advantages—especially as a woman in Morocco. People revere their mothers. I let my hair grow out its natural grey. Doors opened to me as an older American woman. I was also a novelty—a curiosity. With men, I had a lot of latitude not true for younger female volunteers. Village women would avoid the cafés, as it was presumed that only prostitutes went there. As a foreigner, I was granted a pass—I could sit in the café below my apartment—and Moroccan women visiting from Fes or Rabat would join me, as the same presumptions do not apply in the cities. Women didn't have places to meet, so the weekly souk, *hammam* (public bath), and weaving cooperative were important for the women to get together to enjoy each other's company and share stories, problems, and gossip."

Being an Older Peace Corps Volunteer*

Advantages

Respect that comes with age
Credibility
Business experience
More experience figuring out how to get things done and problem solving
Less harassment from kids and young men
Access to authorities, including government officials
More patience with and tolerance for others
Setting realistic expectations
"It's not all about us," knowing the best solution is the one that the person doing the work believes in
Confidence and the ability to bounce back from circumstances that could shake your confidence

Challenges

Weather extremes
Lack of water and electricity
Loss of privacy—your life is open to all in the community
Learning the language after being out of an academic classroom for a long time
Physical requirements, with walking being the primary means of travel
Other volunteers are mostly in their 20s and make up your key network, which some other, older volunteers had trouble with.

Common Challenges for Younger and Older Volunteers

Missing significant events in the lives of loved ones far away (Skype, email, and packages help)
Being prepared for personal and invasive questions, such as "Are you married? Do you have children? Are you fasting for Ramadan?" Chances are they are treating you like everyone else by wanting to know your business.

**(From Lynn's blog, 8.14.2009)*

"I thought of myself as being incredibly fortunate," Lynn said. "Joining the Peace Corps was an opportunity to give back."

Things Learned as a Peace Corps Volunteer*

I can have more patience than I ever thought possible.
People are people—we're basically all the same.
Friends are invaluable to happiness.
Extreme heat is harder than extreme cold.
Walking helps you see the world.

Music soothes.
Morocco's generosity is world-class.
I can learn a new language at my age.
To sit back and go with the flow
I don't need much, just friends and family.
I won't melt in the rain.
Most NGOs are well meaning, but bring Band-Aids.
I don't like to cook.
Long hair is easy.
I'm not ready for grey hair.

**(From Lynn's blog, 10.14.2010)*

While she was gone for over two years, Lynn's best friend and the friend's son stayed in her house in Southern California, a "win-win" for each of them. Lynn returned to her home in Huntington Beach, California, at age 54, explored options, and decided that having a flexible schedule was a priority. She helped Fatima from the Cooperative visit the United States and nominated her as a visiting delegate for the Peace Corps' fiftieth anniversary celebration at the Smithsonian in Washington, DC. Fatima was selected and Lynn joined her there. In a role-reversal, Lynn said, "I got to observe her reaction to being in America for the first time—for example, riding the escalator and watching groceries get swiped through the automated cashier system."

Fatima and her sister Hind traveled to the United States and sold the women's weavings from the Adwal Cooperative at the prestigious Santa Fe International Folk Art Market. A fellowship paid their travel and most expenses while in New Mexico, supplemented by funds raised through a GoFundMe campaign organized by Lynn. They also visited California—to identify additional marketing opportunities and to meet

Lynn's friends and family. They sold all the weavings, participated in the Handweavers Guild of America's Biennial Convergence Conference in Long Beach, and attended workshops on natural dye techniques to share with the rest of the Adwal Cooperative members.

Hind returned to the Santa Fe International Folk Art Market the next year to represent the Adwal Cooperative. She didn't sell everything, though Lynn flew her to California, where she sold products at different parties hosted by Lynn and friends. Hind later returned to Morocco, where she is now a language teacher working for the Peace Corps.

Back in California, Lynn met Asbjorn and married for the first time at age 58. Three years after leaving Morocco, she returned with her husband for a two-week visit. "He didn't know he had so much family he'd never met!" Lynn said. The Peace Corps has since dissolved the artisanal sector in Morocco—leaving English teaching only, though the women are helped with selling their wares through software that works with phones to take orders in remote villages.

Lynn stays busy volunteering with nonprofit organizations, including the Executive Service Corps; Heifer International; Gold Shield Alumnae of UCLA, an honorary group for which she served as president for two years; and as a board member of SCORE's Orange County chapter. She has given talks, including "Weaving My Way Through Morocco," for the Textile Museum Associates of Southern California.

Each year, she enjoys a fun and productive girls' weekend with a close-knit group of seven who have been gathering annually for more than twenty years. Everyone shares updates, reports on personal and professional goals made the prior year, and makes new goals. "We're accountable to ourselves and each other."

Lynn looks forward to enjoying more activities with her engineer/information technology husband. She never saw herself riding a motorcycle, but since her husband is a motorcycle aficionado, she rides on the back with him. She's not interested in getting her own motorcycle.

Thoughts and Advice About Risk

"I never thought of myself as a risk taker. People said I was crazy and nuts for going into the Peace Corps. 'Why would you do that?' they asked. It was a personal test. You need to stretch yourself to grow. Just do it! You get so much more back—this was no exception. You're never too old to learn something about yourself.

"It's good to keep the brain working. You'll live longer. And the Peace Corps can be as stimulating as you want it to be."

From her Peace Corps service, Lynn believes, "Your experience is what you make it. Don't wait for someone else to tell you what to do. Make it happen. Life *is* a self-fulfilling prophecy."

Lynn in Morocco

Photo by Unknown

REPRESENTATIVE PATRICIA HYMANSON, MD

From Neurologist to Elected State Representative at 57

BIRTH YEAR: 1957

Raised in a suburb of New York City, Patricia "Patty" Locuratolo enjoyed school, liked sports, and was a natural leader and musically inclined. As a Yale undergraduate student, she took pre-med classes, and then she went to medical school. Patty worked in clinics in India and Morocco, decided to specialize in neurology, traveled, married a cardiologist, and had three children. As a longtime volunteer community advocate, and wanting to delve into and help with local and statewide issues, Patty ran for state representative in Maine.

Earlier Years

Patty's mother struggled to get pregnant, adopted a girl, and fifteen months later, became pregnant with Patty. From an Italian heritage, Patty lived in a mixed immigrant neighborhood in Yonkers, New York. Her mother, "a wonderful, kind woman with an engaging spirit," was an obstetrical nurse and her father, a furrier and artist. As a young girl, Patty played the piano and liked gymnastics and ice skating. She excelled at and enjoyed school, and was at the top of her class. A natural leader, she was elected to posts throughout her school years. Liking sports in the era before Title IX, Patty was a cheerleader, one of the few girls' "sports teams." During vacations, her family traveled through the Northeast and drove to the World's Fair in Canada—their car filled up with kids (seat belts didn't exist then).

To earn money in her teens, Patty waitressed near her home, walking to her first job at a restaurant that featured ice cream, hamburgers, and a ragtime piano player, and later worked in local steak houses.

Patty was encouraged to apply to Yale by her mother and a teacher who said, "You're just the kind of student Yale wants—a smart leader." Women had just been admitted to Ivy League colleges. She was accepted. "It proved to be an eye-opener and a candy store experience," she said. Students were encouraged to experiment by taking different classes.

She tended bar at campus events and, during several summers, worked as a phlebotomist, drawing blood from patients at a local hospital where her mother also worked. "I worked the early morning shift and walked the halls with my cart, visiting patients just as they were waking up," Patty said. "It was a quiet time of day, and I enjoyed the intimacy of working with the patients. Though I didn't like poking people, I was good at it. The challenge was finding the veins. When off duty, I noticed people's hands and arms and thought about how I would draw blood from them." She took her first European trip, hitchhiking with a friend across England, Scotland, and Wales the summer after her junior year.

Her public-health professor encouraged her to pursue medical school. She was accepted into New York Medical College in Valhalla and was interested in public health. The summer before medical school, she worked at a Navajo reservation near Albuquerque, New Mexico, with an obstetrician who was studying herbs the Navajo women took to induce miscarriage. This physician was an adept deer hunter. The skins of deer killed with one arrow were considered sacred, so he gave them to the Navajos in exchange for information about the herbs the medicine woman collected and how they were used. They also worked with several communes in the area as those groups used herbs in a tea to induce miscarriage.

At a free clinic in Santa Fe they obtained information from a patient survey in which women reported the type of herbs they used, how they prepared them, how much they consumed, and if they or anyone they knew had successfully caused a miscarriage. In a lab, the herbs were put with HCG (human chorionic gonadotropin, a hormone produced in the body during pregnancy) in test tubes. If the HCG disappeared, they knew the herbal tea had destroyed it. In the body, this could result in a miscarriage. However, the tea needed to be very potent, and women had to drink a lot of tea to get a reaction. Women in the commune said they drank a ton of herbal tea.

Patty's first year of medical school was intense. "It involved a lot of memorization, we were tested quickly on our knowledge, and I enjoyed it." Introduced to clinical work, she wanted to go to an Arab country where Americans were accepted, and traveled in Morocco for a short time.

While doing rotations at Tufts University, she met Alan, a cardiology fellow, who later became her husband. During her fourth "design your own experience" year, she worked in rural clinics outside New Delhi, India. "Despite abject poverty, people were lovely, kind, and peaceful," Patty said. "Their spirits were dominated by the Hindu sense of rebirth—that is, the belief that if you're a good person in your current life, you'll be reborn to a higher level or caste. I saw the beauty of the human spirit."

Eager to be part of a community and realizing that the "work of public health is nomadic," she examined different specialty paths. As a girl, Patty grew up understanding that her sister's learning and psychiatric issues were diagnosed as biological. When her father was in his 20s playing around with guns in his backyard, he was shot by a bullet that went through his stomach and ricocheted off the bone around his spinal cord. He recovered after four years, but suffered from "spinal shock," which caused him to have a spastic hitch in his walk. Witnessing these effects with her family, Patty was curious about the neurology field and decided to pursue this longtime interest. She did her residency at Boston City Hospital, the Lahey Medical Center, and Beth Israel Deaconess Medical Center, and interned at St. Luke's Hospital, New York City.

Wanting to travel around the world when no one took a "gap year" off,

Patty requested a year's leave of absence. Her medical program director insinuated that this was a woman thing—she would get married and never return to the medical field. The residents she worked with discussed her request with the chief of medicine, and she was grateful to them for their support. During her year away from being an emergency room physician, she went to Southeast Asia and returned to India. Though the trip was intended as a break from medicine, she carried antibiotics and bandages in her backpack and treated children with skin infections and a man with an ear infection as she traveled on her own.

She was then granted a three-year neurological fellowship at Boston City Hospital and was an instructor at Harvard Medical School. HIV/AIDS was just emerging in the midst of a heroin and crack cocaine epidemic. Seeing drug-addicted patients made her think about the health risks people take and question why people do heroin.

At age 31, Patty married Alan, and the two lived in York, Maine, where she worked as an emergency medicine physician at York Hospital and later opened a private neurological practice. Along the way, she had twin sons and a daughter and went on a service trip to the Dominican Republic. While in Maine and always interested in community issues, she ran for the local school board, serving six years, three years as chair. She also helped start several nonprofit organizations—the York Diversity Forum and healthcareGives. She chaired the Portsmouth Regional Hospital's ethics committee, in New Hampshire, and was immersed in end-of-life decision-making discussions.

Having her own practice, she was increasingly subjected to mandates—such as using a computer system over which she had no control. She found this distracting and had little time to take care of patients. "There was a medical shift in 2013 that was different from the way I practiced medicine," she said. "While I felt secure I was a good physician, I didn't find a system that would allow me to be who I was. Wanting to incorporate my medical world into what I was, I thought about other options."

Transitioning to Politics

As a community health advocate, Patty introduced a bill regarding medical treatments for epilepsy. She testified and followed it through, gaining knowledge and experience about the legislative process. While presenting this bill on medication safety, she learned that not all bills need to become laws. That particular bill changed into a "resolve," which meant the stakeholders needed to meet and figure out a process requiring caution with an anticonvulsant medication going from a brand name to a generically available drug. The experience sparked her interest in politics.

Patty was invited to a meeting at the home of Democratic activists and was asked to apply for a vacant political seat in the Maine legislature. She immediately said no. The speaker of Maine's House was there and offered to have her shadow him, and she did.

At age 57, after years of being "on call," she decided to pursue a House seat in 2014. Concerned that the general population might struggle to remember and pronounce her Italian name Locuratolo, she used her married name when seeking office. She ran as a Democrat, recruited volunteer campaign managers, and won a two-year House term representing District 4, York County (southern) Maine, including Ogunquit and portions of the towns of Wells, Sanford, and her residence in York. Maine has "clean elections" as part of campaign finance reform. Patty opted to be a "clean election" candidate and received funds from the state, but was prohibited from accepting money from individuals or corporations.

"Patient care is intimate—it's about what is going on in people's lives," Patty said. "The medical process now requires spending less time with patients. There are pre-populated questions. I wanted to take the big view. Maine is the patient now, with lots of organs pumping at the same time. I now focus on the health of Maine."

Being a physician is an important attribute in dealing with community health issues. "I like to take care of people and the community," Patty said. "Neurology is a cognitive specialty. It is problem oriented and requires strategic thinking." There are similarities between her physician experience and skills and her political work. She serves on numerous committees and boards, including the board and strategic planning committee of the community health center Families First, and is a trustee of Portsmouth Regional Hospital. She also served on the advisory board for local radio station WSCA-FM.

"I enjoy the political process. Early on before policy development, you need process—it's important, and you need buy-in. There are 1.3 million people in Maine—the population of a moderately sized city. Maine is a huge landmass and is poor, with an older population. We need to figure out the middle and northern Maine economy, which has struggled." She is proud of the bipartisan budget and bills that pass despite officials who get in the way of good governance.

Passionate about singing since childhood but having no available outlets then, Patty auditioned for a Yale singing group while a student, and didn't make it. In her 30s, she became a first soprano with Voices from the Heart, a two-hundred-member women's chorus in Portsmouth, New Hampshire, "singing a rich mix of soulful music from many cultural and musical traditions" (voicesfromtheheart.org). Locally, they perform concerts in New Hampshire, drawing women from that state, Massachusetts, and Maine. Patty sings with a portion of the chorus on humanitarian tours to different countries. They traveled to Northern Ireland and the Republic of Ireland, raising money for women's shelters and a children's peace camp. Standing on the edge of a minefield where a mother and her three sons had been killed in the small village of Perusic in Croatia, they sang in a farmyard and raised $75,000 for Adopt a Minefield, which was matched and resulted in 150 mines being cleared. Filmed by a crew, it became an award-winning documentary, *Many Voices, One Song*, by Nancy Pollock. In Cuba, they sang with the Cuban National Chorus. Patty looks forward to singing her heart out on other humanitarian concert trips.

A music lover, Patty started playing the violin at age 55. Her daughter had to drop her violin lessons, which were paid for, and the violin was rented, so Patty took to playing. "When I play with the music association at a recital in front of people, I get a tingling feeling. It's wonderful," she said.

"I love to write, especially about Maine and life on my street. I write every day and want to see what it all looks like in the future. I compose Zen-like snippets—just about the moment. I like to cook too." Cutting vegetables, she makes soups and has thought about owning a soup restaurant.

She thinks about end-of-life issues. "If Medicare allows billing for these services, that might be a direction I could take. I would be involved in crisis at the end of life—such as family dynamics, maybe patient care, I'm not sure. I am learning about technology and health communities. We need to evaluate telemedicine and monitoring the health of people. Small industries are making wearables, but when they come out, they're obsolete. Cost is a factor. It's a systems and health care management issue, and people want to age in place. Maine is a rural state, so it is a challenge to deliver care to people who want to remain in their homes."

Patty ran again for political office and was reelected. "There's a learning curve," she said. "In the beginning, I felt like I was drinking from a fire hose—there were people to meet, issues to understand, papers and bills to read—there was an overwhelming amount of material to assimilate. With experience, it is easier." There was also the physical challenge of working from the state capital in Augusta, an hour-and-forty-minute commute from her home each way.

House representatives serve two-year terms and are eligible to be elected to four terms, or eight years maximum. In between her political life, singing, and playing the violin, she gardens, reads, and enjoys taking family trips.

Thoughts and Advice About Risk

"I think of risk as traveling down a road that doesn't have certainty to it, but where the end matters. You can choose different options—for example, walking home over the hill or around it. You have to be clear you won't get hurt—for example, in skiing, deciding to take the easy or hard way down. Pushing it a little is good.

"Risk is important to keep in your life to make you feel a little uncomfortable. Traveling internationally where no one travels is risky in a fun kind of way. It has to have excitement too." Patty would not want to do anything that would hurt her reputation, integrity, or family. Living a long time in the same community has provided her time to think about risks she has taken. "Running for office is a huge risk—I could lose, which is not a familiar feeling to me. My name was on posters on streets."

Patty's advice for people thinking about taking a risk is "Sit peacefully with yourself for a while. Think about things that make you happy. How can you bring things to life you do every day? You have to have faith. If you do, good things will follow. Plan, plan, plan." She cites the truth in the often-quoted Roman philosopher Seneca, that "Luck is what happens when preparation meets opportunity.

"I always try to be happy in a simple way. If I'm happy, it means I am doing something that speaks to my strengths and the core of my being, which includes adventure, love, spirituality, artistry, music, risk-taking, and intellectual stimulation."

Representative Patricia Hymanson, MD

Photo by Rob Karosis

CHAPTER 3 — EDUCATORS

MARCELLA MORAA OGEGA

Academy and Children's Home Founder in Her 50s; Community Organization Co-Founder at 67

BIRTH YEAR: 1944

Born into poverty as the oldest of nine children in southwestern Kenya, Marcella defied tremendous odds. She toiled hard and went to school, graduated from college, married, and endured horrific physical and verbal abuse from her alcoholic husband. Considered a social outcast for having only daughters, Marcella taught school and in her 50s, founded two academies and a home for needy, desperate children. At 67, she co-created Mpanzi, a dynamic organization supporting women and girls.

Earlier Years

Growing up in the rural village of Keumbu, near Kisii Town in the Gusii Highlands—a lush green, beautiful region of Kenya surrounded by avocado, mango, and banana trees and hillsides covered with shiny-leafed tea bushes—Marcella lived in a mud hut with a grass-thatched roof. As was common in many homes in the area, their house lacked running water and electricity.

Her family was poor—her father was a farmer who used oxen in the fields (while the women used their hands). Marcella's mother worked hard in her *shamba* (garden) and grew maize (corn) and *wimbi* (millet). Walking a long distance while balancing a large heavy pot on her head, she sold her food at the market. Coins could fit in the slits on the bottoms of her torn feet from years of walking many miles barefoot.

The family ate the dietary staple *ugali*, a thick, sticky starch made from maize flour cooked with water and eaten with the hands. It was often dipped in sour milk or vegetable or beef stew and accompanied by greens, usually kale (*sukuma wiki* in Kiswahili). The colonialists, before Kenya became independent from Great Britain in 1963, promoted maize rather than the more healthy millet. People became accustomed to eating ugali, which was a popular dish—typically the only food eaten daily by many Kenyans. Not owning any glassware or mugs, Marcella and her family drank from carved-out gourds.

Working hard to help her family, Marcella hauled water from the river, cleaned, cooked, gardened, took care of their cows, and looked after her brothers and sisters. Her brothers did not do any chores—that work was left to the girls and their mother. She attended day school, and her mother worked hard to earn money for the fees. After completing her evening chores, with no electricity or candlelight, Marcella held small bits of lit charcoal to do her schoolwork before bedtime.

At 10, Marcella went through the traditional female circumcision ceremony with other girls in her village. Performed in a group during the August or December school holidays, it was considered an important rite of passage—for girls and boys. Before the genital cutting, girls were immersed in the cold river to numb their bodies, as an antidote to the pain. Celebrated by family members and villagers, it was a festive occasion with much singing, ululating (a loud, powerful, high-pitched tongue trill), and dancing. "I felt very happy going through circumcision then, because of the songs, ceremony, food, visiting relatives, and drinks—porridge, sour milk, and local beer," Marcella said.

Around this time, Marcella's father died. He had returned from a beer party complaining of stomach pains and was rushed to the hospital, where he was operated on and died the same day. They suspected he was poisoned, but in retrospect, Marcella thinks it was appendicitis. At the time of his death, he had sired seven children, six of whom were living (one daughter died as a toddler). Per Gusii tradition (Marcella's family are from the Gusii tribe in the Kisii region), her father's brother "inherited" her mother and moved into their home. "I was naughty when my uncle showed up after my father died," Marcella confessed. "I didn't want him there and refused to budge from our hut until being forced out." From the time of circumcision, girls are not permitted to sleep in their parents' home, so she slept at her grandmother's nearby mud hut from then on. Her mother had three more sons by her brother-in-law. There is a twenty-two-year difference between Marcella and her youngest half brother.

When her oldest brother was about to be baptized a Catholic, the church asked whether there were other siblings in school and insisted that Marcella and her sisters attend their school. Marcella and her three sisters had already been baptized with their mother. Their mother, a former pagan, converted to Catholicism to wed her husband, who had already converted during the colonial missionary era. All children were to be registered in the church and receive Christian names. Though it was rare for girls to go to school, especially in the 1940s and 1950s, Marcella went to Catholic boarding school for grades five through eight and excelled in her studies.

"I passed the common entrance examination for boarding school very well, taking the first position out of all the schools, defeating boys and girls," she said. "After my mother was told I took the number one position, she wondered why her daughter couldn't get a bigger number like fifty and above, instead of number one, because she looked at quantity.

"Though illiterate, my mom was a happy woman and never discriminated against girls. She wanted her boys and girls to go to school and have the same opportunities."

While a student, Marcella worked as a housemaid in the nuns' residence—fetching water and wood, cooking, and cleaning. At one time, she wanted to be a nun. After working and observing the nuns quarreling and being mean, she changed her mind. Her mother scraped together money for her children's school uniforms and fees. Marcella's sisters didn't pursue their education past primary school and married young.

Marcella graduated from high school, followed by a two-year college program in education. In college, she lived on campus and had to bring bedding—not having the requisite supplies was grounds for dismissal. Her mother promised to purchase and deliver the sheets to her dormitory. Not knowing what sheets were (they used only blankets), her mother went to a fabric shop and bought two small pieces of material. She walked many miles, as she had no car or money for public transportation, and arrived at her daughter's school late at night. "I panicked when I realized the sheets were only small scraps of material but didn't say anything to my mother," Marcella said. "We had nightly bed checks and I didn't want to be expelled. My classmates told me to tuck the fabric over the blanket so it looked like they were whole sheets. I did and never got caught the entire school year."

In college, Marcella met Casmir Ogega Mabeya and married him at age 21. He was educated, a "learned man," and smart in business. He was one of the first Africans, and the first Kisii Kenyan man, hired as a banker with Barclays Bank of East Africa, under British colonial rule at that time. Soon after marrying, her husband started drinking heavily and lost his job.

Marcella and Casmir had three girls—Jane, Pam, and Jackie. It is a terrible stigma for men not to have boys, and Marcella bore the brunt of her husband's drunken brutality for bearing no sons. Ostracized by the villagers, men without sons are derogatorily called "uncircumcised women" (*egesagane* in the Kisii language), a major insult. Marcella was blamed by her husband, mother-in-law, and community members for having only girls. "I was humiliated and abused endlessly by my husband's relatives and mother-in-law, who called me a witch, screamed at me in public, and pooped on our property and made me pick it up," she said. She endured regular beatings from her husband.

When her oldest daughter, Jane, was an adult, she told Marcella about an abhorrent act by her father that she had witnessed as a little girl. Marcella hadn't been home at the time. They had a young live-in house girl who shared a bed with Jane. One night, Jane woke up to find her father chasing the young maid around their bed. The girl screamed, and Jane yelled to her father to stop. Whacking Jane hard on the head, he knocked her out. She recalled waking up to the cries of the young girl being raped by her father in his bedroom. Jane didn't dare tell her mother about it when it happened.

Trained in education, Marcella taught in a public, government-run school. She also kept a shamba, planting millet, kale, and maize, and sold vegetables at the market after her school day. She saved a little money and bought a small parcel of land, twenty-five by a hundred feet. Needing more money because Casmir was drinking away her earnings, Marcella opened a shop in the local village of Igare and didn't tell her husband. But he found a spare key and took the supplies to buy beer. With no goods left to sell, she was forced to close the shop and then sold soda. Determined, she still saved money to send her three daughters to school.

Founding Schools, a Children's Home, and an Organization

At age 50, Marcella started a primary school with three teachers and six children. To do this, she needed to get her husband's permission. According to Kisii culture, men are the heads of the family. If she didn't involve him in this decision making, it would lead to further violence in her family and the community. There were no women or men running and directing private schools in the area then—they were all government run. Expanding the property she had purchased earlier with money earned over the years, she converted it to Mercy Academy. On two opposite parcels of land, across a dirt road, large U-shaped stucco buildings house the school's classrooms, meeting space, and her living quarters. Small stone-and-stucco buildings on the other side hold the "baby classes."

The school grew in size as she purchased more land across the road. Initially, the minister of education gave Marcella a tough time, saying that the buildings where the classes were held were insufficient, but later she was issued a formal registration. During 1998–2000, the school grew to a peak of 420 students, and Marcella hired teachers and other staff.

Marcella's husband had a stroke at age 60 and went into a monthlong coma. He was moved to Kenyatta Hospital in Nairobi for better care, but died there. At his funeral, people cried and said it was sad that he hadn't left any sons. Marcella, age 58, stood up and spoke—an unheard-of act for a woman. "God blessed me with three daughters from my own stomach, and now I have three sons as well." Her daughters had married, and attended their father's funeral with their husbands, whom she considered sons. Marcella took in her ailing, elderly mother-in-law and cared for her until she died—despite having been relentlessly abused by her for many years. The former custom of a deceased husband's male relative assuming the role of the widow's new husband (whether she wants him or not) is no longer practiced. Marcella remains a widow.

Her husband's only worth was serving as a bodyguard, Marcella said. He wouldn't pay his daughters' school fees, and he stole money she saved for their tuition and spent it on alcohol and prostitutes. But he was proud that they excelled. Casmir had been the first person in his family to pursue higher education. After the funeral, Marcella's brother-in-law asked, "How will the properties and schools be maintained now that your husband is gone?" The truth was that Marcella was handling all the business transactions and running the school. Casmir had had three brothers and four stepbrothers. Her father-in-law was also a drunkard and abusive. After Marcella's husband died, one of her brothers-in-law went to the Land District Office. He wanted his brother's inherited property divided among the three brothers-in-law, land that had been passed down through many generations of Casmir's family.

Before dying, Casmir told Marcella he wanted his property divided among his three daughters. It was highly unusual for a man to give any land to females. Marcella had the other land deeds in her husband's name and rightfully inherited this property according to the law, which had changed to benefit women by that time. She created a second school on a property up the road from her home and Mercy Academy. That school was named Bitengo—after Casmir's grandmother—as the property formerly belonged to Casmir's ancestors.

"I was interested in starting two primary schools, having been a primary school teacher and observed that the children from kindergarten and lower primary levels were not being taught well," Marcella said. "I wanted to provide quality education for children so they could read and write at an early age. When I started Mercy Academy, the children came from very far away, so Bitengo Academy was started to cater to those children who were traveling from very far to search for the quality education I was providing at Mercy."

Marcella also founded a children's home, converting two large downstairs rooms below her living quarters into separate girls' and boys' dorms. More than a hundred orphans and needy boys and girls have lived in her home, ranging from 3 to 20 years old.

Some are "complete orphans" (both parents were deceased); others have one parent who often is mentally ill or living with chronic disease such as HIV/AIDS or is a single, landless mother; and others have extremely poor parents. The children have suffered many challenges—including rape or sexual assault for the girls, physical violence, hunger, stigma, and neglect. One girl, "P," the third of thirteen children born to extremely poor landless squatters, arrived with her grandmother, who begged Marcella to take her into her home and school. She was about 9 and very scared and timid, and spoke little Kiswahili and no English. Being too old for a lower class, she began in grade two and did well. She became more confident, led the children in singing, spoke fluent Kiswahili and good English, and excelled in class.

Though faced with significant deterrents, Marcella perseveres and has helped many needy children get an education. Young girls who can remain in school have avoided early marriage. In addition to directing two schools, she works tirelessly every day and night, running the children's home. "Madam Director" is strict, good natured, and kind, and assigns the children chores. Devoted to providing for and educating these children, Marcella distributes supplies, gives money to buy food at the market, handles disagreements, helps with homework, says prayers, sings songs, and even does aerobics with the students to a Hollywood DVD on a fuzzy screen in a dimly lit classroom at 5:00 a.m. "Most of my students passed very well; most of them went to secondary school and then to university," Marcella said. "Some are doctors; some are teachers and highly achieved people now. I am very proud of them."

Resilient and positive, Marcella is seen as a leader in her village. Unafraid to speak up about violence against women, she has gained the respect of local and regional officials. With other women, she co-chairs the women's nonprofit group Mpanzi, which she founded, at age 67 in 2011, with her three daughters. Mpanzi ("to nurture from a seed" in Kiswahili) has three primary programs: (1) educate needy children, especially girls, and sponsor family caregiving programs; (2) conduct peace-building programs and trainings to eliminate female genital cutting and prevent violence among ethnic groups; and (3) promote livelihoods and microenterprise programs. These programs have included seed grants and microloans for women to launch businesses; buying goats and hens for food and eggs to sell, with the chicks distributed back to the women so all benefit; distributing solar lights, which are less expensive and more healthful than smoky, smelly kerosene lamps and light dirt paths at night for women and girls traveling in the dark; and managing a chair and tent rental business to generate revenue for the group.

Starting with a handful of women, Mpanzi has increased to hundreds of women meeting weekly. It is seen as a role model organization, and neighboring Maasai women have joined the Kisii women as well. It is a strong form of support for rural Kenyan women, and the group leverages its purchasing power to buy products at a discount to improve their lives—like solar lights and a simple and natural water purification system that saves both money and time and is revolutionary to their village.

"I am proud of my three daughters and grandchildren because they went to school," Marcella said. Her daughters are successful, which makes her happy and gratified. Receiving good educations launched them toward advanced degrees and professional careers. Each daughter has a master's degree; Jackie has a PhD in peacekeeping studies and published *Pervasive Violence*, a book about female circumcision documenting her and her sister's personal stories. All have been teachers and administrators.

"Girls have been viewed by men as 'property,' not people to take to school," Marcella said. "That's made me more determined than ever to support children, girls especially, in getting an education to better themselves." In one generation, her daughters' lives have improved significantly. "Education is key to a healthy, better quality of life for girls today," she believes. "My hope is to grow the schools, and I dream of having a college or university. This is because I like education. It is the means for people to live a quality life."

Quick to laugh, Marcella is an exceptionally strong woman. She is an uplifting role model to many young girls, her daughters, her grandchildren, and the women and men in her area. "My mom always encouraged us to be anything we wanted to be in life," Jackie said. "Each of us knew we could bring to Mom our wildest dream and she always would embrace it and make it better. She instilled in us the importance of getting educated."

Thoughts and Advice About Risk

Purchasing land was not socially acceptable for women, but Marcella defied all odds to purchase land, expand it, open a shop, sell soda, and later, start two private schools and a children's home. No female or male was running any private school in this area at the time. There were only mission and government schools. Founding and directing the schools and children's home required overcoming numerous obstacles, as well as incessant abuse from her husband and shunning by the community. Ostracized by her husband, his family, and the community, Marcella risked failing and being scorned for creating a school. Ignoring her husband's and others' verbal and physical abuse, she went from having a very low status to becoming a highly regarded community member and gained the respect of male officials. Marcella also persevered to save money for her daughters' education, determined to make sure their school fees were paid and they stayed in school.

Private schools are harder to run, as poor people have a difficult time paying the fees. Student and teacher retention is challenging. New technologies, computer instruction, Internet access, and equipment critical to education are costly. Government schools are free, though the quality of education is often mediocre. The government has instituted incentives to attract more students, including paying caregivers.

"The main risk was that I knew I could not make money out of it," Marcella said about launching and directing two academies and a children's home. "But I was very passionate about education, and I sympathized with the children who needed quality education. I feared that Kisii men would not send their children to my schools because I am a woman, and women, especially like me who have no sons, had no say in our culture. But I took the risk, and earned their trust. I love my work, because through education, I have produced great men and women in the community."

All of the women Mpanzi members have been or are still being abused (many by polygamist husbands). Sharing their stories of abuse is a big risk. Abuse of women and girls in rural Kenya is still rampant. Marcella, beaten and abused for many years by her husband, told her story and provides support and empathy to other abused women who now share their stories and are working together to help prevent violence against women and girls.

"It is very helpful in healing the trauma of the women like myself who have endured different forms of violence in the community, to provide economic empowerment so they are able to educate and care for their children," Marcella said. Marcella is educated and well read, and has traveled to visit her two daughters living in the United States. Hearing that domestic violence is pervasive in America, she says, "I did not know that white people are also abused. I think that all forms of abuse must be stopped."

Although female genital cutting was outlawed in Kenya in 2011, it is still practiced today on the majority of girls in Marcella's village. It is a complicated issue. Marcella's daughter Jackie said, "Grandmothers who believe in and practice female circumcision in rural villages have no idea it was outlawed in 2011. Criminalizing circumcision by putting grandmothers in jail for continuing this practice is not the answer." The practice is commonly referred to as "circumcision" for both girls and boys in Kenya.

Marcella now believes female genital cutting (FGC, the politically sensitive term, rather than "female genital mutilation") should be stopped. In Kisii culture, it does not play any important role. Initially, it was there to help transition children to adulthood, but now, children are taught life skills in school.

"I support the government to stop this practice," Marcella said. "I am very pleased that my granddaughters have not gone through this practice." Grandmothers play a major role in taking their granddaughters for FGC, especially those who did not go to school. Mpanzi encourages members to preach to others against taking their children to undergo FGC. They launched the "*Nasema La*" (the Kiswahili phrase for "I say NO") campaign against FGC in the community. "We as Mpanzi women have taken a stand; we have T-shirts we wear as a symbol of our stand, and we spread the word in the community.

"Growing up in severe poverty and my belief in God has helped make me strong," Marcella claimed. Raised Catholic, she is a leader in her local church and is friends with the area priests. Her widowed, gracious, independent, and determined mother, who has lived into her 90s, has been a major influence in her life.

"I think women pursuing their dreams have a specific set of challenges," Marcella said. "They should not rely on their husbands, because they might hinder them. I would advise women to go ahead and pursue their dreams—at any age."

Marcella at home in Kenya

Photo by Norah Moturi

MARIANNE BOCKLI

Teacher in Switzerland and America to Mentoring Kindergarten Teachers in China at 57+

BIRTH YEAR: 1953

Tall, tan, and lean, Marianne Bockli's wholesome, outdoorsy look matches her love of nature. Born and raised in Switzerland, she attended a teachers college and taught kindergarten in Swiss public schools. She was well traveled and community minded. After moving to America, Marianne taught French and later, an outdoor kindergarten class at a Waldorf school. With her Waldorf experience, she was recruited to mentor kindergarten teachers in China. Knowing three Mandarin words, she went to China for the first time at age 57.

Earlier Years

Having lived primarily in Neuchatel, in the northwest part of Switzerland, when younger, Marianne is multilingual. She spoke French (her mother was from France) and German, and learned English in high school. Her family lived on the top floor of an old restored village house—a family with four children lived underneath. Marianne was the middle child between a sister and brother. Her mother was a homemaker; her dad, a supermarket manager. In her youth, Marianne biked, roller-skated, hiked, skied, and helped plant and weed the family garden. For their family's food, her mother raised rabbits, sheep, ducks, and hens, which Marianne helped care for. They grew vegetables (lettuce, leeks, carrots, radishes) and fruit and nut trees (plum, pear, quince, walnut, and hazelnut). Marianne's interest in gardening and natural foods blossomed at a young age.

As a girl, Marianne enjoyed playing outdoors with the neighborhood children. "My childhood was happy, and I was involved in all kinds of activities—helping around the house, working in the garden, caring for the animals, and swimming in ponds. I was free. My freedom as a child made me a stronger adult, more willing to take risks. We were allowed to explore. From around the age of 10, we left notes for my parents saying we'd be back for dinner, and off we went on our bicycles."

Spending a year post–high school in New Jersey at 17, she received more English instruction and worked as a volunteer assistant in a Head Start program with 3–6-year-olds—her first institutional experience with children.

"I resisted teaching because that's what most females did," Marianne said. "I didn't know what other career to pursue." Graduating from École Normale, a teachers college, Marianne taught kindergarten in Switzerland's public schools for three years. In between teaching jobs, she hiked through Europe; hitchhiked with her brother through the Andes, Peru, Ecuador, and Bolivia; and, after saving money from working one season at a ski resort in the Alps, took a three-month driving trip across Australia with her sister, camping by the side of the road. Returning to the United States in her late 20s, she married an American man living in Maine and then had a daughter. (She divorced later, and she and her ex-husband shared custody of their daughter, who was then a young teenager.) Marianne worked in a health food store in Bath, Maine, and began substitute teaching at a Montessori school, launching their French program.

Moving to midcoast Maine, she became the traveling French teacher for several independent schools before joining Rockport's Ashwood-Waldorf School—initially teaching French, then kindergarten and grades one and two. The Waldorf educational philosophy, founded by Rudolf Steiner in Germany, emphasizes the head, the hands, and the heart—incorporating the arts, movement, and foreign language using practical applications. The emphasis is on wholeness in body, soul, and spirit.

Teachers typically stay with the students from grades one through eight for the two-hour daily "main lesson" exploring different subjects.

Leaving the Waldorf school more than fifteen years later, Marianne traveled and spent time with her elderly mother in France. Returning to Maine and wanting to do something different with her early childhood teaching experience and skills, she contacted the Association of Waldorf Schools about new opportunities. "We need you to mentor Waldorf kindergarten teachers in China," she was told. There are more than a thousand Waldorf schools worldwide, including more than two hundred in China.

A New Cultural, Work Experience

Having never been in China before and not knowing Mandarin, the official language, Marianne said, "I was excited and scared. I always had a smattering of a language to get by in previous travels. I also thought, *Wow, this is what I always hoped for—traveling and working internationally with expenses paid!*"

At age 57, starting with a six-week assignment, she assumed a volunteer mentor role. Her work was split between Shenzhen, across from Hong Kong, and Tianjin, south of Beijing. She stayed with a young, divorced Chinese woman with no children, who lived in an apartment and spoke good English. Bonding with her hostess over television dating games and soap operas, Marianne gained a good understanding of mainstream, contemporary Chinese culture through shows and commercials. "We had fun judging the dating show contestants and making irreverent remarks," Marianne said. "We looked at the contestants differently. Seeing my tan, ruddy face, my hostess said my color was not good, it wasn't white enough, so she applied thin paper face masks that stuck to my face. We laughed and had fun wearing our face masks and peeling them off during commercial breaks."

Wanting to be hospitable to their American guest, her hostess and school coordinators bought milk, white bread, and peanut butter, which

Marianne normally doesn't eat. Liking natural foods, she diplomatically explained that she wanted to eat what they ate. The food was good and plentiful. Breakfast was broth with noodles, seaweed, mushrooms, dates, ground millet, and a hard-boiled egg. Lunch and dinner choices were plain or red-bean-paste-filled steamed buns, rice, fish, vegetables, meat, and dumplings. "Eating fish with chopsticks—picking bones daintily off the flesh without reading glasses in a dimly lit room and retrieving the bones that ended up in my mouth—was challenging. Touching food with your fingers was considered rude," said Marianne.

No sweets were served. She enjoyed huge grapefruit, dragon fruit, and durian, a popular fruit with a potent smell but fine taste. Beverages were rose or chamomile flower tea (no black or green tea) or water. Women did not drink any alcoholic beverages. When traveling on her own, Marianne tried and liked Chinese beer and wine.

"Everyone uses English and Chinese names interchangeably, making it confusing to identify who's who," Marianne said. In the kindergarten classrooms, she communicated with the teachers by demonstrating the Waldorf way of role modeling techniques to show the teachers methods to interact with the children—playing with puppets, for example. Though an interpreter was present, their English pronunciation was sometimes difficult to understand.

After Shenzhen, Marianne had a week to sightsee. A hiking tour to the Great Wall with people from many different Western countries was the highlight. Because it took three hours to walk to the wall and another two hours to return, it was not touristy or crowded. En route, they passed through villages with mud huts—a contrast to the high-rise buildings in nearby cities.

Arriving in Tianjin, Marianne was given a small spot on the floor of the school's office to sleep during her three weeks. "There was a board with a quilt surrounded by supplies and equipment with no room to open my suitcase. After spending one night, I discovered I had displaced a young woman teacher who had moved into an even smaller space on the kitchen floor. I requested different accommodations for the rest of my time there and was given a hotel room nearby. I wanted to be treated as a colleague and felt guilty moving into a hotel, but knew it would be difficult to work effectively for three weeks while trying to fit my five-foot, nine-inch body into a cramped space to sleep."

The Waldorf schools are private—the children of affluent families attend, but the teachers are paid a pittance and have no money for apartments. They squeeze into small spaces in the school to sleep. Many schools are in apartment buildings with small courtyards. Students go outside every day—usually to the courtyard and, once a week, to a large park. During the frigid, gray-sky months from November through April, it is cold inside the classrooms. Children wear their winter coats indoors throughout the day.

Marianne was happy to walk the forty-five minutes to school. Parents took turns making her breakfast, which they delivered in steamed baskets to the school each morning. She ate delicious, prepared lunches with the students at the school. Dinners were eaten in a home with a family of five—two grandparents, a father who worked in a bank, his wife, and their daughter, age 6. Only the mother and young girl spoke some English. "We smiled at each other a lot. The grandfather made jokes about foreigners in a nice way. His daughter played translator and seemed embarrassed interpreting her father's jokes. The family was warm and kind to me. In China, I was often asked my astrological sign, never my age, though you can figure out someone's age by their sign. I was born in the year of the snake, the same sign as the father's. We bonded when we realized we were the same age. At the dinner table, we talked about fashion, comparing our dress and haircuts. I complimented the mother on her straw hat, which she gave me. The family laughed when I clumsily served myself using chopsticks, moving the food from the bowls to my plate. They compared my skills to those of little children—with good humor, though.

"We ate a lot of green, cooked vegetables—peas, cabbage, bok choy, green beans—lots of noodles, sweet potatoes (which were also sold on sticks by street vendors), and chicken, pork, and some beef. Dessert was never served."

On three other assignments in China ranging from four to seven weeks, Marianne returned to Beijing and went inland and northwest of Tianjin by bullet train to Hunan Province, where there were no foreigners and she had her own apartment. Braving trips to the market by herself, she didn't understand the language. "It is hard to know the cost of items. I don't know if I paid the right amount. Everything is inexpensive, though, so I didn't worry.

"Seasoning in foods was different and good, ranging from spicy to mild, depending on the region. There was lots of ginger. When I complimented people on the food, I was told, 'You must have been Chinese in a previous life.' One time, not far from Beijing, I was taken to a fancy restaurant with some of the school's administrators and teachers where I worked. An assortment of foods was ordered, and they eagerly watched me taste everything. A meat dish covered in sauce wasn't particularly good. I didn't care for the sauce. I was told that 'dog feet is good for cold weather.' That was the dish. Different foods are served according to the weather. This was winter food. There are many excellent vegetarian restaurants throughout China run by monks."

Families took her to visit temples and museums on the weekends when there was no school. If Marianne expressed interest in seeing a place, people wanted to take her, even if it was far away. Realizing this, she was careful not to mention certain places, because she didn't want to inconvenience people eager to please her.

Adjusting to primitive conditions in some rural areas was challenging. Some bathrooms had a hole in the ground; others had a long, narrow trough to squat over. "Pollution is a major issue in China, and the air quality threatens everyone's health," Marianne said. "It's hard to breathe. After walking outside, even without touching anything, the water turns black when I wash my hands." Cities are crowded—even small cities have eight million residents.

Marianne has enjoyed sharing her Waldorf experience with the young teachers. "Their eagerness and openness to learn from my teaching experience makes me humble. It's a true cultural exchange. It isn't me just spewing my knowledge, but rather giving them the freedom to develop curriculums to fit their culture." For example, after Marianne engaged the teachers in a discussion about their festivals, classes created puppet plays for the Dragon Boat Festival.

"When you don't speak the language, you are more observant and develop a different way of understanding," Marianne said. "Adapting to a new environment with what you have expands my world. These new experiences are enriching. Any challenge or experience I've overcome has been enriching anywhere."

Fond of the outdoors and an environmental advocate, Marianne, in her 60s, teaches a novel Forest Kindergarten curriculum at the Ashwood-Waldorf School in Rockport, Maine. This year-round class is held on the thirty-two-acre wooded campus. The children spend half a day outdoors in warm weather, and on cold, snowy days take walks through the woods, learning about plants, trees, and wildlife. Once her students found a sleeping porcupine in a tree—it is now known as the "porcupine tree." The children learn through play and by doing. Once a week, they cook soup. "They pick herbs and wild asparagus for soup, drill holes to tap an old maple, dig for crystals, climb rocks, gather berries for snacks, pick leaves and flowers for teas, fell rotten trees, and saw branches for firewood." Through stories, she teaches the children about the outdoors. During the frigid Maine winters, Marianne introduced hot, soothing footbaths for each child, which was enthusiastically welcomed.

"I want to be the best I can be with the children. My teacher role makes me conscious of my words and actions—I want to be sure I state facts correctly. They trust me and I want to be worthy of their trust.

It's a responsibility. The children have a sense of wonder—they bring freshness to looking at things. It makes me observe and appreciate little things."

Marianne looks forward to more work assignments in China and is helping to coordinate a teacher-mentor matching program. She is also receptive to new teaching and mentoring experiences in other countries and around the United States. Loving the outdoors, she is becoming a specialist in nature education programs, including one designed for adults and children.

An active, adventurous woman, Marianne likes physical challenges and enjoys hiking, biking, canoeing, cross-country skiing, snowshoeing, and swimming. In her late 50s, she did manual labor for three months and fulfilled a fantasy of learning how to drive a harvester to collect the wheat, oats, and barley crops on her sister's farm in Western Australia.

Supplementing her income with gardening work, Marianne also runs errands for, and takes walks with, elderly people needing help. She is interested in hospice and end-of-life care. Community is important to her. "I believe in helping to make things better as a responsible member of the area I live in." Participating in a community shared agriculture program at a local farm, she helps cultivate fruit and vegetables using non-chemical methods in exchange for a share during harvest. She has volunteered for a land trust, an abused women's support program, and the annual film festival in Camden, Maine.

At one time, she was interested in biking across the United States. This interest has morphed into a possible walk across France someday.

As a mother, Marianne is proud of her daughter, Zoé. "My daughter believes in social justice and sustainability by gardening, purchasing local foods, recycling, and maintaining a low-carbon footprint. She enjoys the outdoors like I do and likes to ski, hike, and camp. I admire and respect Zoé and credit her with helping me become a more open adult through our conversations, her encouragement and example."

Thoughts and Advice About Risk

"Jumping into the great unknown" is Marianne's definition of risk. She doesn't consider herself a risk taker. "I like to play it safe," she says. She doesn't see going to China to mentor kindergarten teachers as a risk, since she works under the auspices of Waldorf's education program.

Marianne likes "little" challenges, pushes her boundaries, steps outside her comfort zone, and learns new skills. Creating and being responsible for teaching a new outdoor kindergarten class and going to China she sees as little challenges. "I wouldn't want to do anything that is harmful to others or myself. I probably will not jump out of an airplane or bungee jump." She takes "little" risks, like jumping into the Atlantic Ocean off Maine's coast in frigid January.

Reflecting on her life, Marianne says, "I've shaped a life that suits me. I've had a good life—I've fallen into good places, have good health, and met good people." She is strong and independent, and values her freedom being on her own. Marianne has friends who died young—one at age 50.

"My friends who died encouraged me to live fully, not to postpone important things, and to value the relationships I have—my friends and family."

Marianne, on right, with host and colleague Grace
Forbidden City, Beijing, China

Photo by Unknown

MIMI O'HAGAN

Volunteer Fundraising Leader for Five Schools in Rural Ethiopia in Her 70s and 80s

BIRTH YEAR: 1930

Mimi (Eugenie) O'Hagan was born in Brooklyn, New York, and later moved with her family to a farm in Virginia. After college, she launched a career in public relations, working for others and then starting her own firm. She lived frugally and traveled annually to Europe and Asia. At 70, Mimi volunteered doing manual labor in Bangkok, Guatemala, Tanzania, and South Africa. From age 76 through 84, she raised funds to build desperately needed schools to enable girls to get an education in rural Ethiopia.

Earlier Years

The youngest of three girls, Mimi was living in Staten Island, New York, when her businessman father lost his job during the 1930 stock market crash. Fortunately, he regained his footing and the family moved in 1944 to a farm in Charlottesville, Virginia. Mimi recalled that when she was a girl living on a 65-acre farm, "My father thought he was Noah." He bought Hereford cows, Shropshire sheep, chickens, and pigs to raise. As a businessman, he traveled a lot. "My brave, born-and-bred New Yorker mother ended up learning to throw slush to the pigs and hay to the cattle." Introduced to manual labor with farm chores, Mimi developed a lifelong passion for physical work.

An Irish Catholic, Mimi attended Sacred Heart Boarding School and Newton College, part of Boston College. Sacred Heart education fosters an expectation of helping others. After college graduation, Mimi worked in the early 1950s for Eisenhower's campaign. She then became the public relations manager for Schweppes beverage company, and later managed communications for Project Hope, a floating medical center that brought care and health education to communities around the world. She did the advance work and public relations in Nicaragua, living on a ship for two months. This assignment led to a career of promoting nonprofit organizations, including the American Museum of Natural History, the Association of American Publishers, Oxford University Press, and Danbury Community Hospital. "I was a career woman at a time when female competence was not adequately recognized." She was careful with her money and took annual vacations to Europe and Asia to explore and understand other religions and cultures.

Retiring at age 70 after forty-eight years in communications, Mimi decided to stop traveling for pleasure. She volunteered with Cross Cultural Solutions for a variety of assignments, including teaching Buddhist monks to speak English in Bangkok; working at a homeless shelter and with a microfinance program in Guatemala; helping with newborn HIV babies in Cape Town's townships; and assisting with a women's microfinance program in Tanzania, where conditions were appalling. Enjoying the satisfaction of physical labor, Mimi volunteered with Habitat for Humanity constructing homes in Malawi. "I love manual labor," she said.

At age 75, she helped build a home in Ethiopia and visited a Save the Children school. After witnessing a young boy whose face was covered with sores, wearing a ragged shirt and crying by a dirty stream as he tried to fill a rusty enamel plate with water, Mimi was haunted by the memory. Seeing many destitute, uneducated children, she created Mimi's Building Blocks to raise funds for a school in northern Ethiopia's Tigray region.

A Fundraising Leader with a Mission

Committed to raising funds among her family and friends, Mimi believed in helping those in need. Seeing poverty firsthand inspired her to mobilize her network to provide education for children. Working in partnership with the nonprofit international humanitarian aid organization Save the Children, Mimi was a dynamic force in making schools a reality in Ethiopia's rural northern Tigray region. Her handwritten, compelling Mimi's Building Blocks letters with photographs requesting support were effective and generated significant contributions.

The first school was named the Two Mimi School, with major funding from Mimi's dear friend Mimi Meehan's family. The village women carried rocks cut by hand for the men to build the structure and dig a well.

The opening celebration of this first built school in Afgol, a desolate area in northern Ethiopia, was in 2007. About a thousand people of all ages walked eight to nine miles to witness this significant event. From a hillside overlooking the valley far in the distance, the horizon was covered with a winding throng of adults and children and a hundred priests in flowing, colorful gowns and turbans heading toward the cinder-block school.

The women ululated (making a high-pitched tongue-trilling sound) while holding homemade woven baskets as sun shields. Girls wore long, brilliant green dresses hand designed by the women to be let out as the children grew. An elegant, stunning teacher glowed in her white dress and graciously welcomed all to the school. She had grown up in the village, left to get an education, and was proud to return as a teacher. Everyone was swinging and swaying to the music. Laughter and happy tears flowed. All joined in gratitude to show their appreciation to the tall, thin, strong white woman and her American women friends dedicated to helping children get an education.

Huddled under tree branches, the children previously learned in "classes," sitting on rocks in a circle in the dirt. Largely uneducated parents had taught them. Because girls are the water gatherers, they typically weren't allowed to attend school. Save the Children helped to ensure they could make a difference in girls' attendance by building wells adjacent to schools. Girls can now go to class, carry their jerry cans (usually dirty plastic containers), and fill them up (weighing about 25 pounds) before walking over the rough terrain to their homes.

Encouraged by this first overwhelming success, Mimi vowed to raise more funds through Mimi's Building Blocks: Building Ethiopian Children's Futures Through Education, leading to seven years of fundraising, more than $800,000 donated, and five schools in Ethiopia.

Initially built as grades one–four primary schools with fresh water and latrines, these education centers in the Tigray area (Afgol, Maichecka, Dagia, Adi Gogol, and Mahago) have expanded with extra classrooms to provide a grades five–eight middle school education and reading and comprehension skills for the community.

Each center uses solar panels and has a playground, library, and health clinic. Illiterate family members benefit by learning to read books with their children at home by candlelight.

The schools are transforming the community, providing girls a chance to be educated like boys. The campaigns' success was a tribute to Mimi's tenacity and compassion. Her realized vision is making people's lives better with the gift of education.

After working years to build structures in remote regions of the world, Mimi formed a volunteer group, the Seven Working Ladies, to help restore homes for Habitat for Humanity in the United States. When Mimi was 82, they went to New Orleans, where she broke her neck. She was painting while standing on a ladder propped against a locked door. The door somehow opened, and the ladder crashed to the ground with her on it. Recovered and with good-natured perseverance, Mimi went to Santa Fe the next year on another building project and tore her meniscus.

Undaunted by her physical setbacks, she returned to Ethiopia later that year to visit the five schools built as a result of her fundraising campaigns. "It was rewarding and heartwarming to see the many students being educated," she said. But at 84, she said, "My trips to Ethiopia are probably over now."

A lifelong single woman with no children, Mimi was her family's "matriarch." She had a niece and four nephews from her two now-deceased sisters. Each nephew had four children, blessing her with sixteen beloved "grandees."

With Mimi as a philanthropic role model to adults and youth, Saint David's School, a private boys' elementary school in New York City, partnered with Mimi's Building Blocks Campaign and Save the Children. The young children raised funds to build Saint David's Kalina School in Tigray, Ethiopia, culminating with a delegation of students, fathers, and administrators attending the opening in 2014. Affiliated with the school through her grandnephew Liam, Mimi was proud that the younger generations are giving back and helping those less fortunate.

Not one to rest, Mimi worked as an outdoor volunteer two days a week, year-round, for the Central Park Conservancy, which was close to her former condominium in Manhattan. She weeded and planted bulbs, raked, and, when snow descended, happily shoveled the paths and cleared the benches. Her love of manual labor kept her energized. Her lovely apartment had mementos and photos of places worldwide. A shelf held fine porcelain that she lovingly restored in earlier years to generate additional income.

At age 86 in 2016, Mimi moved to a care facility in Washington, DC, close to many family members.

Thoughts and Advice About Risk

To those interested in charitable fundraising and volunteer work to make dreams come true for those in need, Mimi said, "Go for it! Don't be timid! You'll learn far more and be more gratified by helping others. Sponsor a Save the Children project of your own—a playground, health clinic, school, etc.

"With the help of the many donors who responded to the dream of bringing schools to remote, northern regions of Ethiopia, I wanted to help those who have so little and need so much. Mimi's Building Blocks has truly been a miracle in my life."

Mimi's dedication to community service continues to inspire adults and youth. A strong woman with a great sense of humor and warm laugh, she advised, "Instead of going to the beach in the summer, volunteer, help, and learn about people. You will *love* it.

"It's a miracle that I had this success and life-changing work."

In May 2018, Mimi died peacefully at age 88. An extraordinarily altruistic woman, Mimi touched many lives. She is greatly missed, and her legacy of helping others lives on.

Mimi in Ethiopia

Photo by Diana Coleman

CHAPTER 4 — ENTREPRENEURS

CLAIRE WEINBERG

From Teacher to Botanical Skincare Entrepreneur at 54

BIRTH YEAR: 1958

Claire spent her childhood romping around the great outdoors in Missouri. Later, she studied in New Hampshire and Vermont, and then moved to remote Gott's Island, Maine, where her husband's family had property. She taught in Maine and South Africa, but Claire, her husband, and her daughter dreamed of launching a botanical skincare products business. Dealt a major blow, Claire persevered through shock to become an entrepreneur.

Earlier Years

The second oldest with two brothers and a sister growing up in St. Louis, Claire swam, bicycled, climbed nearby bluffs, and indulged in A&W root beer floats and ice cream. She enjoyed going to movies and plays—sports were not her thing. Admitting she started school too soon with a September 2 birthday, she fell a beat behind as the youngest student in every class. "I knew how it felt to struggle to keep up with my classmates. I think this prepared me to be a good teacher," Claire said.

Her dad was a high school history teacher and later, an education administrator; her mom was an art teacher. Hearing about New England from her father, who was from there, Claire dreamed of visiting and living on the East Coast. She attended Franconia College in New Hampshire, which went bankrupt during her sophomore year. The doors closed, and the students were left to figure out what to do next.

She reconnected with a guy she knew from high school and married him, and they moved to small, one-mile-wide, remote Gott's Island off the coast of Acadia National Park and Mount Desert Island, Maine, onto land owned by her husband's family. Gott's Island was once a thriving fishing community, but people gradually moved off the island, leaving only summer visitors. Their property was down the hill from where the Moore family formerly lived—home of prolific author Ruth Moore.

Enthusiastic about an experiential school, Claire enrolled at Johnson State College in Vermont, which permitted her to attend classes on a flexible weekend schedule and attain a degree in elementary education while she worked as a caretaker for one of the Rockefeller family's estates.

When they moved to Gott's Island in the early 1980s, Claire and her husband were about the only people living there year-round. They lived in a handmade log house with only solar-powered electricity. Water came from a well, supplemented with rainwater collected in barrels. There were no stores, cars, or roads. Without ferry service, they went back and forth to the mainland in a small boat. They grew potatoes, salad greens, and vegetables for their food; chopped wood for their stove for heat; cooked using LP gas; raised pigs, chickens, and ducks; and had a pony. Everything was either grown on the island or purchased on the mainland. Throughout her life, Claire sewed—making clothes, aprons, and pillows. Her mom was "big into sewing," and she followed suit. "My sewing projects and things I made remind me of the different phases of my life," Claire said. She also designed sweaters and sold them on the island during the busier summers.

Claire was pregnant with her daughter and without health insurance when she and her husband got in their boat the morning she started having labor pains. After landing in Bass Harbor, a mile from the island, the car they kept on the mainland broke down en route to the midwife's house an hour away. It couldn't be fixed after a delay, so they borrowed a car. They arrived in Blue Hill, where, fortunately, Carly waited to be born. At one day old, Carly returned to the island with her parents.

Eking out a life year-round on Gott's Island was hard. They had to be totally independent. "We were poor," Claire said. Through snow, ice, and rain, their lives and crops revolved around the weather. After seven years of island living, with little money and no financial security, Claire, her husband, and their three-year-old daughter moved to Belfast, Maine, where she worked as an elementary school teacher. Her husband was also a teacher. At a job fair, Claire looked at teaching positions and thought about Europe as a destination. Hearing about openings during Valentine's Day weekend, she felt, was a good omen. The International School in South Africa beckoned. Claire and her husband got teaching jobs there, and the family moved to Johannesburg.

"Life in South Africa was fun. The food was fabulous," Claire said. "Lamb was abundant—*braai*, barbecued grilled lamb, was delicious. There was lots of good wine too. I loved the people, who were friendly, and the weather never got too cold." They lived in a gated complex in Johannesburg, which added some stress to their lives—it was very different from being in rural Maine, where they never locked their doors. Crime, such as robberies at the ATM, was a problem, but otherwise they felt safe where they were. Later they moved to Pretoria, where the pace was slower. They lived in a house surrounded by a fence and grew most everything—fruits and vegetables. Carly went through high school in South Africa. During the summers, they returned to Gott's Island for their six-week school break.

Launching Dulse and Rugosa

Claire was fascinated to learn about healing herbs and lotions at a botanical farm workshop. Seaweed's healing properties were demonstrated. Having had problems with an itchy scalp since her teens and tried fancy prescription shampoos that never worked, she discovered that adding powdered seaweed to regular shampoo cured her dry scalp. Claire and her husband dreamed of starting a business back on Gott's Island using the resources there, but they weren't sure what it would be. After looking at options, they decided to develop natural skincare products by harvesting the abundant island seaweed and growing herbs and flowers. At this time, Carly, following her parents' careers, also taught. She was in Texas and wanted to go into business with her parents. Knowing they needed income while launching a business, the three of them decided that Claire and Carly would quit their teaching jobs in South Africa and Texas, and her husband would continue teaching in South Africa during the school year.

Moving back to Gott's Island after teaching for thirteen years in South Africa, the family began fulfilling their dream from "the ground up." They worked together in the summer, adding a large garden to grow herbs and flowers for their botanical skincare line. It was hard work—moving rocks, preparing the soil, and carrying up the forest earth. Seaweed was added to the loam they brought over from the mainland. They built "sod mountains" from the compost of tough grasses. Needing to replace the log house, they built a wood home.

In the fall, Claire's husband returned to South Africa, and mother and daughter split up the work to get ready to launch the business. Buying a house on the mainland in Rockland gave them a place to operate part of their business and provided alternative housing to island living.

At Christmas, the family spent their holiday together in a rented apartment in England—halfway between South Africa and Maine. Back to work, Claire and Carly continued to put in long hours.

Six weeks after their family holiday, Claire received an email from her husband declaring he wanted a divorce—he was in love with someone else. Stunned, crying, angry, and distraught, Claire said, "I had to figure out what to do and how to survive." She signed the first divorce papers on Valentine's Day. "I hate February now," she confessed. Her ex-husband gave the Gott's Island property to Carly.

Needing money, Claire and Carly determined that one of them had to get a job. They decided whoever found a job first would be the income generator; the other would grow the flowers and herbs. Carly found a position first—working for the Puffin Project, a nonprofit organization in Rockland, Maine, launched by the National Audubon Society to restore puffins to historic nesting islands in the Gulf of Maine.

"It was scary," Claire admitted. "I hadn't lived on my own, and yet, I didn't want to give up our business idea." Heading to Gott's Island, she worked by herself. May to October is the season for planting herbs and flowers, growing, and harvesting—it's a "farm rhythm" schedule and is slower from the post-December holidays until March.

Carly worked hard to help her mom when she wasn't working for the Puffin Project. Besides growing herbs and flowers, seaweed had to be gathered; flowers dried; formulas created and mixed for the soaps, balms, lotions, perfumes, and other botanicals; the packaging and website developed; promotions put in motion; markets and stores approached for sales; and all other functions of running a business taken care of.

Mother and daughter thought carefully about what to call their business. "We wanted a name that captured the landscape of Maine islands and in particular Gott's Island, our home," Claire said. Loving seaweed and roses, they decided on Dulse, an abundant seaweed with many varieties on the coast of Gott's Island, and Rugosa, a fragrant and therapeutic pink and red rose. Both seaweed and roses are used for their special, organic lotions, body butters, sea salt scrubs, facial oils, bath teas, and soaps. "Seaweed was the spark that ignited the product development," Claire said. Growing and selling vegetables wasn't practical because of the transport challenge. Regulations were a major consideration in determining the type of products to offer. Food-based products required inspection. They needed to determine what was available, what they could produce, and what was realistic and practical to market, as well as create products they were excited and passionate about.

Dulse and Rugosa launched in spring 2013. "What started as a passion to grow and produce our own food turned into a desire to create natural skincare," Claire said. "Pure, straightforward skincare infused with island goodness" is the description on their dulseandrugosa.com website. With enticing names, their organic offerings include Lilac Sugar Scrub, Breathe Easy Balm, Bring on the ZZZ's Sleep Balm, Bug Be Gone Balm, Baby Belly Balm, Gardener's Scrub, Island Body Butter, Rosehip Lip Balm, Seaweed Shampoo Bar, Island Salt Soak, and Sea Lavender Solid Perfume. Branching into the "man market," there is Calendula and Thyme Aftershave, a Men's Shampoo Bar, and even dog shampoo.

Growing herbs and flowers and collecting seaweed for their lotions, scrubs, lip balms, and soaps is an arduous process with many steps. Their five-acre property has yellow, red, and orange calendula, blue bachelor buttons, lavender, and hedges of rugosa roses. St. John's wort and rose hips are gathered from the meadows, and the women keep a large vegetable garden and greenhouse. Carly has a seaweed harvester license and picks the seaweed along the shoreline, including dulse, nori, and sugar and finger kelp. All of the botanicals are air dried. Claire also maintains a large garden at her Rockland home, growing roses, lavender, straw flowers, thyme, and other herbs. Determining which products are prepared and sold depends upon the harvest.

"The challenges of starting and operating a business are many," Claire said. "Understanding the finances, for example, is hard—especially when my eyes glaze over looking at reports and numbers." Figuring out how to promote their product and make money is key. "I took some business seminars, which were somewhat helpful, but many things I learned I already had figured out by trying."

Mother and daughter split the business work—growing, harvesting, gathering seaweed, marketing the products to stores and the website, and maintaining inventory. They hired outside help to manage the books. Carly writes a blog on their website and enjoys making all kinds of delicious food from scratch.

One blog entry reads, "I made ricotta for the first time while I was waiting for the coffee water to boil. SO COOL!!! The ricotta is going to be turned into morel and lion's mane mushroom ravioli with, you guessed it, homemade pasta. Another fun food project was making fruit leathers out of canned pineapple. They are still in the dehydrator but they look amazing, pictures coming soon. This was as easy as opening a can of pineapple, pouring it into a blender, blending for a minute and spreading it out and turning the dehydrator on. Easy peasy."

A big believer in the healthy, soothing, and edible properties of seaweed, Carly promotes this multipurpose sea vegetable in her blog. Seaweed is high in vitamins, minerals, and amino acids and is great for detoxing in the tub; as a food additive when the dried flakes are sprinkled on potatoes, pasta, popcorn, and in soups; and even for dogs, houseplants, and gardens.

Claire and Carly live on Gott's Island periodically throughout the growing and harvesting season and may also live there during the winter. Carly was mentioned in the *Bangor Daily News* for seeing a moose munching on apple, maple, oak, and horse chestnut trees on their property. Since there are no moose on the island, it probably swam the mile over from Mount Desert Island and would likely swim back. Carly and a friend affectionately named the moose Virginia after Virginia Woolf because she "seemed to need an island of her own and they were a little afraid of her."

Dulse and Rugosa specialty products are "higher end," requiring customers who can afford them. Lotions, oils, and soaps are sold online via their website and in a variety of distribution points, including midcoast Maine's health food and gift stores. They've tried marketing at different farmers markets—some do not pay off, because there isn't the heavy traffic needed to make it profitable to transport and "person" a booth. The South End Boston Market has proven to be a good venue for them. They are constantly looking for new, cost-effective selling methods with a limited inventory. They are capable of producing only so many items. There's a lot to determine for the future.

Claire enjoys "being on her own" with the business she and Carly run. "I like spending time in my garden gathering the plants, and I love the smells." Gardening is a way of de-stressing for her. With smooth skin and a tanned face, Claire sports a healthy, wholesome, natural look—a believable model for their skincare botanicals.

"I want to do more meditating to help me respond better when things happen," she said. "The negatives can get to you!" She cited an example of a customer complaining about not liking a lip balm—Claire takes it personally and it can get to her. However, she said, "When I'm in my groove and meeting people at Boston's South End Market, for example, I love it—especially when people exclaim over our products."

In thinking about future goals, Claire would like to be more business savvy, that is, self-sustaining, and make the Internet work better to increase sales. She and Carly are always evaluating what pays off. Making a profit takes time.

She would like to go someplace warm during the winter months and have Dulse and Rugosa earn profits that would enable her to do that. Carly runs the inventory from her place on Mount Desert Island. They are open to exploring other products to cultivate and market.

"I'm super proud of my daughter, Carly," Claire said. "I'm also proud of how I've been able to survive, given my personal challenges. I'm stubborn—I don't like to give up. It keeps me going."

Thoughts and Advice About Risk

"Risk is the opposite of doing what's comfortable," Claire said. "I call myself a reluctant risk taker." Yet, she maintains, "You have to do things you're afraid of." Living by herself admittedly was "scary" for her. Starting and continuing with the business was a huge risk. "I've been spite successful," she said.

She mused, "I'm not sure I would have launched this business, looking back, if I had known I was going to be divorced. Would I have done things differently? Going to South Africa, living on remote Gott's Island for seven years—three of them with a child—were also risks."

To women considering starting a business, especially at 50 or older, she says, "Make sure you have a passion for it and people behind you for support. You need to be okay with your finances." Claire had quit her teaching job in South Africa and her daughter left her teaching position in Texas, so they had no income once her husband delivered the news that he wanted a divorce. "Financial stress leads to bad decisions. There's a huge difference between being in your 30s versus being in your 50s and taking a risk with little money. When you're younger, you can do something else, like get a job. If your dream doesn't make it when you're older, you can't suddenly do something to make money. It's not as easy."

She laughs a lot, though, and Claire's humor helps her persevere.

Claire selling Dulse and Rugosa products
Camden, Maine

Photo by Vicki Harner

DENISE DAVENPORT

Insurance Executive to Hot Dog Café and Dog Treats Bakery Owner at 55

BIRTH YEAR: 1958

Raised in a small Rhode Island town, Denise endured a grueling youth as the middle child between a brother and sister. Her father was a builder-contractor. Her mother died when Denise was young. Working a series of jobs out of high school, Denise married and had three children. Interested in laws protecting employees, she became a paralegal and worked her way up in the insurance industry. At 55, she bought a small run-down building and launched a hot dog café and dog treats bakery. Two years later she closed it.

Earlier Years

Denise lived with her family in the old mill town of Coventry, Rhode Island. Her father was a hard worker but an abusive, mean drunk. Her mother was a warm, open-minded, and positive woman. She became seriously ill when Denise was 9 years old.

One Thanksgiving, her mother returned home from a hospital stay, and a neighbor brought over a home-cooked turkey dinner. Her father launched into a tirade. "He yelled, 'We don't take charity.' He made us kids carry the food back to the neighbor's, and the neighbor's house became a safe place for us," Denise said. Her mother died of congenital heart failure when Denise was 13.

Attending Catholic schools, Denise did well, and after high school, had a series of short-term jobs. She folded Christmas tree skirts at a furiously fast pace in a factory and was paid by the piece. The company then reduced the price-per-piece rate. At 18, she was an entry-level shipfitter for General Dynamics in a sprawling complex where submarines were built. She interpreted blueprints, hauled heavy equipment, and welded brackets onto hulls. "I worked with a bunch of guys who laughed at me while I climbed sixty feet high with my tools. They'd take my tools and harass me. It was uncomfortable, so I quit." She became a waitress, married, and had three children.

As a young mother, she sold Tupperware and had an in-home child care business. A serious work injury put her husband out of a job for three years. Determined to fight for workers' compensation, Denise contacted a renowned lawyer and waited weeks for him to respond. When she grew tired of being put off, she took her three children, all under age 4, and sat in his firm's waiting room, determined not to leave until he met with her. With her restless children and her youngest screaming from hunger, the attorney acquiesced, took on her case personally, and put her in contact with the advocacy group Injured Workers of Rhode Island. This organization brought her family a welcomed food basket. Other nonprofits and the church also helped them cope during lean times. Denise educated herself about workers' compensation law. She joined protests to lobby for workers' benefits. Becoming the executive director of the all-voluntary organization, she earned little pay, but gained experience and knowledge. Advocating for workers' compensation rights launched her interest in laws protecting employees. "It was fun to be part of changing things. I learned you can fight city hall and win. I was driven out of a need to feed my children."

Because of her work success, she was offered a paralegal job and began college part-time at night, learning about personal injury law, business law, and probate and estate law.

When Denise and her husband divorced, she stopped going to college six classes shy of graduating to spend more time with her adolescent children. As a paralegal working for a solo practitioner, she found she enjoyed business law the most, because it provided opportunities to bring together people with divergent views. But the position lacked the financial security she needed as a single mother, so she moved into the corporate world, working for several insurance companies throughout her career. Denise capitalized on opportunities to grow, and advanced in the field. "However, making changes in larger firms was like moving the *Titanic*," she said. "The bureaucracy was a killer. By the time you could effect change, the need for change had passed."

While a senior executive, Denise became disillusioned with corporate America. "The level of greed bothered me," she said. "Executives were arrogant, people were fungible, and the focus was on short-term profits. My health suffered." After ten years, she needed to come up with an exit strategy and had no idea what to do.

Near her home was a run-down building that had been for sale for more than a year. Formerly an ice cream shop, it had deteriorated and needed a lot of work. She considered buying the building but wasn't sure what for. She prayed for guidance. "I had a strong feeling in my gut, which I sometimes get, that told me to move forward," Denise said. "It was as though an inner spirit spoke to me."

The next morning, she had a message from the real estate agent she had contacted previously. He asked her, "What is your dream?" A compassionate man, he worked with Denise to determine how the building could be fixed.

She bought the building with funds from her 401(k) plans, not knowing what she was going to do with it. It was in a great location in Coventry, Rhode Island—adjacent to a bike path, a park with baseball and softball fields, and a community and recreation center.

Denise had previously taken her grandson Damian on a "baseball odyssey" around the country to Fenway Park, Yankee Stadium, and other ballparks in Minnesota, Wisconsin, Atlanta, and Baltimore. An 8-year-old Boston Red Sox fan, he talked to his grandmother about her building. "Why don't you sell hot dogs named after different baseball stadiums?" he asked.

Creating a Café

Denise continued working in her insurance job for another seven months. Her blood pressure went to a sky-high 190/120. She thought her home blood pressure machine was broken. It wasn't. She was put on medication. She had remarried, and with her husband's agreement (he would become their sole income provider for a while), she quit her insurance position. Her blood pressure dropped significantly within a week.

Thinking about starting the café, Denise said, "I have to do this. I would be foolish not to." The building she bought needed a total rehab. The plumbing had to be yanked out and the roof replaced. It was a dump, but she thought she had paid a fair price for it. On weekends her husband and daughter helped her fix the building. She hired contractors and installed a new electrical system and plumbing. She figured out building and health codes. Taking classes sponsored by the Department of Health, she learned about proper food-safety techniques. She studied equipment and figured out where to put outlets. Although never a professional carpenter or builder like her dad, she understood how things should be done, which came in handy while working with contractors. "It was a tremendous learning curve," she said.

The DogHouse Café, with its signage advertising Stadium Style Specialty Hot Dogs and Homemade Dog Treats, opened less than a year after Denise purchased it. It was open from March through December, weather dependent. The café was cheerful and inviting: a yellow exterior, interior walls of red, white, and sage green, and decorated with baseball memorabilia. Former ice cream counter stools were painted red, and Denise sewed white seat cushions with red stitching to resemble baseballs.

The café served specialty hot dog combos following the major-league ballparks, players, teams, and baseball themes. Hot dogs on freshly baked buns included the Big Peach, a quarter-pound all-beef dog topped with pulled pork simmered in a root beer barbecue sauce, creamy southern slaw, and pickles; and the Blue Wahoo, an all-beef dog wrapped in bacon, topped with creamy macaroni and cheese, and sprinkled with Fritos. Recipes were original, borrowed, and ongoing creations, and new suggestions were encouraged. If a specialty hot dog was not popular, it got "scratched" and "traded." During the World Series, two specialty competing hot dogs were offered.

Having loved dogs since childhood, Denise baked healthy treats such as peanut butter–oatmeal bones and wheat-free brown rice–and-honey bones for dog friends who enjoyed stopping by.

Because she was community minded, one of Denise's goals was to give some of the café's profits to help others. Liking the ripple effect, part of her sales went to the local food bank and kids' sports teams. The signature DogHouse cookie sales supported the animal shelter. Her young grandson questioned her business sense by asking, "Why aren't you waiting to make a profit before giving some of the earnings away?" Denise explained, "It's like savings. If you start saving at the very beginning, you will always do it. It's important to start my business by giving some of the earnings back to the community." She wanted to make people happy with fresh homemade food and feel good about having a positive effect. She had learned compassion from her mother, and because others had helped Denise and her family when they had had very little, she knew what it was like to struggle to feed her kids and the importance of people preserving their dignity.

The challenges of café ownership included making money, finding a work-life balance, and getting enough sleep. During the first year, Denise worked 70–100 hours a week. Though exhausted, she didn't have the same stressed-out feeling she had had with her insurance job. As one of her "lessons learned," she reduced the café's hours. She hoped to break even in her second year and make a profit the third year. It helped that her husband worked full-time. "Money is not that important to me—only to the degree that I can eat and pay my way."

Two years later, Denise closed her café and put the building up for sale. "The decision to close was very painful," she said. "I spent time reviewing the finances and fixed costs. I had to put aside my pride and make a dispassionate decision when I decided to close. I put my heart and soul into the business. I met great people. I hired teenagers. I loved what I did. It came down to money. I put a significant amount of money into it. Not only did I not turn a profit, it didn't sustain itself." Until the building sells, she incurs the fixed costs of taxes and insurance.

Before launching her café, Denise thought about the consequences if her business didn't work. "Failure doesn't define me. Closing down the café could be embarrassing, but I would view it as a learning experience. You can't fail without trying. Trying something new is a positive attribute." Selling the building was a fallback position. She could also find another job in the insurance industry but would want a less stressful position.

In retrospect, she would have done some things differently. "I would have reallocated funds and spent less on equipment and salaries. I would have ramped up the business more slowly. I fell short in marketing and would have spent funds hiring someone with advertising expertise. Not enough people knew about the café."

Out of financial necessity, Denise returned to the insurance field and used her skills working for another company, but in a different role with new challenges. She no longer directly manages a large team of people, but her job is stressful in other ways. "I'm much more comfortable now telling my boss what my work tolerance level is and that quitting is an option. My health and family are more important." Ideally, she would like to take early retirement and work part-time.

Denise enjoys spending uninterrupted quality time with her grandchildren, family, and friends. She likes watching movies, cooking, developing new recipes, and playing games with her grandchildren. She does remodeling jobs around her house and finds it relaxing. A reader, she enjoys books and crocheting.

"Going to the Galapagos would be wonderful," she says. She has been to Bangalore, India, to attend her son's wedding to an Indian woman; visited Stalybridge, England, to see the house her great-grandfather grew up in—a stone building with apartments and a tavern, in a little village with mills reminiscent of an earlier Rhode Island; ridden white horses on a beach in southern France; and gone to Arles, France, the hometown of her favorite artist, Vincent van Gogh. In Sorrento, Italy, she met a glass artist she commissioned to create several pieces for the café, including a baseball-diamond clock with a hot dog pendulum.

Denise harbors a fantasy about being a weather forecaster. Though afraid of heights, she would like to try skydiving, because she loves the idea of flying and the feeling of freedom.

Pleased with her life, Denise says, "I've actually done a lot of what I've wanted to do so far. If I get run over by a Mack truck, I would die a happy person."

Thoughts and Advice About Risk

"Engaging in an action where you're unsure of the outcome" is Denise's definition of risk. Coming from the insurance industry, Denise analyzes risks. "I always thought of myself as more of a checkers player than a bungee jumper. I don't think I seek out risks. I did a risk analysis with this new business. I examined what I would lose and what I could fall back on. I asked myself, *How secure is my insurance job?*" She witnessed layoffs and thinks no job is guaranteed, and in large firms, older employees are expendable.

"I took a leap of faith," Denise said. "Buying the building and starting a café and bakery was a great unknown. This was a pretty big risk for me, coming from a healthy six-figure salary with benefits. I raided my 401(k) plans and was in a deficit income mode.

"I tried, I failed, and I moved forward. I'm at peace with it. I knew it was risky, and if I hadn't tried, I most certainly would have regretted it."

For those who are thinking about taking a risk but are fearful, Denise recommends prayer. "Without sounding preachy," she said, "I believe

God provides, he listens. I prayed. I didn't know what to do. Then I jumped in with my eyes wide shut."

She further advises people contemplating starting a business to "weigh your options carefully. You need to ask yourself, What's your failsafe? Your tolerance level for risk? I asked myself two questions: *If I fail, will I regret it?* and *If I don't try it, will I regret it?*"

Denise's mother died before she was 33. "During my 32nd year, I was fearful about my life ending," she said. "Because my mother died young, I instilled a sense of independence in my children to ensure they could do things for themselves—cooking, laundry, filing taxes, and so on." Denise's father and stepmother had their own businesses. Both died in their early 60s and never enjoyed retirement. Her aunt and uncle went to Miami, where her uncle slipped and fell. His fall led to a serious infection, his kidneys shut down, and he died within the year. He never got to retire and realize his dreams together with his wife. Denise has had friends die early who didn't do what they hoped they would in their later years.

"It doesn't matter how safe you think you are—some things are not in your control. You never really know what will happen. Life is precious," Denise believes. "Your life can be deceptively comfortable. There is no guarantee that the life we are living today will be here tomorrow."

Despite a rough childhood, Denise chooses to be positive. "Starting a café is the first time I took a risk *for myself*. In the past, I've taken risks when someone else's survival was on the line. When younger, I went after my father to protect my sister, who was being hit by my dad. I was bold and took risks to stand up for others. As a single mom, I had to take care of my kids. My difficult experiences during my youth were part of who I am, but they don't define me. Alcohol, addiction, and abuse hurt and have a far-reaching impact. I was lucky enough to be able to separate from my father's actions and develop empathy for the man who turned to alcohol to cover up his inability to relate to his family—or any human being—in any meaningful way. I don't believe people wake up thinking they're going to hurt people. I believe in the inherent goodness of people. I like to be happy.

"I have zero regrets about starting the café and bakery. I wanted to give it a shot and go for it. I'd rather die happy than die wishing I had done it."

Denise in the DogHouse Café
Coventry, Rhode Island

Photo by Diana Coleman

DIANE ELLIOT

Community Activist and Healer to Restaurant Owner at 62

BIRTH YEAR: 1946

Born at home in Indiana, Diane raised a family in Virginia and was an active community volunteer, developed a healing practice, and was initiated as a Western Sufi. At 58, she was ordained as a Universal Worship minister. Passionate about working for Mother Earth, Diane spontaneously bought a restaurant at 62 with no business background. Her farm-to-table restaurant was named one of Open Table's "Top 100 Foodie Restaurants" in the country.

Earlier Years

Diane, her brother, and her sister were home-birthed intentionally. Her mother's first child died in the hospital, and she opted from then on to deliver her babies at home. Though not the attending physician, Diane's physician grandfather remained close by during the births. A general practitioner, he was taught to evaluate patients through the five senses and rode his horse to make house calls when his car couldn't run on rough roads outside his Nashville, Tennessee, home.

Growing up in Indianapolis, Diane loved school and swam competitively year-round from age 6. Educating women was important in her family—her father's grandmother went to Mount Holyoke Female Seminary (now Mount Holyoke College) in the mid-1800s. Diane attended a girls' college prep high school; was an exchange student in England, meeting her future American husband aboard the

Queen Mary on the trip over; and graduated in the last all-female class at Vassar College. "While my family told me I could do anything I wanted, society didn't agree," Diane said. She found this out while doing cold calls for Manpower during college. When she called on a male bank employee, he said, "Banking is no place for women." Diane believed him. Feeling strongly that she shouldn't marry right out of college, she was a department store buyer/trainee for one year before marriage.

Living a full life as a wife and mother of three children and active in her Roanoke, Virginia, community, Diane was a childbirth educator advocating for women to take charge of their own experience through natural childbirth. She helped support a day shelter for people with AIDS and was one of her Roanoke Episcopal church's first women chalice bearers, lay readers, and governing board members. She did craniosacral and mind-body energy work and started Dances of Universal Peace, which uses sacred names, phrases, movements, and music from the world's spiritual traditions. "This provides an understanding of oneness in the web of life—that we're all connected," Diane said. She led inner-growth classes in her home that included chanting and spiritual practice. Becoming a Western Sufi, she embarked on a mystical path based in Islam but much older—it is a process of becoming who you really are and understanding that all is One. "Deliver us from the differences and distinctions that divide us" is one of the prayers. Since being ordained as a minister in the Universal Worship of the Western Sufi order at age 58, Diane continues to officiate at baby and house blessings, weddings, and funerals.

When Diane was 62, her son, who had used his college money to start a restaurant in Roanoke, decided to go into a different field. Asking his mother if she knew any potential investors for the restaurant, she said, "I'll buy it!" Believing in the restaurant's Sustainable, Organic, Local, and Ethical food mission, she would not have started it herself, but wanted to see it continue.

Owning and Operating a Restaurant

"I felt as if I were jumping off a cliff when I decided to buy the restaurant," Diane said. She never would have imagined doing it. As a young woman, she had not been allowed to work in a restaurant and had no business experience. Growing up in an academically oriented family with a father who ran a printing firm, she was raised with the belief that restaurant work, like waitressing, was not proper employment for someone with an education. When her son created and ran the restaurant, she was not involved in the business by her son's choice.

However, Diane was committed to the restaurant's mission and wanted to ensure it continued to thrive. "Food was always an important part of my life." Though not a hippie as a teen and young adult in the 1960s, she read a lot about and respected the "back to the land" movement. For many years, she frequented one of Virginia's oldest farmers' markets in Roanoke with her young children. She felt good about eating seasonal food and getting to know the farmers. From them, she learned what produce was in season when, and guided her family in accordance with the rhythms of the earth—such as no fresh strawberries in January in southwest Virginia.

Her son had refurbished a former day care center, a large old house, for the restaurant. After she bought the restaurant from him, it became clear that the infrastructure, including water and electricity, was not adequate to support the business. She decided not to put any more money into that location and looked for another place. Though moving would be expensive, she realized she couldn't afford not to move.

"There have been very dark moments combined with good fortune," Diane said about operating the restaurant. Four blocks away was a burgeoning artsy area—charming Grandin Village—a revitalized 1920s business district with an eco-friendly clothing store and an independent movie theater, yoga studio, and natural food co-op. A long, rectangular space that had formerly housed a record, clothing, and appliance store opened up for rent. "It was unattractive," Diane said, "but it was in a great location, and I knew we could make it look appealing." To do so, she hired an architect and a contractor, remodeled the space, decided on the colors, and bought proper kitchen equipment. It was a large capital outlay. She poured more money into her venture. "I told myself, *I am in it too far now. I cannot go back. I must go forward.* I've recovered since then, but it was hard.

"You need to decide how much money to put into a business and how much is too much." With exposed-brick walls and pressed tin ceilings, the space was transformed into an attractive dining area, a bar with wood and painted golden earth tones, local art on the walls, and sustainable/organic food books and publications on shelves near the tables.

Local Roots, A Farm-to-Table Restaurant opened in its new location in Roanoke sixteen months after she became owner.

"Being in the restaurant business was foreign to me. I knew less than nothing about the many aspects of running a restaurant. The restaurant has stretched me and made me face things I didn't like—working with bureaucracies, for example. I had to learn everything business-wise: working with the IRS, finances, how to fire someone, and how not to trust finances to the hired bookkeeper." There was a time she was going to give it up because she was running out of funds. "I bled money for three years and planned on closing it."

Since doing healing and spiritual work for an alcohol and drug rehabilitation program with residents court-ordered from prison, Diane says her training and inclination was always to see the best in people and not judge them. "I had to be discerning in this business journey. I learned how to call the restaurant staff on their stuff, how to determine what kind of person is on the team versus those for whom it is just a job."

Finding responsible, team-focused, conscientious people fostering harmony makes working together a pleasure. A shared-tips policy for the servers helps promote teamwork. "For many months, I felt like hell had opened up and spit out people incompatible with our mission; then heaven opened up and sent beautiful and harmonious people."

Diane runs the highly acclaimed restaurant, "serving food grown sustainably and in harmony with the earth, people, and animals, as one big connected web." Committed to being part of the local, organic food movement, she enjoys working with neighboring farmers who supply the restaurant's food. "The meat served comes from animals that are treated humanely—for example, the chickens are raised on pastures where they eat natural diets and wander about freely, chickens the way God made them to be." The restaurant's garden provides some of the herbs and vegetables and is overseen by the chef and staff. Diane also grows flowers, herbs, and vegetables for the restaurant in her home garden.

Only fresh food in season is served. "Nothing comes in frozen and is then reheated in a microwave! One man walked out of our restaurant because we didn't have a fresh tomato to serve on his hamburger. It was winter. We don't serve tomatoes then (unless they are preserved in a sauce from the previous summer), because they're not grown in southwestern Virginia in the cold months." Diane thinks that situations like this are educational opportunities to explain seasonal eating—for example, root vegetables are served in the winter and berries in the summer. A limited amount of food, like strawberries, is frozen or dried to serve at other times.

Local Roots, A Farm-to-Table Restaurant has received numerous, overwhelmingly positive reviews. Open Table named Local Roots one of the "100 Best Restaurants for Foodies in America," and *USA Today* recognized it as one of the "10 Best Slow Food Restaurants That Are Sustainable and Scrumptious."

Lunch, dinner, brunch, and Sunday supper are served. Menu items have included handmade fettuccini with butternut squash, lacinato kale, shiitake mushrooms, and garlic bread crumbs; ancient White Park beef rib eye with parsnip-potato puree, braised greens, black radish, and black garlic; spring soup, a chilled blend of asparagus, broccoli, and house-made whey poured from a tureen at the table into a bowl over fennel and bread crumbs; and warm chocolate chunk brownie with crème Chantilly and oat streusel. Beverages, including wine, beer, and liquor, are from "small-batch, family-owned, rare and unique purveyors." Small-scale catering services are available.

"Our food is local, organic, sustainably produced, and made from scratch, so the prices are somewhat higher than most restaurants' industrial agriculture food, which is government subsidized so prices are artificially deflated," Diane said. "Our farmers get a fair price for their hard work." She is sensitive about offering excellent healthy cuisine at a good value. The Sunday brunch and family-style supper menus reflect less costly options.

Incorporating an educational aspect into her restaurant, she likes giving people a dining experience that they won't have elsewhere. Even the paintings on the doors of the restrooms have been a teaching tool to show people the difference between a hen and a rooster! She found it rather shocking that many people do not know the difference. Visiting colleges and groups, she provides programs about food, where it comes from, and the many benefits of eating locally. Passionate about offering high-quality, locally grown, delicious food, a pleasant atmosphere, and excellent service, Diane feels joy in owning the restaurant and working with amiable people. She takes pleasure in talking to her guests.

"I enjoy being in the restaurant—it's like being at a party without having to cook the food."

Someday, Diane may sell the restaurant, perhaps to an employee who will continue the mission. She would like to travel with her husband, do things as a couple, and spend time with her grandchildren. It has been a balance between her family and the restaurant. One daughter, a chef, had a restaurant in Brooklyn and does catering. Diane plans to launch a Local Roots foundation to provide grants to those who want to contribute to the local food web—through farming, community gardening, education, food distribution, journalism, and other ways.

Interested in food politics, such as the issue of genetically modified organisms, toxic pesticides, and Monsanto, she signs petitions and writes letters and could see herself more involved in this area, such as with a regular radio show focused on food and food politics.

Before the restaurant, she embraced her Cherokee ancestry as the storyteller for the Red Feather Medicine Singers. Influenced and guided by her Cherokee background and beliefs, Diane thinks about the seasons' meanings. Winter, the season of the North, is a time of small tests, learning about outer and inner endurance strengthening and resources. Spring, the season of the East, marks a new beginning. Summer, the South, represents fruition and creativity. Fall, the West, is a time of transformation and great challenges. Diane intentionally took over the restaurant during the spring equinox, on March 21, 2009, in keeping with honoring the seasons.

Thoughts and Advice About Risk

"You can be comfortable in your own box or risk going outside the box and growing," Diane maintains. "The future is here. If you don't do it now, you may never do it. Some people might think you're kooky, but you are doing something you are motivated to do and have a passion for. Go for it!"

For anyone thinking of owning a restaurant, Diane recommends knowing your limits. "Buying the restaurant was a super big risk. It takes money and requires financial resources, which will almost certainly be more than you expect. Talk to other restaurant owners. Give me a call! Ask yourself, Do you really want to do this? Is this a mission for you? What's your endurance? It's not about ego. Are you physically well enough to do this work? Are you in decent shape?"

The image of "dancing bear," the Cherokee Adawee, Wise Protector of the West, a healer who stomps out fear and ignorance, helped her. "I needed to stomp out and move through my fear, acknowledge my ignorance, and be shown what I needed to know," Diane said.

"There's no failing. You always learn, especially in the United States, where risk-taking is approved of. People pick themselves up and start over, but you need to be realistic. There's stupid risk and there's why not? risk.

"I would not jump out of a plane or bungee jump. I'm not a physical risk taker. I am an emotional, psychological, and spiritual risk taker. Move outside the box to have a broader, deeper experience as a human being."

Liking challenges that cause her to grow and trying new things to see where they go, Diane said, "Change is growth; even what appears to be negative change requires deepening within yourself to be able to do something to deal with it. We become stronger.

"I'm glad I did this. I have never looked back."

Diane at the National Heirloom Seed Festival
Santa Rosa, California

Photo by Bill Elliot

CHAPTER 5 — FAMILY LOVE

CAROLE LINK FLEMING

Reunited at 55, 36 Years After Giving Her Baby Up for Adoption

BIRTH YEAR: 1945

Coming from "an awful, crazy, mentally ill family," as she described it, Carole, raised primarily in New Hampshire, became pregnant at 18 and gave up her baby at birth. Throughout her life she imagined what her son must look like and be like. At 55, her life changed profoundly when her child, at 36 years old, found her.

Earlier Years

Surviving a rough childhood in New Hampshire (with short stays in Idaho and California, where her military father was stationed), Carole was the second of five children. Her parents were verbally abusive to each other and shoved each other around. Carole was terrified of her father. He put a gun to her head when she was a little girl. "I had no idea what I did wrong," Carole said. When she spilled her milk, she was forced to lick it up off the floor. Her father—and mother—beat her regularly—swinging a belt or slamming her to the floor with a cast iron skillet. As a child and teenager, she often hid in her closet to avoid being abused.

Creative and artistic, Carole won a scholarship from her high school to take an art class at the Boston School of Fine Arts. She graduated at 17 and, interested in fashion, was accepted into New York's Fashion Institute of Technology. She never attended, however, because she couldn't afford the tuition. Her father offered to give her $200, but only if she would go to secretarial school. Then her father was transferred to

South Dakota, where she was forced to move with her family. Soon after turning 18, she moved back to New Hampshire on her own and worked for an art supply store, where she enjoyed creating window displays.

Discovering she was pregnant at 18, Carole, who was single and not ready for a relationship, was taken into the home of an older woman friend when her pregnancy began to show. She managed to avoid running into kids she knew from school. Carole feared she might perpetuate the abuse she had lived with if she kept her baby. She thought the child would have a better chance if adopted by a two-parent, loving family. The baby's father offered a small amount toward the delivery expenses. Delivered by C-section at Portsmouth Regional Hospital, her baby, whom she never saw, was whisked away and given to a couple in a private adoption. Carole never knew whether her baby was a girl or boy, though she felt strongly it was a boy.

"It's better you don't know," she was told.

Needing to regroup after giving birth, Carole moved to her family's home on a military base in Tucson, Arizona, to work and take college classes. When she found the courage to tell her mother about the baby, her disapproving mother said she had dreamed that Carole had given birth to a child on her birthday. In fact, Carole's baby was born the day after her mother's birthday. Her mother, fearing that someone in the "small national military community" had heard about her daughter, wanted her out of sight when company visited. Carole was prohibited from being at the house when her mother had guests over for mahjong. Surprisingly, when Carole told her father what had happened, "He took me in his arms and said he was sorry I had to go through this."

A few years later, lured by the 1967 Summer of Love, Carole, at 21, moved to San Francisco on a Sunday. The day after arriving, she met Myles, a wonderful Irish guy who was visiting a friend of hers. "By Wednesday, we were a couple, and we've been together ever since—living together for a while and marrying in 1973. He's the love of my life. I'm so lucky to have him as my husband."

Carole dabbled in watercolor painting and drawing. She dressed up work spaces and her home, which, she said was "overdecorated—new ideas are always popping into my head." Her talent extended beyond the artistic world. "My ability to come up with creative solutions to problems did me in good stead even in noncreative data processing and collections positions when I worked for Crocker and Wells Fargo banks." Later, as a receptionist for Project Open Hand, a nonprofit organization providing meals and groceries for people with AIDS and other sick, homebound people, Carole greeted everyone in her friendly, outgoing manner and magically decorated the office.

Pleasant and funny, Carole loved people and was well liked. Despite her childhood abuse, she was unusually optimistic. "I knew in my heart abuse was wrong. As kids, we shouldn't have had to go through it." With the exception of Carole and her mother, mental illness ran rampant in her family. Two of her sisters died—one an assumed suicide.

Carole stayed in touch with her parents when they retired to San Diego. She and her mother talked by phone after her father's death, but Carole could never forgive her mother for allowing her father to abuse them. When Carole finally confronted her mother about it and asked why she hadn't protected her children from him, her mother said that with no money and no job, she hadn't seen a way out, though she confessed she found her husband's abuse "exciting." "I did the best I could," her mother said. Carole replied, "It wasn't good enough." Still, their relationship continued until her mother's death.

Throughout her life, Carole wondered what her child was doing but didn't want to initiate a search. She felt it too intrusive. However, she thought it was important to give her personal information to the Adoptees' Liberty Movement Association and the International Soundex Reunion Registry in case her child was looking for her. These nonprofit organizations maintain registries for people wanting to find relatives.

Once, while watching the *Oprah Winfrey Show* on TV, Carole thought she saw her son among a group of hunky, eligible bachelors. Though she didn't know the sex of her child, one of the men looked very much like the handsome father of her child and had a similar background. She ordered a tape of the show so she could study it more closely, but she never did anything more about it.

Then in July 2001, a certified letter arrived at Carole's house. Myles signed in seven places to receive it. When Carole saw it was from New Hampshire, she immediately thought it was about the death of an older nurse friend. She started to shake as she read the letter. The letterhead was from a social services agency. Signed by a social worker, the letter included Carole's maiden name and birth date and said, "At times, we are asked to locate people by individuals who are searching for relatives. We have such a request from a woman born in June 1965, who we believe may be related to you." Carole and Myles were stunned, worried, and then jubilant. Carole called the phone number immediately, but the office was closed for a week of remodeling. Desperately wanting to connect, she left several messages. "YES! I'm her mother! Please call me!"

Connecting with Her "Child"

Carole was ecstatic upon hearing about her "baby"—a 36-year-old woman. She and Myles discussed their concerns. What were her daughter's circumstances? What if she was mentally ill? What if she was contacting them because she needed money? Carole was thrilled despite the uncertainty. She wanted to take the risk of getting to know her daughter. She sent the social worker an email about her life, included photos, and said her daughter could contact her by email, not by phone, requesting that they "go slowly."

She talked to the social worker the following week. Five days later, Carole received this email (edited) with photos:

> Hi,
>
> My name is Susan ... I am 36 years old ... I was adopted at birth ...

My mom was a "stay-at-home mom," however she passed away in February of 1994. My dad will be 81 in September and my mom was 72 years old when she died. I have a brother who is 20 years older than me who is their natural child. I was told from the beginning that I was adopted and that I was "chosen." I have always felt being adopted was a special thing. They wanted another child, and after many miscarriages, believed adoption was their only alternative. I also always believed that my birth mother gave me up for adoption because she thought it was the better choice for both of us, regardless of the reasons. I can only imagine how difficult yet unselfish that choice must have been.

After my mom passed away I felt very disconnected. Although I have a wonderful husband and his family is great, it isn't the same as having a connection of your own. My dad knows that I have been looking and wants for me whatever will make me happy. I have always been curious about what my birth mother looked like. I've wondered if she thought of me on my birthday. I was surprised to learn that you were never told whether you had a boy or a girl. I was surprised by the pictures! The larger, adult, black and white picture with bangs is like looking at a picture of myself in high school!

... I would love to talk with you, but I do understand if you want to go more slowly and continue writing for a while. I am so glad to have "found" you. I hope you will find this opportunity to be as wonderful as I do ... I look forward to hearing from you.

Sincerely,
Sue

Sue grew up ten miles from where she was born. She married her high school sweetheart. On their honeymoon, she and her husband stopped at the Cliff House in San Francisco, not knowing then that they were less than four miles from Carole's home. She was a stay-at-home mom with three children—a girl, age 7, and fraternal twin boys age 5.

Euphoric, Carole screamed in her empty house. She tried printing the message and photos to show her husband, who was at work. (This was before smartphones.) The printer was out of ink. She ran to the store to buy ink, flew home, printed out the message, and hurried to Nag's Head Tavern, where Myles was tending bar. He was exuberant too.

Carole and Sue began emailing daily. "The excitement of receiving one of your emails is right up there with that feeling you have when Santa is coming!" Sue said. They discovered they looked very much alike. Sue admitted being concerned that her birth mother wouldn't accept her. Her fears soon evaporated.

Carole's Christmas gift to Sue was calling her—their first conversation. Seven months after Carole initially heard from her daughter, Sue and her husband flew to San Francisco to meet Carole and Myles. They left their three children at home.

Arriving at Carole's door, mother and daughter stared at each other. They looked astoundingly similar—the same small mouth, round face, and body type.

"You have my mother's hands," Carole said.

They were dressed alike—in turtlenecks. Sue also wore a scarf and vest—exactly what Carole typically wore. For a week, they talked and toured around San Francisco. Carole brought Sue to Project Open Hand, where she worked. Everyone commented that they looked identical. At a gas station, someone asked if they were sisters.

The following Mother's Day, Carole received a card and thirty-six long-stemmed roses— "One for every year we were apart."

The next year, Carole and Myles took a trip to Ireland and stopped in New Hampshire on the way back to California. They met their grandchildren for the first time. Their granddaughter was 9 and their twin grandsons were 7. "The kids ran and hugged their newly found grandparents as if we were forever grandparents," Carole recalled. She also met Sue's adoptive father. "Thank you for giving us Sue," he said.

It had taken three years of sleuthing for Sue to find her mother. New Hampshire is a closed-adoption state, and information is not released to anyone other than the state. She had filed a petition with the court to open her adoption records. After she'd been granted a judge's approval, her case was assigned to a social worker. Sue called frequently, eager to have an answer, and was frustrated by how long it seemed to take. "I had always been curious about what my birth mother looked like," she said. "I wondered as I got older about my own medical history. I always had to answer 'I don't know' during appointments with doctors. I never wanted to do anything that would hurt either of my adoptive parents, particularly my mom, so it wasn't until several years after she passed that I initiated the search. I was never really curious about my birth father." Sue's adoptive parents had given her the notes from the nurse who worked with the obstetrician who delivered her. None of the birth mother's and father's details were correct except for Carole's brown hair and brown eyes. Clearly, the notes were about another baby's parents.

The only correct information the social worker had was Sue's birth date and birth hospital and Carole's Social Security number, birth date, and birthplace. Key to the search was finding the military death records for Carole's father, who died in 1988, and later, her mother's obituary in 1999, which listed Carole as executor. The social worker contacted a California social worker friend who tracked down Carole.

"I thought, *I could be no worse off than I am now if she is not interested in meeting me, and I can only gain and be reconnected with my mother if she is willing*," Sue said. "Either way I would have an answer, more than I had without searching. I wanted to be respectful that she had a life—possibly a family and children who may or may not know about me. My biggest worry was she would not want to be found."

Carole developed serious health problems in her 60s and had to leave her job at Project Open Hand after thirteen years. She had two fractured vertebrae; ruptured quadriceps from a fall after a knee replacement; lymphedema, which required her to wrap and elevate her legs; diabetes; and psoriasis. Despite these conditions, which limited her ability to travel and prevented her from driving, she made the most of every day. Recalling a reference letter from a former boss in Tucson, he wrote, "Carole can do *anything* she *wants* to do." It became her mantra—she believed she could do anything she wanted and everything would be okay.

"My DNA is full of optimism," she said.

Asked what she was most proud of in life, Carole said, "That I came out of my family alive and sane is a big deal. I've made the right choices: marrying Myles, buying a house in San Francisco, and working for Project Open Hand."

She enjoyed spending time with Myles and visiting with her newfound family. "Sue is mentally sharper witted than me and has lots of friends," Carole said. Sue is creative, as was Carole. Sue made wonderful costumes for her children when they were young. Carole was always immersed in artsy projects for friends, her home, and charity. She made wreaths from magnolia leaves, feathers, and dried flowers; sewed curtains; and repainted garden figures. Carole found pleasure from caring for her cat, reading, decorating, being on the Web, taking little walks around her block, and gardening.

Thoughts and Advice About Risk

"Go for it!" was Carole's mantra.

"Risk is doing something without knowing the outcome. There's a chance it could go wrong, but is outweighed by the potential for something great to happen. Women age 50 and over have fifty-plus years of experience! You weigh the good and the bad. If your life has been good, why not assume it will continue to be good? By this time, you know who you are, and that should give you the fuel to go forward. Myles and I used to take huge day hikes, often getting into dangerous situations, but it was worth it!"

Carole was grateful to have her daughter and family in her life. The two talked regularly and saw each other every few years. Carole and her daughter were together to celebrate Sue's 50th birthday—the first they had shared since her birth and the first time the grandchildren visited San Francisco.

After discovering she had a daughter and not a son, Carole said, "Frankly, I was neither surprised nor fazed—probably not unlike a new parent. I just thought *It's mine!* Looking back, however, I don't think a boy and I would have become as close as Sue and I have. Girls have much more in common."

About reuniting with Sue, Carole quoted the hymn "Amazing Grace"—"I once was lost, but now am found."

Sadly, Carole died unexpectedly in October 2017, at age 71, and is greatly missed. A kindhearted woman who loved life, she was pleased to share her story.

Sue, 50, and Carole, 69, September 22, 2015, at The Boulevard Café, Daly City, California

Photo by Sue

ELIZABETH BANWELL

Single Foster Parent at 50; Adopted Two Children at 52

BIRTH YEAR: 1962

From birth to early childhood, Elizabeth lived in other countries before moving to the United States at age 6. She was an imaginative girl, and her creativity blossomed with fantasy play, writing, performing in a children's theater, and music camp. With two college degrees, Elizabeth launched a journalism career, later shifting to nonprofit work and then real estate. Single and wanting children at 50, she fostered a boy and his sister and adopted them at 52.

Earlier Years

Born in Kampala, Uganda, Elizabeth spent ages 2 to 4 in England, and was 4 when she, her younger brother, and her parents moved to Calcutta, India, where her father, a gastroenterologist, researched and treated cholera with a team from Johns Hopkins University, in Baltimore. In India, her parents adopted a 4-month-old girl and a 6-year-old boy.

From age 6 to 12, she lived in Baltimore, then Lexington, Kentucky, until graduating from high school. Elizabeth played the violin and piano, enjoyed writing, loved imaginative play, and acted in children's theater. In the summers, she attended a music school in Bennington, Vermont, run by a family who owned a cabin on Deer Island, Canada, off Eastport, Maine. Through her formative relationship with that family, Elizabeth became attracted to Maine and eventually to Colby College. While in college, she came out as a lesbian.

With an English degree, she wrote for and edited several newspapers until entering the nonprofit sector. Through her work with nonprofits, and her growing interest in facilitating organizational change, Elizabeth decided to pursue a master's degree in organization development from American University. She spent a short time in Sierra Leone, working at the United Nations Special Court with staff hired to protect victims of war crimes who were to testify before the war crime tribunal. "I had always wanted to return to Africa, and this project gave me an opportunity to see another African country," Elizabeth said. "The Sierra Leoneans we worked with were courageous, welcoming, and warm. And to be able to see both the beauty and the devastation of Freetown was eye-opening and, all in all, a remarkable experience." Later, she worked for the Maine Association of Nonprofits before becoming the chief of strategy and impact officer for the Opportunity Alliance, a health and human service agency in Portland.

Elizabeth's journey to adopting children was a result of reconciling two personal challenges that shaped her early life. One was her biological family's experience of adopting two children. "My parents are very loving and generous people, and did everything they could to integrate our family and help us each become successful. But in the 1960s and '70s, there was not the cultural understanding or support there is today for the issues that can result from blended families, adoption, or the impact of adverse early childhood experiences on attachment, development, and family systems. Additionally, there wasn't acknowledgment or support for the particular issues facing interracial families. The experience of adoption was hard on every member of my nuclear family, and therefore adoption seemed like a very risky way to create a family."

The second personal challenge Elizabeth faced was healing and reconciling internalized and societal homophobia. Doing so enabled her to embrace her desire to pursue parenting and to be a partner. "Although I knew I wanted children in my late 30s, it took me another ten years to do the personal work to give myself permission to create the life I wanted.

Being in therapy and joining women's groups where I met wonderful friends who found the courage to be themselves was helpful. It was a long, hard, painful struggle to fully accept myself and my dreams."

Pursuing Adoption

Elizabeth registered with a private adoption agency as a single gay woman. She knew she wanted two children, but the idea of raising two children alone seemed formidable. Although she received three calls from the agency over three years, she was traveling frequently for work and was not settled enough to be a single parent.

A friend recommended that she become a foster parent through the Maine Department of Health and Human Services (DHHS). Elizabeth completed the application process, the required home study, and a foster parenting class. She simultaneously changed jobs, relocated to Portland, and bought a house. She was uncertain whether her desire to have children would materialize. But in August 2012, she received a call from DHHS about a brother and sister needing foster care. Ten days later, she became a foster parent of two siblings—Lily, a 9-month-old girl, and Liam, a 2-year-old boy—thanks to a DHHS caseworker who insisted the children remain together.

The road from foster care to adoption had significant hurdles, but nineteen months after Elizabeth became a foster parent, she was able to adopt the children. Maine's child welfare system allows biological parents whose children have been removed to have supervised visits with their children twice a week, as one step in the state's "family reunification process." These visits continue until the parents meet reunification requirements or the state terminates parental rights. The process, although important for the parents who are able to make changes to meet their children's needs, is very hard on foster children, because they are in limbo—unable to fully attach and transition to their foster family, and unable to truly connect to their birth parents. "It was a very difficult and stressful time for everyone," Elizabeth said. "It's been a miracle.

"I didn't know how to change a diaper when I first met them," she confessed. "I had a crash course in parenting—probably not that much different from any new parent."

Elizabeth was only six months in her new job at the Opportunity Alliance when the children came to live with her. "The Opportunity Alliance began as a child welfare agency, and my colleagues could not have been more supportive of me as a mom," she said. She also gets a lot of help from her partner, who lives close by, and from her mother, who moved to be near Elizabeth and her grandchildren. (Elizabeth's dad died at age 73, four years before she became a foster mother. Her father's mother had died when he was 7. Elizabeth fondly recalls her father as "parenting with a kind eye—from a distance. He was a powerful role model to me, and very loving.")

A proud and caring mom, Elizabeth enjoys parenting and providing for her children. She gets pleasure from meeting their needs, as well as playing and reading with them, and watching them grow and develop. She and her partner have a great time introducing them to new experiences, including camping, and traveling. "We enjoy each other's company. Of course, with young children, moods and energy levels can turn on a dime, depending on exhaustion and hunger and the need of the moment, but despite the ups and downs, we have a very full life and a lot of fun together." Swirling Hula-Hoops; kicking soccer balls; listening to guitar music; climbing on playground equipment; making faces; dressing up in costumes; eating ice cream; digging in the sand; jumping in the ocean; taking care of their three dogs, a cat, and a goldfish; picking strawberries—they are happy sharing good times together.

As a mother, Elizabeth sees how others are more natural at certain aspects of child rearing. "It's both a humbling and affirming process," she said. "I am the parent who is good at establishing routines in a comforting way and minding the big picture, but I don't innately have the gift of spontaneity that my partner does. Both are important, and no one person can provide everything."

She good-naturedly recalls that when Lily and Liam were smaller and visiting her mother's house, they were allowed to pull out and play with the pots and pans to listen to the different sounds they make. Although her mother didn't mind, Elizabeth wasn't too keen about that level of chaos in her house. She does, however, think about each child and what she can do to ensure they are getting what they need—and tries to stretch beyond her established comfort zone.

Elizabeth's life is hectic with two children fifteen months apart, a partnership, and maintaining relationships with her mother and close friends. Her children require special therapy sessions because they are dealing with sensory and eating issues from their earlier backgrounds. Initially, her daughter's height and weight were only 2 percent of expected growth for her age; she is now on par with her age group. It was especially busy when Elizabeth was working in a traditional full-time position. "I'm learning how to parent and meet my children's needs while also doing the things I need to do. Any given day, the balance can be thrown off!

"People have been amazing throughout this process," Elizabeth exclaimed. For the first month the children lived with her, caring friends prepared suppers for them. Friends who are mothers shared clothes, tips, enthusiasm. "My mother and partner have been fully engaged as well, developing their own relationships with the children. It's been a wonderful celebration in my life."

As a happy and contented mother, Elizabeth's creative challenge was figuring out how to be a good parent while having a job with flexibility. "It's a dance. A lot of women throw themselves into their careers in their 50s and take on more responsibility and leadership. I have always loved my work. Now I love my children as well, so I have to balance both as effectively as possible. I am working on being present in my life."

To adapt her daily life to her children's schedule and her community, Elizabeth secured a real estate license and became a real estate agent in the Portland, Maine, area, a position with flexible hours. "My goal is to create a life that really supports the family," Elizabeth said. "That means being connected to other families and the community. I have a fantasy of eventually owning or co-owning a local business that would enable that level of flexibility and availability."

Living in a gay-friendly area, Elizabeth has not experienced any discrimination as a lesbian parent. She continues to do volunteer work in her community as time permits and enjoys reconnecting with friends. In the past, she rented houses for vacations in places like Provincetown, Massachusetts. Now, she and her family take camping trips and stay with friends, and have fun without spending much money on vacations. She hopes to travel again outside the country as her family's schedule and finances permit.

Thoughts and Advice About Risk

"I don't see myself as a risk taker," Elizabeth said. "It took me a long time to make the decision to adopt children. I had many concerns. Will I have support? Will I have enough money? Will I be able to work and meet the needs of my children? None of my fears have come to pass thus far. It's been a remarkable experience."

When it comes to risks she does not wish to take, Elizabeth said, "I wouldn't choose to take physical risks like jumping out of a plane, bungee jumping, or rock climbing.

"The 'risk-taking' of parenting shows itself most in the metamorphosis that has happened since I started parenting. I read a quote that went something like this: 'Children start off as an intrusion into your life, and then become your life.' I spent the first year of parenting actively trying to preserve my life as it was pre-parenting, and then at some point in the second year, I completely oriented myself to the role of parent. That role required much adaptation, risk-taking, and dealing with the challenges of responding to and assisting another person who is revealing themselves right before your eyes. As any parent knows, your heart is on the line all the time."

For older women interested in fostering or adopting children, Elizabeth recommends being honest about what you truly want to do with your time and energy as you get older. "Be as intentional as you can about the decision. Some of my friends are writing novels and poetry or have pursued the career they couldn't have when they had children as younger mothers. Most people want to take on more meaningful, purposeful activities as they get older. I just happened to want to spend my energy as a parent. Children are just one way to demonstrate devotion.

"I have benefited from being a mother," Elizabeth said. A warm, friendly, compassionate woman, she is determined to be a good, loving parent. "They've saved me. If you're a parent to young children, you are tested every second." As children grow older, parents are faced with different challenges. Outside negative influences such as television, which exposes children to guns, and violence-themed video games require monitoring as is feasible. "Being a parent requires you to be open and adaptable. Just like children, a parent is continually picking themselves up off the ground, so to speak, and trying again.

"It's been the best thing I have ever done because the currency is love—and true love requires presence, strength, courage, and commitment."

Elizabeth, Lily, and Liam

Photo by Angela Crabtree

SHELLEY COTTON

Took Up Motorcycle Riding at 52 After Divorce

BIRTH YEAR: 1952

An exuberant, outgoing woman who laughs easily, Shelley lives in the small, historic town of Longmeadow, Massachusetts, and has been a hairstylist, a profession she loves, since age 24 and co-owner of a hair salon since 46. Formerly married, she has two children and divorced at age 41. She has faced significant challenges, including breast cancer. As a single woman, Shelley took up motorcycling at 52.

Earlier Years

The oldest of four children (three girls, one boy) from Springfield, Massachusetts, Shelley, a self-described "purebred Armenian," has fond memories of playing in the woods after school and jumping off high, soft sand dunes in her neighborhood. She played dodgeball and softball—there were no girls' sports teams then. One summer when Shelley was 10, her family piled into their station wagon and drove cross-country. They slept in the car en route to moving to Fresno, California. Deciding the area wasn't for them, they moved back to New England within two months. Her parents worked together in different coffee shops that her dad owned. When she was in high school, Shelley's family moved to Longmeadow, where she has lived since.

After one year of college, she and her cousin decided to go to hairdressing school during summer break, and she never looked back. She was a stylist at four places and met her best friend, Sharon, when they were working together. They decided to open their own place, Duets Hair Salon in East Longmeadow.

"I get great satisfaction in making a woman look pretty," Shelley said. "When a client tells me I've made them happy, I feel good." The environment is cheerful and warm, and Shelley enjoys spending time there. "We all respect each other. It's proof positive of a supportive atmosphere."

Shelley married at age 26 and had a son and a daughter.

When she was in her late 20s, a doll-collecting salon customer purchased a Marilyn Monroe doll in New York City for Shelley at her request after she admired it in a *National Geographic* magazine advertisement. Shelley was intrigued by Marilyn Monroe's persona, and the doll launched her collection of items related to Hollywood's sex symbol starlet. She obtained another doll, and has two pairs of earrings with Marilyn motifs, a movie script, photos, books, and a tea set with the actress's image on the cups and creamer.

After learning about Monroe, Shelley says, "She had a jet-set lifestyle, seemed insecure, was a warm and kind woman who took up drinking. I felt sorry for her." (Reports indicate Marilyn was an intelligent, well-read woman who loved dogs, was concerned about civil rights, and helped charities. She died from a barbiturate overdose at age 36.) Later, when Storrs Library in Longmeadow heard about Shelley's Monroe collection, they created a temporary exhibit of her Marilyn memorabilia, which was well received.

Following sixteen years of marriage, Shelley divorced her husband. That year, at 41, she received a diagnosis of breast cancer, had a mastectomy, and three years later developed tumors at the site. Her chest wall muscle was excised at Dana-Farber Cancer Institute in Boston, followed by chemotherapy and radiation. *Thank God it's me and not my kids,* she thought.

As a breast cancer survivor, Shelley volunteered for ten years as a devoted patient advocate for the breast cancer organization Rays of

Hope at Baystate Medical Center in Springfield, Massachusetts. She comforted women and men undergoing breast needle localizations before having surgery to excise the area to be biopsied. Her work ended when needle localization was replaced by radioactive seed localization and advocates were no longer permitted in the room with the patient during the procedure.

Taking Up Motorcycling

Shelley's son rode motorcycles and worked as a mechanic in a cycle shop. Knowing his mom was interested in riding a motorcycle, he called her about a beginners' 1981 Honda CM 400 on sale that he thought she might like to check out. At 52, she bought the motorcycle and her son taught her how to ride it in the local parking lots.

"I loved the excitement and freedom of riding a motorcycle!" Shelley said. "It was a personal best for me to master shifting gears. I've always been a car person by nature." She bought her first car at 17—a Toyota with a stick shift. Although she didn't know how to drive a manual transmission, she bought it anyway and learned how to shift later.

After learning how to ride her motorcycle, she rode around with her son and brother. "Once when my brother and I were riding on a steep hill, I had my bike in neutral instead of first gear and ended up rolling backward down the hill and then fell over. I was lucky not to get hurt. Only the mirror cracked."

When her son and brother moved away after a few years, she rode on her own. "I never joined a motorcycle club—that wasn't my thing. I took some long trips, including Misquamicut Beach in Rhode Island. Highways were easier riding, as you're better spaced and farther apart from other vehicles." One of the women salon customers had a motorcycle, and they occasionally rode together.

"At your age, how could you do this? You are the laughingstock of Longmeadow!" her mother said. "My former husband probably would have said the same thing," Shelley added. "He wasn't into doing anything like this. People looked at me when I rode in my 50s, but no one said anything. My son of course encouraged me, and my daughter thought it was fine too. I never would have had a motorcycle when I was married—I felt too restricted."

As the matriarch in her family with both of her parents deceased, Shelley says, "Losing your parents is a sad part of life." She misses her dad especially—he was the loving, huggy type.

Shelley's daughter and granddaughter live with her, and they're doing well as a trio. They have endured tough challenges together, and Shelley has supported her daughter through difficult times. "I talk about my problems," Shelley said. "It's important to me to be open about my life."

A warm and compassionate woman, Shelley loves her family, and enjoys interacting with friends and hair salon customers who are like extended family members. Duets Hair Salon buzzes with laughter and animated conversation among Shelley, her business partner Sharon, and their loyal, longtime customers. By disclosing the issues she has had to face, Shelley finds that others open up to her and they share stories and support each other.

Shelley would like to travel to Europe on her own. "You have an opportunity to talk and meet others that you don't have when you're traveling with other people. I have met the nicest people when I've traveled on my own to visit my son in Florida." Her travels have usually been with others.

She wants to try skydiving. "If President George H. W. Bush could do it at 90, I suppose I can," she said.

Thoughts and Advice About Risk

"A risk is putting yourself or someone else over the edge," Shelley said. "For example, though I rode a motorcycle, I wouldn't ride with my granddaughter on the back."

Shelley sees herself as a risk taker. Motorcycling was risky, but she never regretted riding one for eight years. "I would regret *not* taking the risk," she said. She wasn't afraid when she started to ride. At age 60, Shelley realized that her responses and reflexes weren't as sharp. "You must be 100 percent aware of who's around you when riding." Though no close call or accident prompted her decision, she gave up motorcycling at age 60 and sold her Honda.

Shelley encourages any woman over 50 who is interested in getting a motorcycle to do it. "However, they should ride a motorcycle only if they're extremely self-confident on the bike. If they have any fears, they shouldn't do it."

After age 50, Shelley went zip lining high up in the jungles of Colombia with her son and his family. Another time in Massachusetts, she ended up extreme hiking after getting lost off of a trail. She walked across a fallen tree suspended twenty feet over water—a treacherous feat. Her son is a triathlete and into lots of physical activities. Her daughter is on a Roller Derby team.

Asked what risky behavior she wouldn't do, Shelley responded, "Saying anything mean about anyone." She is very "opposed to people who spew negativity. I would not Roller Derby skate, as they hurt each other, and I couldn't do that. My daughter is tough and can handle it.

"By being kind to myself and others, I stay positive." Her breast cancer diagnosis was a key turning point in Shelley's life. "I realized the importance of putting yourself first," she said. "Before, I always put everyone else ahead of me."

Shelley describes herself as "very happy, fun-loving, and adventurous." She said, "Life is far from perfect, but I believe in taking the best attitude."

Shelley ready to take off

Photo by Diana Coleman

CHAPTER 6 — SPIRITUAL AWAKENINGS

THE REVEREND CLAUDIA WYATT SMITH

From Health Care Administrator to Ordained Episcopal Priest at 56

BIRTH YEAR: 1949

Claudia spent most of her youth in Texas as the younger of two daughters, raised by a nonpracticing Jewish mother and agnostic father. She had several religious experiences in her youth, pursued social work after college, married and had a son, and later divorced. Burned out from hospital social work and health care administration positions, Claudia discerned a new calling and entered seminary at 53.

Earlier Years

After her first four years in New York, Claudia's family moved to the Dallas area. Her dad, Jack Wyatt, an advertising entrepreneur, also moderated a panel on the television crime/reality show *Confession*, where he interviewed convicted murderers, counterfeiters, and prostitutes about their insights into being unlawful. "When I was young and the TV program aired, you never knew who was going to come to Thanksgiving dinner," Claudia said. "The prisoners felt a connection with my dad and saw him as a friend." On weekends, her father became a "country farmer," plowing the family's fields. Her mother provided the "accounting arm" for her husband's advertising business.

Claudia's family subscribed to the Church of the Month Club, occasionally sampling services from Unitarian to Methodist. A rabbi had advised that the Christian tradition was more suitable for their family. With a Baptist friend in the third grade, Claudia went to a Baptist camp one summer. In the sweltering heat, she lay in her bunk at night praying for Jesus to come into her life. Nothing happened.

Maybe you're just supposed to believe and act differently, she thought. She became a religious zealot at age 8. *Perhaps I should become a nun?* she wondered. Claudia had intermittent religious experiences throughout her childhood and teens. One Sunday, sitting in an Episcopal church, she was deeply touched by the liturgy. "I knew I had come home," she said. She never got the calling to be a Baptist.

During her youth, Claudia loved animals. She had dogs and horses and told them her troubles. She did community work in high school with a nondenominational Christian youth group and went on their social outings, including ski trips. At this time, her paternal grandmother, whom she called Nana, became severely ill. Claudia's father, often away on business, was hesitant to travel, fearing his mother would die while he was away.

He was persuaded to travel because he was told that his mother's bad health could linger for a while. Between meetings in Europe, he found himself in churches believing he had been drawn in by their historical architectural significance. His mother died, and he couldn't return home because he was in England and there was an airline strike. It was decided to proceed with his mother's memorial service in Dallas without him. Feeling the need to be in a church at the same hour as the service, he grabbed a cab. With the time difference, it was not the usual hour for church services in England. Frantic, he told the cabbie his story. They drove to Westminster Abbey, where a priest was locking up. Hearing that Claudia's father wanted to honor his mother at the same time as her service in the States that was starting within minutes, the priest performed a service just for him, translating the Latin into English. The cabbie refused to take any money, stunning her business-oriented father. On his flight home, he sat next to a social worker and discussed what had happened. What did his experience mean? Synchronicity had surely played a role, he concluded. He had a major conversion experience.

"Coming off the plane, my father had visibly changed," Claudia said. "His normally tense face from his 'driven' personality was gone. He looked peaceful."

When Claudia was in high school, her father was baptized and confirmed by a priest at a small Episcopal church in Dallas. He began independent seminary studies in Canterbury, England. At 54, he was ordained as an Episcopal priest in Oklahoma and later was called to his own congregation.

During his ordination, Claudia, a college student, felt strongly that she should be the one being ordained, though she didn't pursue this vocation. Women couldn't be ordained in the Episcopal church until 1979. Females didn't go into the ministry at the time. It wasn't done. "Though it was a fleeting thought, if I had had the opportunity then to go into the ministry, I'm not sure I would have. I couldn't imagine that God would have wanted me to do this—others were surely more holy. I was reticent and believed it was not my calling."

As a nonpracticing Jew, Claudia's mother, who adored her father, was fine with his new calling. "My mother had trouble reconciling that 'the only way to God is through Jesus' until, in a dream, she repeatedly heard 'He is Me,' and realized that it doesn't matter what name one uses. It's still the same God."

After two years at Christian Female College, a women's school in Missouri (later renamed Columbia College when it became co-ed), Claudia transferred to Southern Methodist University in Dallas and spent her junior year in England getting an old tutorial-style education at King's College, London. "Fried" after England, she took a year off and worked in Dallas. With her ordained father in Oklahoma, Claudia transferred to Southeastern Oklahoma State University and finished her bachelor's degree in sociology, with a double psychology and Spanish minor.

Claudia became a social worker with community action and senior care agencies in Arkansas. After meeting her newspaper publisher husband in Arkansas, they married and moved to Texas, where she directed the local hospital's social work program. "I loved medicine," Claudia said. "I would have become a doctor, but I didn't have the brain cells to be a doctor. I liked health care settings." Moving every three years for her husband's jobs, she ultimately moved into health care administration and management.

While working for a hospital in Arkansas, Claudia's marriage fell apart. She became a single mother with a son age 5. They went to Kansas City, where she ran a diabetes center and later oversaw national programs. Changing companies and locations several times, she moved up the ranks. By the time her son, Joseph, was a teenager, she wanted to be home with him rather than traveling extensively with her job. As vice president of marketing and new product development for a firm in Denver, she was required to work during the week at its subsidiary in Florida, and was in Denver on the weekends. "I wasn't a Florida woman, and health care no longer appealed to me." She had found a church in Denver but was never there. Early one morning while walking in humid Florida she prayed to God: "I can't figure this out. You do it!"

At 9:00 a.m., she quit her job. She hatched an idea for herself and a male colleague, who loved Florida but was based in Colorado: "You take my job and I'll take your severance package, and we'll both be happy." It worked. Claudia had a house payment and a son in college. She assumed she would get another job right away. After not working much for a year, she discovered she had the same amount of money in the bank at the end of that year as she had had in the beginning. She did a little consulting, had some severance funds, and was in a lower tax bracket. "I was thankful for having a year to contemplate the future as I turned 50 in Denver."

With time off, she asked the priest at her local Episcopal church for some volunteer work. Completing what he asked, she kept coming back for other things to do and told him, "I think there's something else I'm supposed to do." After a while, the priest asked, "Do you think you're being called into the ordained ministry?" He brought it up three times, but each time she said no because she was terrified by the idea of going to seminary. "Getting a graduate degree after more than thirty years away from school scared the hell out of me. It wasn't until I verbalized it that I realized that was the problem. The discerning process in the Episcopal church is long. I talked to God and was willing to be put on the path. Contemplating entering the seminary, I said, 'Don't let me get to the end and drop me.' My relationship with God gave me courage."

Seminary, Ordination, and Life as an Episcopal Priest

Claudia entered a three-year seminary program at age 53. "The night before beginning seminary at the University of the South in Sewanee, Tennessee, I questioned what I was doing. I didn't know about this—being with all the young students. But in the end, it was about something bigger than me." She wasn't the oldest student—there were others closer in age to her—but there was a generation gap between students. Whereas the younger students typed on computers, she took notes longhand.

Her father was "excessively supportive," Claudia said. "He lived vicariously through me. I had applied and was accepted at two seminaries. He loved getting my papers. We talked every Saturday morning. I used to read my dad my sermons. He journeyed with me.

"I thought the biggest dragon being a student after thirty years would be the academics." Ninety students were living together on a mountaintop in Tennessee for three years, and acclimating to communal living as a woman in her 50s presented even bigger challenges. At Sewanee, they gave sermons—there was a lot of preaching in many settings, especially in small groups with colleagues where their peers critiqued them, so learning to put aside one's ego was a huge part of the process.

"The big bugaboo was the graduate ordination exam during my last year of seminary," Claudia said. Taken using a computer, it lasted five days—from early morning to noon with another section from 1:00 to 5:00 p.m.—with one break each day. "I taught myself to think on paper, but I could think for only so long before I needed to type. I was a slow typist. I still have to look at the keys to this day, which is nerve-racking. During the exam, there was a question which I should have known, since I had taken classes on the topic. I blanked out. Toward the end, I picked up the thread of the question's answer and then ran out of time. After the test, I wept buckets. The younger students thought the exam was easy."

The exams were scored on a scale of 1 to 5, with 5 being outstanding. It was recommended to "Aim for a 3," considered a good, solid theologian score. Claudia had to wait eight weeks for the exam results. She didn't know who would be reading her exam—readers were from all over the country. "I thought I flunked. I ended up with two 5s and nothing less than a 3. Some of the younger students did horribly. It affirmed for me that the test measured, 'How do you assimilate information?' not what you parrot back. As a priest, a key question is 'How does your life experience communicate to the parishioners in their journeys?' That's the gift and benefit of age."

Claudia received her Master of Divinity degree and was ordained as an Episcopal priest at 56. "My dad was ordained at age 54 and I thought he was ancient then." Because they were in poor health, her parents could not attend her graduation. In retrospect, they realized her mom had Alzheimer's, and her father was her primary caregiver. Claudia gave her dad her first videotaped sermon. After working in Oklahoma, he retired to Texas and was an interim rector for several churches. He died of cancer at 86, three years after Claudia's ordination. Her mother died six months later at 83.

"I didn't realize it at the time I was discerning my 'call,' but my father was opposed to women being ordained as priests in the Episcopal church. Years later, I discovered that my journey had changed his mind. My mother said, 'You're not going to become a priest, are you?' My mother was concerned with my taking this risk in my 50s and giving up financial security."

Claudia got out of seminary in 2005 during a serious economic downturn in the United States, and jobs as an assistant priest weren't available. The bishop in Colorado helped create a vicar position and partially underwrote her salary for two years—at St. Benedict's Episcopal Church in La Veta. Afterward, she became the rector at St. Francis by the Sea Episcopal Church in Blue Hill, Maine.

Known to her congregation as the Reverend Smith, Claudia consoles and counsels parishioners; facilitates educational programs; prepares and gives sermons; works closely with the staff and the vestry, which governs the church; raises funds; and attends regional and national religious meetings. Her extensive writing, public speaking, communication skills, and chutzpah acquired in business have been put to good use in her second vocation. Having a marketing background also helped with reviewing fundraising campaign materials to raise money for major building renovations.

"I thought Maine would be a quiet place to have a congregation," Claudia said. "My first year here our church was hit by lightning; a hundred-year flood twice; and developed a toxic mold, which required remediation work. The most important aspect of church work is 'visioning,' which is not taught in seminary. What is the church's place in the future? The culture is changing so fast. We can't say where the church will be in three to five years. Rather we need to ask, 'Who are we called to be? How are we living our vision today?'"

When delivering sermons, Claudia often uses her experiences to illustrate religious teachings and lessons. As a single parent, for example, she put notes around the house for her young son to find when she left him in the care of nannies while on business trips. She disliked leaving him and wanted to assure him he was loved and not alone. Citing Jesus with his disciples at the Last Supper giving his "farewell discourse," she spoke of "God dwelling in us, healing our hearts from the inside out with messages of love to remind us we are not alone."

She has compared the work and composition of her church with colleagues from churches around the country. Some congregations have active, young parishioners, which helps boost membership and ensure long-term growth. St. Francis by the Sea's congregation is skewed toward the older population. Recruiting younger parishioners for future stability is a challenge. Claudia is grateful to both the seasonal parishioners and the year-round resident members for their generosity.

Claudia is driven to re-language the church for today's population. Her congregation offers summer services in a public park with a Celtic earth-oriented liturgy.

"I am passionate about our Down East Spiritual Life Conference and can see myself continuing along this path. I enjoy engaging largely unchurched people who wish to talk about spiritual growth. I think people are hungry to be in this conversation about how our spirit journeys make sense with the craziness of life."

A widow once called her church and asked Claudia if Jack Wyatt was her father. When Claudia affirmed that he was, the woman told her that her husband had been one of the criminals featured and interviewed by her father on the TV show. "My husband turned his life around. He recently died, and I wanted you to know the impact and ripple effect your father had on him."

"It made me aware of the legacy Dad left and the impact people can have on another's life, even though they may never be aware of it," Claudia said.

Personal tragedy struck her family when her first grandchild, born to her son, Joseph, and his wife, died of a rare genetic disease when she was just over 2 years old. Holding fragile Rosie in her arms for the last time several months before she died, Claudia said to her, "I think there is something special I am supposed to tell you, but I have no idea what it is." Nothing in her sixty-four years had prepared her to say goodbye to her 2-year-old grandchild. In the end, all she could say was "You be watching for me, 'cause I'll see you later."

A month after Rosie's death, Claudia returned to Avebury, England, a village known for its prehistoric henge monument of stone circles, wishing trees, and female energy—a place she had visited earlier while on sabbatical. She carried a forest-green knitted bootie in which she had tucked a small picture of Rosie, enfolded in a small ball of colored yarn from each of the different outfits she had made for her, and placed it in a small hollow of a large three-trunked beech wishing tree. Women traditionally hang bright-colored prayer ribbons from the enormous wishing tree's branches. "I felt at peace doing this, as though I was giving her back to the 'Mother,'" Claudia said. Drawing from the tree of life, with its aboveground trunk and branches, and its underground roots, she added, "There is a relationship between the seen and unseen which I continue to explore and celebrate—a connectedness that death of our bodies can't undo.

"The Episcopal church has a mandatory retirement age of 72. I am not sure when I will retire. I am also interested in doing artsy, creative things like making pottery. My calling to something hasn't changed. I'm not sure what the future will look like. I continue to ask, *What feeds me?*" Though she has no idea what the future holds, she has learned over the years that it is okay to not know.

Thoughts and Advice About Risk

"There were times in my life when I associated risk with the ability to provide—for example, for my son as a single mother," Claudia said. "In hindsight, I probably didn't need to do all the things I did. I took jobs to make money. My world would have been better with less money and a smaller house to feel secure.

"I guess I have been a risk taker when I look back over my life. I've taken calculated risks. I was a plotter and planner. I didn't arbitrarily take risks like friends who became hippies did. I found that idea attractive but couldn't do it—it wasn't who I was.

"What has given me the courage to overcome the fear of taking risks is when I'm connected to God or the divine—something bigger than myself—whatever name you call it. When I put aside fears and the negative voices in my head, I said, 'Show me and guide me.' Episcopalians have lots of hoops in the discerning process. I asked God to be really clear and send me a postcard. I needed to know I was not in this by myself.

"In thinking about risks, I wouldn't jump out of a plane—that doesn't hold any attraction for me. It's more about personal preference. The underpinning of risks taken has not been my arbitrary decision. Rather, it felt like part of a larger plan beyond my plan—something bigger."

Claudia's advice to other women interested in pursuing the ordained ministry in their second half of life is "If it is a job choice, don't do it—it's too hard. This is not a job change. It is something you are called to do. What gives you life? If you feel compelled, and are drawn into something bigger than yourself, then trust that. If you're making a decision based on feeling a calling, don't let the negative voices get you down. Pursue it!"

The Reverend Claudia Wyatt Smith, St. Francis by the Sea Episcopal Church, Blue Hill, Maine

Photo by Judy Rountree

PATRICIA WEAVER

Hairdresser and Motel Maintenance Worker to Widow at 57 and Hospice Aide at 64

BIRTH YEAR: 1950

A Mainer and the youngest of ten children, Pat Weaver grew up on a dairy farm. After high school, she fixed people's hair, ran a day care program, and worked for a motel. Married with one son, Pat became her husband's caregiver when he received the diagnosis of a chronic disease. Interested in a health care career, Pat became a certified nursing assistant at 57. At 58, she began work as a health aide and burned her house down. At 64, she started her dream job—caring for dying people.

Earlier Years

Born with a "wry neck" deformity (a painfully twisted and tilted neck), Pat spent a few weeks in her early childhood at the Pine State Hospital for Crippled Children, followed by home treatments, to correct this condition.

On her family's farm in rural Warren, Maine, she tended to the calves and cows and did lots of haying and gardening. She remembers her mom's annual spring cleanings. "Every item in each room, one day at a time, was carried out to the lawn for a proper airing—including the mattresses and bedsprings." Pat loved swinging from an old oak tree on their property. "My brothers pushed me so high, I could touch the house chimney."

Though an introverted child, Pat was active in 4-H, learning how to cook and sew. As a young teen, she entered a bread competition in Orono, Maine's State Championship. It was an extraordinarily hot day, so she packed the yeast dough in ice, but it still didn't come out right. She vigorously floured the dough, but it was sticky and ruined by the heat. "It was a memorable, embarrassing time," she recalled.

All through school, Pat hung out with her classmate Susan and Susan's cousin Ann. Called the Three Musketeers, they did everything together. Ann's brother, Brian, who was two and a half years younger than Pat, used to hang around them when they were in their early teens. "He drove us crazy," Pat said. When she was at her high school's Jolly Junior Record Hop, another guy was "making advances toward her" and she wasn't interested, so she began flirting with Brian. He called later to ask her out, and they began hanging around together, later becoming "an item." Though Brian's mother thought Pat was "robbing the cradle," they got married in a small wedding and had a large reception when Pat was 22. "Brian's mother came around, and treated me as another daughter," Pat said. Brian's family was from a long line of Mainers.

As a young mother of a son, Pat took fifteen to twenty children into her home for day care, in addition to fixing people's hair and doing manual work at a motel. Together Pat and her carpenter husband built their home from an old chicken barn and salvaged lumber, windows, and doors from other places. They planned to live there temporarily—no more than five years—which ended up being more than thirty years.

Active in the local Grange, an organization that helps improve farmers' lives—for example, they acquired electricity and gained rural mail delivery in her town—she held officer roles as an ambassador, master, and secretary. Afraid to speak in public and still involved with the group in her 30s, Pat overcame her shyness and voiced her opinion about the inept way that voting was handled. She was rewarded with a standing ovation.

When Pat was interested in exploring different job options, her sister Phyllis, a head nurse at the local hospital and an important role model to her, suggested she become a nurse, but Pat didn't have the confidence to pursue nursing.

Later, when her mom underwent extensive rehabilitation for a broken ankle after falling in her bathtub, Pat enjoyed interacting with her caregivers and learning about their work. She was motivated to help sick and dying people.

A New Career

Pat enrolled in Maine's nine-week certified nursing assistant (CNA) course at Midcoast School of Technology, which included two hundred hours of classroom, laboratory, and clinical experience. Annual continuing educational and work requirements must be met to maintain CNA credentials.

"My mom was so proud I was going to become a CNA." She died two weeks before Pat, age 57, began class. Most of the students were in their early 40s; there were a couple in their 20s and a few in their 50s. It was reassuring to Pat to be in school with some older people.

"I was scared to death to take these classes, because I had no confidence I could do anything more than manual work," Pat said. However, she knew she wanted to work with people needing care. She was afraid of tests and hadn't been to school in a long time, with the exception of a computer class. Her teachers gave her confidence. Pat asked one of her instructors if she thought she could be a CNA and was told, "Go for it!" She froze when taking an essay exam but managed to do fine. "There were wonderful people behind me, and my husband encouraged me when I thought about getting this specialty training."

While enrolled in CNA school, Pat's husband received a diagnosis of chronic inflammatory demyelinating polyneuropathy (CIDP) and small cell lung cancer. She applied what she was learning to take care of him. "CIDP is like amyotrophic lateral sclerosis or Lou Gehrig's disease, but ten times worse," said Pat. It's a neurological disorder, which leads to progressive weakness and impaired function of the legs and arms. Brian suffered from hallucinations. Once when Pat was driving, he yelled at her to pull over and untangle the barbed wire caught around his legs. Pat stopped the car. There was no barbed wire. Moving her hands across her husband's legs as if she was removing the wire, she calmed him down and assured him the wire was "no longer there."

During Brian's last year, he went from his normal 200 pounds to 70 pounds. Given hospice information later in his illness, her husband insisted he wanted no part of it, saying that "hospice was only for dying people." He was told he had six months to live after his CIDP diagnosis. Meanwhile, Pat received her CNA certification. Near the end of his life, Brian accepted palliative care and hospice. A nurse predicted he would die on a particular Tuesday night and was amazed when he didn't die until that Friday at 4:00 p.m. Determined to live a full six months, he had died at age 55 from respiratory failure at the exact hour and day from his six-month prognosis. In addition to losing her husband and mother, Pat saw four other family members die that year—a brother, a cousin, an aunt, and a brother-in-law.

Widowed, Pat began her CNA work at 58 with sick, elderly people in a local retirement community's long-term care unit. "It was a bit scary at first because I didn't know the people," she said. She experienced humorous incidents with residents such as getting her arms tangled up in their legs when moving them in bed. "If you have the mind-set, you can do it," she believes. She kidded around with the residents. Men sometimes made inappropriate sexual advances—she handled them firmly, keeping her perspective. Sometimes patients were violent—she got help from others in handling them. Job hazards also included being pulled and pinched. "It's inevitable and you deal with it," she said. By establishing a good rapport with her patients, Pat felt comfortable talking with them directly. "If I can make people laugh and smile, they make me laugh and smile, and we both forget our problems for a few minutes." She likes knowing that people are helped through her soft words and touch. One resident said he appreciated having her around—for her compassion, love, and understanding.

A month after starting her new career, Pat burned down her home.

It was an intentional, huge bonfire—the year after her husband died. The fire department approved it, although they made Pat remove all the glass first. Newspapers and a tire were put in the center of the house. Pat struck numerous matches that immediately went out. "I felt my husband was preventing the fire." She appealed to him in the heavens. "Let me do this!" The next match started the forty-five-minute conflagration—her "phoenix rising," she said. "It was my new beginning." She drew house plans, got input from her son, Chris, and hired a contractor. A resourceful woman, Pat saved considerable money by doing a lot of the work herself—painting the walls, laying the bathroom tile, and staining the kitchen cabinets. After staying four months in her mother's empty house, she moved into her new house on the same site as her prior home.

At 64, Pat was thrilled to be hired as a CNA for the Sussman House, a hospice facility, when it opened in Rockport, Maine.

In providing personal care, Pat imagines being the person lying in the bed and asks herself, *How would I want to be dealt with?* Loving her work, she glows when talking about it and tears up recalling the last moments of people's lives.

"CNAs are the eyes and ears to the nurses to help them manage people's pain. I have the greatest respect for nurses. I couldn't be an RN—I don't like needles and I wouldn't want the responsibility. However, I can care for and talk with patients and enjoy it." Nights are hard for her because she misses her husband, so she works the 7:00 p.m. to 7:00 a.m. shift.

"People ask me all the time, how can I be around people who are dying? Isn't it depressing? They're dying. It's gratifying to see people who are pain-free and watch them die in calmness and peace." She accepts death as inevitable, believing that people die as part of God's plan.

Pat recalls her first experience with the death of someone she knew. When she was young, an aunt had multiple sclerosis and lived with her family until moving into a nursing home when Pat was in her teens. Pat hated going into that place, with so many drooling people. Near death, her aunt was moved to a hospital. Pat prayed her aunt would die and she did—one week later. She blamed herself for causing her death by wishing it, although she later understood that she was not the cause of her aunt's demise.

Pat reads about the care of dying people and has observed other caregivers. She admires Father Richard Rohr, author of *Falling Upward: A Spirituality for the Two Halves of Life*, and Dr. Ira Byock, a physician and international palliative care leader. One of the hospice nurses who took care of Pat's husband posed the questions often asked of people who are dying: "Do you have any unfinished business? Do you need to see and talk with specific people? Is it okay to leave? Do you need to be forgiven or forgive someone?"

The hardest part of her job is interacting with grieving family members and friends. She assures them that they have helped by being there for their loved ones. At times, she gets teary eyed when leaving a dying person's room. "I cry for the family," she said. "The dying patient will be in a better place. They're not living." A widow who has experienced the death of many people close to her, she understands what people are going through—dying and watching their loved ones die. She is a strong advocate for palliative and hospice care.

"I wanted to do something to make a difference for people—as opposed to motel maintenance work, cleaning, and painting." During her 40s, Pat was devastated when her sister, nurse Phyllis, died at 60. "My sister would be proud of me for being a CNA. As I think about my new profession, I believe my CNA work is a way of honoring my sister."

Pat takes great pride in her home—it's sunny, pleasant, and filled with relatives' paintings and family photographs. Her master bedroom has a beautiful quilt made from her husband's work shirts—a Christmas gift from her son and daughter-in-law after her husband died. She dedicated a playroom for her granddaughter Kiah's visits—a cheerful space with multicolored painted stripes and color splotches on the concrete walls. Pat takes care of her large, nearly seven-acre property, mowing, weed whacking, and tending to her rose and flower gardens.

Active with her Congregational church, Pat has a strong faith. She's participated in Habitat for Humanity community builds and was thrilled to use a chop saw to cut moldings for the house she volunteered for.

Going on a missionary trip with her church interests her—perhaps to Haiti. Other places she would like to travel include Australia, New Zealand, Scotland, and Ireland. "I don't know if I have the courage to travel by myself or if I have the desire to do it alone," she said. "If I really wanted to do something and put my mind to it, I could probably do it."

Time permitting, she occasionally styles hair for women in their 80s and 90s—traveling to their homes.

She has learned to look at things that really matter and not be concerned with things that don't. A while ago, she lost a debit card. In the past, she would have panicked. She no longer does.

In planning for the future, Pat reviewed her finances and health issues. After suffering from headaches, fatigue, vertigo, and anxiety, she received a diagnosis of chronic Lyme disease and is being treated holistically, which helps "take the edge off." Her health is a top priority.

Though she enjoyed her hospice work, she officially retired and looks forward to spending more time with her family in Nova Scotia. In "retirement," she hopes to continue working periodically with hospice patients and their loved ones.

Thoughts and Advice About Risk

"Going out of your comfort zone" is how Pat describes risk. She talks about the difference between knowing you can't do something because of a physical limitation, such as arthritic ankles, and being afraid to do something.

"I couldn't do anything that involves a lot of height—like mountain climbing. I don't like closed-in spaces like elevators." Working with dementia patients in a locked unit was difficult for her. Hearing about women in their 50s and 60s playing Roller Derby, she said, "No way, no how could I play Roller Derby!"

Her greatest fear is giving up her independence since finding it. "I have transitioned from relying on other people for advice to relying on myself." But she feels lonely and credits, and is grateful to, her pastor and personal counselor for their help and support.

Despite her dislike of heights, she thinks she would like to try skydiving and parasailing. "I may be killed skydiving, but the benefit may very well be the greatest experience of my life." Watching a video of her son skydiving, she wondered if she would have the courage to try it. She would only want to tandem skydive out of fear she would forget to pull the ripcord. "With a good-looking hunk on my back, why not?" she said.

"Putting our lives on hold for others is one of my biggest regrets. My husband and I had all our ducks in a row, bills paid, life going well, then came his CIDP diagnosis and he died six months later."

For others thinking about taking risks and trying new things, Pat says her husband, Brian, used to say, "Do what you want to do. Do not put it on hold. Live your life like it's your last day. Do what you love."

When her brother-in-law had a limited time to live, he wanted to go on a road trip. His wife, Pat's sister, was reluctant and nervous about it, but they went and spent a month traveling. He died about a year later. They were glad they took that trip.

"I live for being happy and being the best person I can be. I'm happy with myself now. I want to try and make my patients' last few days more comfortable—maybe with a smile and a laugh, and to help the families through the death of a loved one.

"To do end-of-life care is a privilege."

Pat, CNA, at Sussman House, Rockport, Maine

Photo by Diana Coleman

SISTER VIRGINIA PECKHAM

From Artist, Writer, and Widow to Joining a Convent at 61

BIRTH YEAR: 1951

Raised a Unitarian in upstate New York, Virginia became a writer and artist in New York City. She married her former art teacher and they moved to Maine. In her 50s, Virginia had a conversion experience and joined a Baptist church. She became a Catholic at 58, was widowed at 59, and went online to research convents.

Earlier Years

As a child, Virginia romped about New York State's countryside playing made-up games with her sisters. She enjoyed reading, drawing, camping with her family, and skating and skiing during the snowy winters. Her family moved from Averill Park to Mount Kisco, outside New York City, when Virginia was 12. Ready for adventure after high school, she enrolled at the State University of New York at Binghamton and lasted one semester. She dropped out because she felt she was drifting and wasting her parents' money. Her parents made it clear that if she wasn't going to go to college, she should find some kind of work. They paid for her to take secretarial classes. Bored with being a secretary in her 20s, she took up writing and graphic design to make her work more stimulating.

Virginia describes herself as depressed and shy as a young woman. Sketching in cafés and other public places brought her closer to people; drawing the human figure was a spiritual experience for her. Through her art, she grew to love people in all their variety. She spent twenty years in New York City, and studied at the National Academy of Design School of Fine Art, the Art Students League, and the School of Visual Arts. She was an editor for an art magazine and for the Paley Center for Media (when it was called the Museum of Broadcasting). As a freelancer, she wrote and edited articles and reports, primarily for nonprofit organizations.

When Virginia was a secretary in her 20s in New York City, she had an unusual encounter. Her calm disposition and her interest in wanting to understand all types of people undoubtedly helped her during this surprise visit.

One morning, while working for a couple of men who owned a small movie production company in a shabby building on Broadway, near Fifty-Fourth Street, Virginia heard a knock at the office door. She was by herself. Looking through the peephole, she saw what she thought was a messenger boy and opened the door. A scared-looking teenage boy about 14 said, "This is a stickup!" and shoved his way into the office. He carried a gun and a very large hunting knife. The gun was bad, but the large knife was terrifying, Virginia thought. She saw him as a frightened guy who was probably high on drugs and desperate for money. He opened the office desk drawers and demanded Virginia's purse, taking her $11 total cash. He told Virginia to lie down. Not wanting to be in a vulnerable position, she half sat up, looking "faintly defiant" to watch him and try to figure him out. Cutting the phone wires with his knife, he told her to get into the next room.

"Can I get my cigarettes?" she asked, thinking that might break the spell and humanize the situation by showing that she was a real person—perhaps like his mother or aunt. He hesitated, then said, "Okay." She went to her desk, grabbed her cigarettes, and sat back down. "He then told me to go into the room, pointing to the inner office." She went into the other room, and he closed the door. Seeing another secretary at the window in the building across the way, Virginia pantomimed making a phone call and mouthed the words "Call the police!" She knew the woman couldn't hear her but hoped she got the message. She waited a good twenty minutes, then ventured out of the room. The guy had left. The police arrived later, having been called by the woman in the office building across the alley, who had managed to lip-read. The police asked Virginia for a description. She could say only that the boy wore black pants and a blue shirt, and had a gun and a large knife. She focused on the enormous knife and visualized being sliced into pieces. Looking back on the incident, she realized she shouldn't have opened the door, but it was a weekday morning. Having a robber show up and threaten her at gun- and knifepoint was totally unexpected!

At 36, Virginia married her former art instructor Hugh Gumpel, twenty-six years her senior—a prolific and experimental artist from the National Academy School. Enjoying vacations in Maine, they moved to the midcoast region after deciding it would be a good place to live and make art. Virginia experimented with art mediums under Hugh's tutelage, painting, among other subjects, a series of colorful and whimsical depictions of children. She also wrote marketing material and grant proposals for the local health care system. After the 9/11 World Trade Center tragedy in 2001, Virginia was drawn to, and inspired by, theological readings. She became a believing Christian over the next few years and was initially drawn to a Baptist church. Four years later, she became a Catholic. Hugh died at age 85, leaving Virginia a widow at 59.

As a newly converted Catholic in her late 50s, Virginia became interested in learning what it would be like to join a convent. She found vocationmatch.com and took an online survey to locate convents in harmony with her religious feelings and longings. Asking herself, *What kind of life do I want to live as a Catholic sister?* she tried to envision the kind of life she would lead. Would she wear a habit? Work with the poor? Nine convents were a match.

The Little Sisters of Jesus and Mary, one of the nine "matching" convents, followed up with her. They suggested she find a spiritual director to help her discern whether she actually had a vocation. A local priest was willing to provide direction, and after they met and corresponded by email, he encouraged her to take the next step. Virginia visited the Little Sisters' convent in Maryland—initially for a week, and soon after, for a month. During her stays, Virginia and the community's sisters felt they shared a mutually beneficial relationship.

Within days of returning home to Maine, she decided to return to the convent, and several weeks later, began the long process of becoming a religious sister—starting as a postulant the first year. After her five-week experience of living, working, and praying with the sisters, she said, "It isn't always easy, but at times, it can be like heaven to be with people who are looking for a closer walk with Christ."

Life in the Convent

Moving into the community to begin her life as a postulant didn't require much packing. She brought books and sketchbooks, watercolors and brushes, her computer, her cell phone, nature guides, juggling balls, and books about how to juggle, hoping to share the art of juggling with the sisters. She had learned the basics at a juggling conference and taken it up when working at a computer job to keep her body limber and her mind stress-free.

Virginia's most prized possession was her beloved Charles—a gorgeous black cat with white feet. The convent cannot take animals, so Virginia found a loving home for him—with a man who had lost his cat and missed the companionship. She returned to Maine after six months in the convent and saw Charles in his new, loving environment. Now an "indoor cat," Charles recognized Virginia immediately and sat purring next to her while she petted him. "It pleases me to know Charles appears very content in another loving home and looks beautiful with shiny fur without fleas!"

The convent's combination of prayer and community service appeals to Virginia. Her daily schedule includes private meditation, prayer in common, adoration, and working with the poor at their local crisis center for men and women in need. "I've led a life of self-indulgence, and it is a chance for me to give back now," she said. "When I became a Catholic, I took Saint Clare as my saint because she was so different from me—she was so self-sacrificial and worked with lepers, which would be a real challenge for me and way out of my comfort zone. I thought I would see what service is like. This community's devotion to prayer and service is the right mix for me."

Daily Schedule (from "Are You in Love?" brochure, Little Sisters of Jesus and Mary)

5:00	AM Rise
5:30	Private meditation
6:00	Liturgical prayer and adoration in common
7:00	Mass at parish church
7:45	Breakfast, then work with the poor
12:00	Lunch, then work with the poor
	During the afternoon—Make a Holy Hour
5:00	PM Liturgical prayer in common
5:30	Supper, then free time
7:30	Recreation
8:00	Free time

Nine months after entering the convent, Virginia returned to her apartment in Rockland, Maine, to terminate her lease and get rid of her remaining possessions. She admitted that the act of "de-possessioning" her clothing was difficult and intentionally done first. "Donating all my clothing to Goodwill was a shock for me—much harder than I imagined. Though I am not a very materialistic person, and didn't think of myself as caring about clothes, my clothes reflected my personality. Every article meant something even though many were purchased at thrift stores." It was only after disposing of every item of clothing (with the exception of a jacket for Maryland's cold weather) that she felt comfortable visiting the office where she formerly worked. Virginia, now Sister Virginia, feared that she might be tempted to return to the safety and familiarity of her former position—feeling some doubt then about continuing in the convent.

Virginia owned many sketchbooks, paintings, and drawings—hers and those of her late husband. She held an exhibition and sale of Hugh's art, and disposed of her own art, as her convent room is simple and devoid of many personal effects. "My art class nudes especially would not be appropriate in the convent," she said. Her seventy-one sketchbooks, along with acrylic and watercolor paintings and drawings, were given to friends and acquaintances. She gave her furniture and kitchen items to her landlord and friends.

The Little Sisters of Jesus and Mary say in their "Are You in Love?" brochure, "The upper age limit is 50, although exceptions may be possible." The community would like to grow; there are currently fewer than ten sisters, including Virginia. Most of the sisters are over 60. The brochure explains, "Widowed and divorced women are welcome. (An annulment is required by the Church for a divorced person to be professed in religious life.)"

The sisters live in two Maryland locations a half-hour drive apart. Virginia resides with several sisters in their rural convent in Princess Anne; the other sisters are in the Salisbury city convent. They share household duties. All goods are communal. Virginia has always embraced the simple life and never regarded herself as materialistic. She believes artists typically live simply.

Virginia was issued a habit as a postulant for her first year—a plain blue denim jumper, a white blouse, a blue veil (a simple kerchief) for her hair, and blue knee socks worn with sensible navy or black shoes. As a novice for two years, her habit became a three-quarter-sleeved, blue dress (no blouse), a leather belt, and a white veil. Entering her fourth year, she was given a navy blue kerchief for her head and a wooden cross necklace with a picture of a crucified Christ on it. Her habit is comfortable to wear, though it makes her conspicuous. "I fight the instinct to hide at times, but I think of this as an adventure, and I end up having conversations with all types of people who stop and ask me questions, about the Catholic faith and God and the Trinity."

Describing the sisters as bright with lots of good humor and shared laughs, Virginia said, "The mission to be a universal sister really appeals to me. We all need sisters." Virginia has three sister siblings and had a wild idea that they might try to stop her from entering the convent—holding an intervention or taking away her car keys. But that wasn't the case at all—quite the contrary. Her family has been very positive about her decision.

Daily life in the convent is tiring, Virginia admits. She had a moment of doubt about what she had done after a particularly stressful couple of weeks as a postulant. "I was totally wiped out and thought, *I cannot keep up this pace*," and so she consulted her wise superior. "She advised me to think about how I was feeling in the moment and to pick a date in the future—days, weeks, or months—and then see how I felt on that particular date." Virginia picked a date a few weeks away, and when the date arrived for her to evaluate how she was feeling, she realized she felt great, energized, and in a totally different place.

The sisters are urged to be in the present moment: "Rather than praying for what kind of person I should be, instead I ask myself, *What can I do right now, today, to respond to the Holy Spirit?*" She drew the analogy with her former husband, Hugh, who, when his painting students were stuck, would say, "Do the next obvious thing."

In thinking about her vocation, Virginia quotes Nietzsche: "Life is not a problem to be solved, but a mystery to be lived."

The Little Sisters' spirituality is based on the life and writings of

Blessed Charles de Foucauld and guided by spiritual authors such as Saint John of the Cross and Father Jean Pierre de Caussade, who wrote *Abandonment to the Divine Providence* to provide advice to nuns struggling with the spiritual life in community.

Virginia spends her time praying, attending church, being with the men and women in need at the Joseph House Crisis Center, helping people manage their finances, cooking and serving meals, doing yard work, reading about religious life and the Catholic faith, and preparing and sharing communal meals. She has helped clean and prepare apartments for homeless women and children.

Always the artist, Virginia has made drawings of some of the people in the day shelter for the homeless and colored them on her computer using a graphic software program. The men and women were pleased to see their pictures on display. She gave an art class, along with another sister, in the Joseph House Workshop, a residential program for men. She also led a class on the inspirational book *Battlefield of the Mind.*

Occasionally, there are tense moments among the homeless men they work with on weekdays. Virginia's good nature and interest in getting to know the inner person is apparent in her interactions with all people. One of the "regulars," distraught because his mother had just died, threatened to kill another homeless man who was hassling him. All she could think of to say was "Please don't kill him in the Hospitality Room!"

Laughing when asked what Hugh would think of her decision to enter a convent, she said, "Hugh always liked nuns—he was good friends with a Maryknoll sister who was a student in his art class. He once told me that if he passed away, I should befriend ladies. 'What would you want with another old man?' he asked."

Virginia was advised by her local priest to go to the convent with an open mind, saying, "Take the direction where your heart is warm and you're serving God. See if you like how the sisters live and pray."

One of the realities facing the Catholic church is the decrease in the number of women becoming sisters. As the small group of Little Sisters of Jesus and Mary continues to age, there is concern about whether their community is sustainable.

Thoughts and Advice About Risk

"A risk is a decision you cannot undo—such as quitting a job that I can't go back to, at an age when getting the same kind of work again is not easy to do," Virginia said.

"Joining the convent is kind of like joining the military—it's a strong commitment. It's not like going to prison, however—you can leave at any time.

"Quitting my job as a grant writer with a good income was a risk for me because I don't think I could find another job like that. It was a risk leaving a beautiful, calm, orderly place in Maine to go to the rambunctious city of Salisbury, Maryland, to work in a converted industrial building that serves as the crisis center for poor people—some with mental illness. My life in Maine was full of improvisation, and the convent life is a structured environment. Not being as free concerned me. I risked spending my money (transportation, meal costs, and vacation time from work) during the discernment process when contemplating a religious, consecrated life.

"Part of joining a religious community is taking vows. These vows are public, and we are encouraged to invite family and friends. While I will be grateful to have loved ones witness my religious calling, it is also a risk to do that in front of others."

Virginia's first year was the pre-novitiate, or postulancy, phase. The postulancy is followed by a two-year novitiate when a sister is known as a "novice" in preparation for public "temporary vows." As the convent's brochure says, "Vows are made for one year at a time for six years and then forever, if it is your calling." Virginia explained, "If a sister comes to the conclusion that she must leave the congregation, she petitions the superior general for a dispensation from her vows." It is a vow of chastity, obedience, and poverty. "This way of life is designed to strip away the extraneous to follow God with all your heart and to love your neighbor as Christ has loved you.

"The biggest risk I ever took up to this point was getting married at age 36. Marriage is a serious commitment—you're responsible for someone else. However, I wanted to be with Hugh all the time and would have regretted not marrying him. I realize I'm taking myself out of the husband pool.

"I risk telling people I'm in a convent, and if it doesn't work out, I'll let others down and have to admit it didn't work. I hope to live up to my expectations and those of others. However, if you listen to the Holy Spirit to follow God's will, you're most true to yourself. If I give it my all and it doesn't work out, then that is God's will.

"It's a liberating feeling to join a religious community," said Virginia. "Though that's not to say there won't be a time when I'll say, 'What have I done?'"

Sister Virginia, Little Sisters of Jesus and Mary Convent, Princess Anne, Maryland

Photo by Diana Coleman

CHAPTER 7 — SURVIVORS

GLADYS DeJESUS MITCHELL

Survived a Massive Heart Attack and Launched a Singing Career in Her 50s

BIRTH YEAR: 1959

Born in Harlem, in New York City, Gladys moved to the Bronx in eighth grade. She loved singing but lacked the confidence to pursue a singing career. As a dispatcher for the New York Police Department on the tragic day of 9.11.2001, she was in charge of sending officers to and from Ground Zero. Having suffered a major heart attack later and not expected to live, Gladys survived to fulfill her impossible dream.

Earlier Years

The middle child between two brothers, Gladys was a shy girl who loved to sing. When she was a little girl, her mother and her second-grade teacher told her she had a beautiful voice. "That had a big impact on me," Gladys said, "but I almost always sang inside my house, not outside."

Her father left the family when she was 10, returning to his native Puerto Rico. She visited him in the summers. Her mother became a single parent raising three children.

Gladys's school community became aware of her talent and asked her to sing "The Impossible Dream" in eighth grade. Practicing with the sheet music her older brother gave her, Gladys mustered the courage to perform the song at her graduation.

Her eighth-grade music teacher encouraged Gladys to apply to the LaGuardia High School of Music and Art and Performing Arts in Manhattan. She never thought she would be accepted. "When the letter arrived saying 'Congratulations! You've been accepted ...' I nearly passed out I was so excited!"

Gladys was a voice major and performed in shows, plays, and concerts. "Everyone encouraged each other. We were all on the same level as students. It was the happiest time of my life."

After high school, Gladys tried out for the leading role of Doris Winter in the stage musical *Mama, I Want to Sing!* based on the life of singer-songwriter Doris Troy and cowritten by Doris's sister Vy Higginsen, who conducted the audition. Doris, aka Mama Soul, became famous for cowriting and singing "Just One Look." "I got a callback and was told when to appear. I was too shy and didn't have the confidence, so I didn't go back," Gladys said ruefully.

With a full scholarship to New York University, Gladys pursued majors in music and nursing—her passion was singing. Her mother hadn't heard her perform and thought music was an impractical career choice. Employed by the New York Police Department, her mom told her the department was hiring. Gladys took a six-month leave of absence to help earn money in her junior year, with the intention of returning to college. Twenty-five years later Gladys was still working for the New York Police Department.

At age 25, she married, and eventually she had three daughters. In her late 20s, Gladys decided to sing at Amateur Night at Harlem's famous Apollo Theater. The audience determined the winners of this popular show, and it was televised later. She asked to sing "If I Could." Another woman from Philadelphia wanted to sing the same song, but was told she couldn't because Gladys had already asked for it. Overcoming her fear and excited about performing at the Apollo, Gladys sold tickets to her family and friends, many of whom were in the audience that night. Wearing a beautiful, glittery gold dress, Gladys came out on stage, rubbed a good luck piece of wood, and announced her name. Before she began to sing with the band, people in the front section booed loudly. Confused and dazed, she started to sing. Loud booing from the front seats persisted. Shocked, she stopped singing and left the stage. The producers tried to persuade her to go back on. She wouldn't. Later, she recalled hearing a woman say earlier in the dressing room, "We won't let her get one note out." The booing had been orchestrated by the woman's family to ruin Gladys's performance. It worked. Gladys was terribly embarrassed. She left quickly and never returned.

Seventeen years later on September 11, 2001, when the World Trade Center was attacked, Gladys was at work. It was 911 Day, the police department's annual celebration, and Gladys had been chosen to sing. (She once sang at a Christmas party, so her colleagues knew she could sing.) Typically, the mayor, police commissioners, and other dignitaries were part of this awards event. "Taking calls before the ceremony, I got the first call around 8:30 a.m. as a 911 operator. It was an attorney who said, 'I don't want you to think I'm crazy, but I just saw a jetliner go into the World Trade Center.' Lights flashed on our screens, and the board lit up with calls coming in. 'Okay,' I said. 'I got the info. Help is on the way.' The next caller said, 'My wife just called. A bomb went off—she can't get out of there! I will give you a million dollars if you get her out safely.' I was swamped with 911 calls and realized these were for real. The head supervisor told me, 'I need you *right now* to go to the dispatch room and dispatch the police to the World Trade Center zone.' While dispatching, I asked a woman police officer, 'What am I hearing? It sounds like a train. What are those thumps I'm hearing?' I was told, 'You are hearing bodies hitting the ground.'

"I never took a break until 4:00 p.m. I mobilized children out of school, buses, and ambulances. By 4:30 p.m., I couldn't talk anymore. I stayed late that night and came home at 2:00 a.m. I got no sleep and returned the next day."

From that day on, Gladys suffered periodic heart palpitations but kept on working. She figured the palpitations were anxiety attacks. At times when walking, she had to stop, stand still, and clutch her chest while the pain rushed through.

In the aftermath of the horrific 9.11.2001 tragedy, her husband told her that life was short and he needed to pursue other things. He left the family the next year. Their girls were 5, 8, and 15. Gladys was devastated. "I wanted to give up but had no choice," she said. "My mom said, 'You have these three girls. You must take care of yourself so you can take care of them.' I realized I needed to pick myself up and be there for them. I had to set an example. Things are going to happen in life—you can't give up. No matter what happens, you can't give up."

Many years after dropping out of New York University, Gladys decided to reapply at age 47. The entrance examination was scheduled for a Saturday. In the meantime, a friend told her about a special one-night stage performance of the musical *Dreamgirls*, based on the female trio The Dreamettes, and suggested she audition. Tryouts were scheduled for the same day as NYU's examination. Taking the exam meant she was going to be late for the audition. She took the exam, was accepted into NYU on the spot, and was asked to report back on Monday. From there, Gladys drove to the audition along with her niece and daughter, who had encouraged her to try out for the show. En route, she received several calls from the producer urging her to hurry up. Stuck in gridlock, she saw the flashing lights of a police car behind her. She tailgated it when it passed her, flew to the Midtown theater, and arrived late.

She sang "Already Home" from the *Wizard of Oz* and was asked, "Can you give us a little bit of 'And I Am Telling You I'm Not Going' from *Dreamgirls*? You killed it!" They told her to return on Monday for a callback—the same day she was to report to NYU. She showed up thinking she might get an understudy role or be a background singer, but instead, she was offered the part of the lead singer Effie White.

Because the rehearsals were demanding while working full-time as a single mother of three, she did not pursue her degree. Her mother attended the performance and said, "I'm so happy to see you perform!" Thrilled to sing, Gladys considered that show her one-night musical career and continued working for the police department.

Then one of her daughters received a diagnosis of cancer and her mother suffered a severe stroke. Two weeks later, Gladys had a massive heart attack at age 48. Admitted to the hospital where her mother was still a patient, Gladys had angioplasty surgery and experienced several heart attacks during her hospital stay.

The doctors feared that Gladys didn't have long to live after the severity of her heart attack. She immediately retired from the police department after twenty-five years.

Several months later, Gladys's mother died and she endured even more tragedy. Another daughter was hit by a car and nearly died. Her daughter with cancer had surgery. Four months later, Gladys's younger brother went to sleep and never woke up, dying at 45 from a rare medical condition. "These experiences solidified for me that life is for the living," Gladys said. "If you're here, you're here for a reason. You have to live life to the fullest and do your best. I tell my girls, 'You know what you can accomplish. You do your best!'"

Launching a Singing Career

When Gladys was 54, one of her girlfriends urged her to audition for *Alive! 55+ and Kickin'!*, a new production designed to showcase extraordinary voices from women and men age 55 and over who had come through tough experiences. "Inside I was fearful, thought I was going to die and was too young," Gladys said. She was permitted to audition because she was almost 55. The woman producer conducting the audition said, "You look familiar!" It was Vy Higginsen, the same woman for whom Gladys had auditioned out of high school, when she never appeared for the callback.

Two hundred people auditioned for eighteen slots. The candidates were narrowed down to fewer than fifty, who attended a weeks-long workshop where each person told their life story. "They got to know us, our talents, and heard about our lives. It was rough!" Gladys said. "The day the producers chose the cast was my birthday. I said to myself, *I need this present desperately!* I had no idea whether I would be picked—there was so much good talent. When they said my name, I said, 'Yay!' I was *so happy*!"

Alive! 55+ and Kickin'!, under the auspices of Vy's Mama Foundation for the Arts, is about "the healing and transformative power of story and song." According to mamafoundation.org, the foundation was created "to help re-establish Harlem as an artistic and cultural centerpiece of the world. Mama's mission is to present, preserve, and promote gospel, jazz, and the R&B arts for current and future generations." Vy's husband, Ken Wydro, creative director, selected "The Impossible Dream" for Gladys to sing—the song she performed at her eighth-grade graduation. "This song is my life story," Gladys said.

Amazingly talented singers' voices resonate to cheering audiences from around the world. During the performance, each singer tells their story, whether it's about serving time in prison, being abandoned as a baby, or grieving a young son's death. Gladys comes on stage wearing a stunning black dress, tells her story, and belts out "The Impossible Dream" as if it's her last solo. Audiences go wild clapping, standing, and shouting "Encore!"

Performing at the Dempsey Theater in Harlem, close to the Apollo Theater, *Alive! 55+ and Kickin'!* has also toured in San Diego, Atlanta, and Washington, DC, where the cast sang for the Congressional Black Caucus. The group was featured on the CBS show *60 Minutes*, but Gladys didn't appear on the show because only several singers could be selected.

Cast members rehearse three days a week for three and a half hours leading up to a week before a performance, and then every day. To overcome her shyness and fear of performing, Gladys said, "I put myself in a zone. I don't think about my performance and don't have an opinion about it. My response is based on the reaction from people.

"Attendees say to me, 'You made me cry!' and I ask, 'Is that a good thing?' I'm definitely still afraid when I perform. I have a fear of failure, of not being good enough. Ken says, 'You gotta go deep within you.'" Awed by, and having tremendous respect for producers Vy and Ken, Gladys said, "They're brilliant and the other singers are extremely talented." She feels honored to sing among them. "I still can't believe it!" she gushed.

Gladys is proud of herself and her daughters, Tracey, Danielle, and Briana, who are doing well. "I'm pleased with the way I've handled myself in all my circumstances." She tells her daughters, who have gone through tough times of their own, "Out of every circumstance there's a reason. There's a lesson in every experience."

Since her retirement from the police department, Gladys receives health benefits and has fought for a special World Trade Center pension that was allocated for those working during the 9/11 tragedy. "I'm the forgotten hero," she said, maintaining she is entitled to the pension. Her case has been denied three times. Gladys has always fought injustice and helped friends and colleagues over the years with advice and support.

Singing has brought her rewards and commendations. Gladys met her fiancé while singing at the Greater Centennial A.M.E. Zion Church in Mount Vernon, New York, where she also sang in a special one-woman show. While she was in a hair salon one day, a man walked by and came in saying, "I'll never forget you, Dreamgirl!" He had been to the one-night performance years before and asked her to sing Sam Cooke's "A Change Is Gonna Come" at his mother's memorial service. Gladys was amazed and flattered, and couldn't refuse.

Having wanted to sing ever since she was little, Gladys had never found the confidence to pursue it as a serious career. After suffering her massive heart attack, she never dreamed she'd have a singing career in her second half of life—she didn't even think she was going to survive.

She loves singing and performing with *Alive! 55+ and Kickin'!* "I love it so much, I would do it even if I wasn't paid. When I hear about people dying from heart attacks, I think, *Why not me? What is the reason I'm still here? You will not leave this earth until you have accomplished and fulfilled your dreams. There's a reason you're still here—there's something you're supposed to do.* The Bible says, 'Trust in the Lord with all your heart and lean not on your own understanding.'" Gladys believes God shows you the way. "This show came into my life when I was battling the biggest fight of my life."

Thoughts and Advice About Risk

Gladys sees risk as "taking a chance on something or someone that is, or who is, unreachable or impossible. Formerly, I've been a risk taker when it was for anything other than music, and that changed. I've learned after everything that's happened to me that I won't take a risk that affects my family. That's not a risk I'm willing to take. If a risk makes my children detour in other ways, I'd have to give it up. My health is very important. I need to be conscious of my health and need to stay diligent."

She has faced health challenges with an optimistic attitude. While at a rehabilitation facility after hip replacement surgery, she developed a pain in her back and asked a resident friend with two broken legs from a car accident to pound on her back to relieve what she thought was gas. Pounding didn't help, and the pain became excruciating. An ambulance whisked her to a hospital, where multiple clots were discovered in her lungs. She was in intensive care for five days and told that having her friend pound on her back was the worst thing for blood clots. Discharged from the hospital, Gladys returned to rehab for two months and was then released to go home for outpatient rehab. Within one month, *Alive! 55+ and Kickin'!* was starting a new season. "I wasn't sure I would be ready to perform, but with God and my daughter driving me to rehearsals, I recuperated miraculously and I was ready for opening day.

"Sometimes my humility works against me and prevents me from taking steps that I should. I'm now taking a whole other route I didn't expect. I'm afraid of the unexpected.

"I am fearful when I hear things going on in the entertainment industry. They say the music industry is cutthroat. I've been blessed and been prepared. The decisions I've made earlier in my life are not decisions I'd make now. I'm afraid to take risks—I'm not looking for success. I want people to enjoy what I do. This is my passion. My life has come full circle. I'm definitely in a better place now. With grown-up girls, I can focus my time and energy on the show.

"It's never too late for you to accomplish and fulfill your dreams. The song 'Impossible Dream' is like my singing dream. Vy Higginsen says, 'The first fifty years are for learning; the second fifty are for *living*!' and she has made that the motto of the show. Everything seemed so impossible—you try to reach for it and it doesn't happen when you want to grasp it. Everything in its own time. There are endless possibilities in the future."

An effervescent, dynamic woman with an enormous smile, Gladys cannot believe her good life right now. She's fulfilling her girlhood dream and passion. "I can't even imagine what's in store, because I never thought I would be doing this. I'm not doing this for fame or fortune. I'm a simple, plain woman. I may look like a million dollars on stage, but I could have just $5 in my pocket. I'm just as happy looking like a million with $5.

"I don't know what lies ahead. Whatever it is, I know God will let me fulfill it. Everyone can relate to someone in the *Alive! 55+ and Kickin'!* show. I don't even realize how many people the show has impacted. The show uplifts us and makes us realize dreams come true.

"Fear is a natural feeling. Everyone is afraid of the unexpected. You have to take a chance or you'll live another fifty years thinking you shoulda, coulda, woulda. Go for it! Never give up!"

Gladys singing at the Dempsey Theater
Harlem, New York City

Photo by Jeremy Daniel

JOAN VARGAS

A New Body and Image After Losing 100+ Pounds with Gastric Bypass Surgery at 55

BIRTH YEAR: 1957

A petite woman with waist-long dark hair, Joan grew up in midcoast Maine. She struggled through school, worked, and was an entrepreneur and avid volunteer. After marrying her high school sweetheart, she had two children. At five feet, she went from 120 pounds to 240 pounds after giving birth to her second child in her late 20s. Obese and fearing an early death, Joan was desperate to lose 100 pounds.

Earlier Years

Joan's grandmother died from childbirth complications, and though housekeepers were hired afterward, her oldest daughter (Joan's mother), who was 13 at the time, bore much responsibility in caring for a newborn infant and seven brothers. The family lived on a prison farm where Joan's grandfather was a guard. Admiring her mother for assuming responsibility and persevering at such a young age, Joan said, "Most 13-year-olds would have melted in a heap." When Joan was growing up in Thomaston, Maine, with five siblings, her mom sewed her children's clothes, made military uniforms at a factory, and scooped ice cream at a local shop. Her dad worked for a phone company and a union, and became an elected state representative. He died at 62, one year into office.

As a child, Joan played in the street with lots of neighborhood kids. In elementary school, she had to repeat two grades—first grade when she had rheumatic fever, and third grade when she lacked concentration and fell behind. She suffered from sexual abuse by an older male when she was a young girl. With support from her younger brother, she confronted her abuser when she was a seventh grader, which ended the abuse. In retrospect, she thinks being abused made her unable to focus on schoolwork.

Struggling with dyslexia, she scratched numbers onto sandpaper, believing it would etch the numbers in her brain. It didn't work, and gave her bleeding fingers. Recognizing she was smart but couldn't learn from standard methods, her fourth-grade teacher gave her a calculator to figure out math problems and had her explain how she arrived at the answers. It worked.

"I hated school," Joan confessed. "I couldn't sit still. I always wanted to work and had odd jobs from age 13 on—carrying meal trays up and down the stairs in a nursing home, busing tables and washing dishes at local restaurants, and conducting store inventories. I jumped at the chance to join a work-study program in high school." At age 20 she married Richard, whom she had known since she was 12. He was a marine, and they moved cross-country, from Maine to California, several times for his career.

Bored and lonely with her husband deployed overseas for six months to a year at a time, Joan worked several jobs near their San Clemente, California, home—as a cook, a school bus mechanic's assistant, and a custodian at her children's school. Pregnant with her first child, she climbed to 185 pounds, returning to 120 pounds after the birth of her daughter. Six years later, in her late 20s, five-foot Joan went up to 185 pounds again while pregnant with her son, and then to 240 pounds, to size 22. (Her six-foot-three husband weighed 183 pounds.)

"I ate the wrong foods. I craved starches, like potato chips, salt, and bread, more so than sweets. I ate all the time and never exercised. Though I was skinny as a child, teen, and into my 20s, most members of my family were heavy. My overweight mom always made homemade cookies and kept three cookie jars filled at all times."

When they lived in Maine, Joan continued working in restaurants. Skilled in setting up businesses and creating and managing events, she helped friends start a restaurant. Joan also became a successful entrepreneur, launching Local Talents of Maine, in Thomaston. "I always enjoyed crafts, and there were no venues for artisans except high-end galleries and short-term fairs. I saw the need for a year-round venue." She invested $3,000 to launch a business where three hundred craftspeople rented space and sold their work. Ready to start something else after six years, she sold the business.

Joan has always been an energetic volunteer as well. "I see myself as a ferret, a hyperactive woman who is easily distracted." When her children were young, she was a Brownie and Girl Scout troop leader wherever they lived—from San Diego to Maine. Her weight didn't hold her back. She went on many trips, including canoeing. Although she lost her breath at times, she kept on going. She helped start a Girl Scout camp while living in Maine's Presque Isle region. At Camp Pendleton in California, she worked at an elementary school, and was honored with the Volunteer of the Year award. With the Key Wives Club, she supported other wives whose husbands were deployed.

"I have to volunteer. My parents instilled this in us," Joan said. She has volunteered at the local July Fourth parade festivities working at her brother's food booth, and has cooked 40 pounds of squash and rounded up pies for Thanksgiving dinners through Community That Cares. Joan has also coordinated midcoast Maine's campaign for Toys for Tots, a national organization founded by the Marine Corps Reserves. She began working for the group with her husband. "I enjoy the challenge of collecting toys, getting the word out, and running fundraising events, like auctions and train rides." She is proud that the program distributes toys to more than three thousand children during the Christmas season. "I like to make kids happy," she said.

An animal lover, she formerly worked at an animal shelter and drove a red-and-black-trimmed smart car shrink-wrapped as an orange cat.

Her two Irish short-legged Jack Russells, Jack and Lucy, are named after her parents. Since her mother didn't want any animals in the house, their family had only a turtle when Joan was growing up, but she pet-sat for lots of cats and dogs when young.

Sporting a "Born to Be Wild" thumb ring, Joan used to ride on the back of her husband's motorcycle and then decided she wanted her own bike. She bought a Honda Shadow motorcycle without knowing how to ride. Her husband taught her. Later, she graduated to a Kawasaki 900.

A compassionate woman, Joan understands and sympathizes with family members who struggle with challenging mental and physical health problems—Asperger's syndrome, multiple autoimmune deficiencies, and post-traumatic stress disorder.

By the time Joan was 54, she had been overweight for more than twenty-five years and had serious health problems herself. Her blood sugar and blood pressure levels were "migraine high," and she was on thyroid medication from a genetic condition. She didn't want to die early. "I'm incredibly lucky to have my husband," she said. "I didn't want him to end up alone, nor did he wish to be alone. I worried I was headed down a path toward diabetes and fearful for my husband and son especially, who had health problems. I wanted to be there for them. I had a conversation with myself and approached my weight like I do solving problems. The hardest part was putting myself first, but I checked into ways to lose weight."

A Transformation

Weighing 240 pounds, Joan tried every diet and weight-loss program available. She ate Lean Cuisine meals and went on Nutrisystem twice, participating in their weekly phone check-ins and counseling. Though she went from a size 22 to size 16, the weight didn't stay off. She ordered Jenny Craig meals. She joined Weight Watchers and, despite participating in regular group meetings, gained weight. "Weight Watchers made me feel like I ate more, and I gained weight. Maybe there were too many free choices or I was doing it wrong."

Shocked when her physician labeled her "morbidly obese," Joan listened when the doctor recommended exploring gastric bypass surgery, which would also reduce her blood sugar and blood pressure. She researched Maine Medical Center's Weight and Wellness Program in Portland and was impressed by Dr. Roy Cobean's extensive experience with gastric bypass surgeries. He was passionate about doing the surgeries and provided her with many details, which inspired confidence. The program required six months of extensive work pre-surgery: meetings with a psychiatrist, nutritionist, and nurses; support groups; health screenings; and tests. She was grateful that Richard accompanied her to all her meetings and appointments.

At age 55, after six months of work and cleansing her intestines two weeks before the operation, Joan underwent Roux-en-Y gastric bypass surgery in February 2013 weighing 220 pounds. "I had some concerns prior to the operation, like the anesthesia's side effects. I was afraid of the nausea, but mostly, I was very excited the surgery was going to happen." Five laparoscopic incisions were made. Her stomach was divided into a larger part and a small pouch the size of a medicine cup. Part of the small intestine was bypassed. With the smaller pouch and bypassed stomach/intestine, weight loss occurs because people eat less and absorb less. Joan stayed one night in the hospital and the following night in a local hotel because of a snowstorm.

She had pain at the incision site and took Tylenol with codeine for three days afterward. She followed a strict intake protocol: liquids only the first week—water and protein shakes. To acclimate to the protein shakes, she was directed to drink them pre-surgery. "They were okay tasting and came in vanilla, chocolate, and strawberry. I preferred the chocolate. Cream of wheat was the first food I ate, a tiny portion with a baby spoon. It was four weeks before I could eat an egg." Recovery took more than a month. She wasn't tempted by the foods in her home refrigerator or cabinet that her husband ate, because she no longer felt hungry. She also needed to eat small amounts in the correct order. Her lifelong thyroid pill had to be taken first, a half hour before liquids, and then small, solid portions.

Liquid and protein intake was critical. She needed soft, blended foods. Refried beans were one of the recommended proteins. She gradually began eating five times daily.

Breakfast was a cup of Greek yogurt followed by a snack of half a protein bar. Lunch was cottage cheese or refried beans. The other half of the protein bar was an afternoon snack. Dinner was a small portion of meat, fish, or tofu. Fish was hard to eat initially and needed to be moist and chewed a lot. Meat was harder and eaten only after some time. Richard prepared his own meals while Joan adjusted to a new food regimen. Dinners were later prepared in a slow-cooker. She eats half a chicken breast and saves the other half for lunch the next day. Eating apples (with the skin) is okay, but she must chew all foods thoroughly or she gets sweaty and has a painful, tight feeling. She likes and tolerates popcorn.

Three months post-surgery she had lost about 45 pounds. "I could see the weight dropping off me daily," Joan said. Seven months later, she had lost a total of 100 pounds and weighed 140. She told many people about her procedure. When she weighed 115 pounds, those who didn't know she had had the operation were afraid she was ill. Rather than saying anything to Joan, they asked others if she was okay.

"I got down to a size 14 from my usual size 22," Joan said. "One day, Richard told me my pants were too big. I was used to pulling them up and putting a belt around the waist. He said, 'Look!' and grabbed my pants at the waist and pulled them down. They came down with no effort. I had lost enough weight to wear a size 6. *I never thought I'd wear a size 6!*"

Eight months post-surgery, she suffered from dumping syndrome after eating one piece of Halloween candy corn. This uncomfortable abdominal feeling and a rapid bowel movement occurs when food moves too quickly from the stomach to the small intestine, often caused by sugar.

"My husband calls me a cheap date," Joan said. "When we eat out, I order a meal, split it in half, and bring one half home." She cannot drink any liquids a half hour before and after eating because the fluid will fill up her small pouch. Protein first—17 grams per meal, she was taught. She was told not to use a straw initially, because the air intake fills up the pouch. "Some people cannot use straws because of the air intake. I am okay with straws. I have to watch certain drinks containing sugar alcohol, which causes diarrhea. I'm not afraid of food now. Before, I set timers on my phone because I was worried about when I needed to eat. Now there's more of a flow and I'm not as concerned."

Knowing the size portion she is supposed to eat, she's amazed at what Americans eat as a normal-sized meal. Lean Cuisine meals are in proper food portions, she was advised. A healthy portion of meat is two ounces, but most people eat much more than that.

Eating too much food causes her stomach pouch to stretch and enlarge. That's how people who have had gastric bypass surgery regain weight. The program requires attending weekly psychiatrist appointments and monthly support groups for five years post-surgery. "You need to have the right mind-set to lose weight," Joan said. With the help of a psychiatrist, she is exploring how being abused as a child may have affected her desire for food and considerable weight gain. "I saw food as a comfort; a way to push down my feelings. I ate when I felt abused in any way," she said.

As a size 6, Joan gave away her clothes that no longer fit and kept her biggest pair of pants as a reminder of her old self. She needed all new clothes and still heads for the plus sizes when she shops—an old habit. "My husband, Richard, loves to shop for me. I try to wear prettier things now. Before, I just covered up. I didn't care and it didn't matter what I wore. No one was going to look at me anyway."

Joan is getting used to her new body. Over four years post-surgery, she ranged between 135 and 140 pounds. "Initially, I lost too much weight. I thought I looked sick at 115 pounds." It's taking a long time to shed her old fat-body image. She says she still walks like a fat woman, hunched over. "It's the 'I don't want to be seen' posture—bending over and hiding. My mind hasn't caught up with my small size," she said. She doesn't recognize her reflection in building windows.

"One day, I was walking my dog Jim down our neighborhood street and glanced at the shadow on the ground next to me. I thought it was a person following me closely. No one was there when I turned around. When I realized it was my shadow, I did a little dance in the street with Jim."

Joan said she is treated differently as a small woman. She often helps her brother lug fifty-pound sacks of grain at fairs. "No one held the door for me when I was obese. After losing a lot of weight, doors are opened for me. The first time someone held the door after I lost weight, it bothered me. *Fine, help me now that I'm thin—not that I needed help when I was heavy*, I thought sarcastically. I was indignant that no one would help me when I weighed a lot.

"I am concerned about putting on weight now. The surgery has done its work; now it's up to me. It's harder not to eat more during the holidays. I can now eat everything I could before the surgery. Initially, I couldn't—I couldn't tolerate all foods, but with time, I can. I don't want to get complacent and need to return to my initial food list and amounts. I always think I'll go back to gaining weight." Part of her six-month regimen post-surgery included daily exercise—twenty to thirty minutes on the treadmill and an upper-body strength workout. "I hate exercising," she admitted. "It slows me down. I think of all the things I could be doing instead," but she knows she should be exercising. She has the same amount of energy as when she was obese, but she is no longer out of breath.

After losing more than 100 pounds, Joan found she couldn't handle her heavy Kawasaki motorcycle. "It went into a 'slow melt'—I was not able to right the bike back up when it leaned. Fortunately, I didn't get hurt." Needing a lighter motorcycle, she settled on a Harley Davidson

1200 Sports cycle that is 600 pounds lighter. A friend who watched her lose weight bought her a smaller jacket. She also got smaller leather chaps. Even her head shrank: she went from a medium-size helmet to an extra small. Maine's motorcycle helmet attitude is "You ride, you decide," but she and her husband always wear full gear. Calling themselves Old FOBs, or Old Farts on Bikes, they ride their motorcycles regularly with friends throughout New England.

Joan continues to help launch new businesses and create events, which comes naturally to her. Because of her dyslexia, she may misspell words, but she has the ability to visualize a project sequentially for success. She helped a restaurateur start an ice cream shop in Rockland, Maine, and was the front manager of another restaurant. She worked long hours on her feet all day. "My legs hurt even with compression socks. My excess skin made it painful, as it hangs around my knees."

An impromptu vacation to Spain with her daughter helped stimulate Joan's interest in taking trips around the country with her husband. They purchased a fifth-wheel camper and traveled from Maine to New Mexico for a couple of months.

Joan and Richard also plan on going into a retirement home someday. "We do not want to be a burden on our children, so that's in our future," Joan said.

A lively woman who laughs easily, Joan is most proud of "my kids and my 'I don't give up' philosophy." When things get tough, she hangs in there. She loves staying busy and gets involved with lots of projects, although that sometimes puts additional stress on her family. "I become totally enraptured with activities I enjoy."

As a creative woman, Joan enjoys making fairy houses from clay and furtively plants them around the neighborhood—on people's lawns, in planters, in trees. "It makes me happy," she said, laughing.

Thoughts and Advice About Risk

"I see risk as anything that endangers my family or income," Joan said.

"I didn't see gastric bypass surgery at age 55 as risky, other than having a few jitters prior to the procedure because it was surgery. I had complete confidence in my physician."

For others struggling with obesity, Joan recommends doing thorough research if contemplating gastric bypass surgery. "Having a supportive husband was very helpful. Everyone is different and must evaluate whether she or he is a good candidate. The program is designed to help formerly heavy people understand why they gained and kept weight on, and methods to keep the weight off. I think it's critical that people in the weight-loss field address the causes of weight gain. I am glad that having this surgery required me to see a therapist weekly for five years, and I'll probably continue the therapy sessions after that." Although she was one of the oldest people in her group to go through the surgery, there was a person in their 60s who was having the procedure.

An undesirable outcome of her huge weight loss is excess skin. "I have 20 pounds of skin that hangs from my upper arms, legs, stomach, and backside. Sitting is sometimes painful unless I readjust my position, as I end up sitting on a roll of skin with no fat." Removal of excess skin is not typically covered by insurance. For those considering gastric bypass surgery, Joan advises saving money for excess skin removal later. "I am uncomfortable with all my excess skin—especially where it's visible on my arms and legs. Having all this extra skin affects my self-image. I wish insurance covered this. I feel good, but wish I could have this skin removed. It's too costly and has a six-month recovery time—longer than the gastric bypass surgery."

Familiar with TV's weight-loss programs such as *The Biggest Loser*, Joan admitted, "It's painful and sad to watch people trying to lose weight. I'm amazed by the results. These programs are good motivators. There's a story behind every heavy person.

"I love the butterflies in my stomach feeling when I launch a business, project, or event. It's exhilarating! I like starting things, and when they're up and running, I get bored and move on to something else," she said, laughing. She doesn't see her projects and activities as risky.

"One risk I wouldn't take is skydiving!" she added.

Joan likes helping others. "When things happen to you and people come into your path, there's a reason. You need to respond," she believes—and she does. "My favorite saying is from A. A. Milne's *Winnie-the-Pooh*: 'You're braver than you believe, and stronger than you seem, and smarter than you think.'"

Joan is now a small woman, but her heart is as big as it always was.

Joan

Photo by Joan Vargas

LITA TOMAS

Kidney Donor to a Stranger at 56; Early-Onset Alzheimer's Diagnosis at 59

BIRTH YEAR: 1954

A petite, optimistic woman, Lita was the oldest of eight children growing up in the Chicago area. Marrying out of high school, she had two daughters. Later divorced, she enlisted in the army, went to school, and joined the Army Reserves and National Guard. At 50, she retired from the army and became her daughter's caregiver. At 56, Lita donated her kidney to a stranger. Having received a diagnosis of early-onset Alzheimer's at 59, Lita is preparing for the years ahead.

Earlier Years

Born in Champaign, Illinois, Lita moved to Chicago as an infant when her mother remarried and had four sons and three more daughters. Lita considered her mom's second husband as her father, and he adopted her. He had a dry-cleaning business, then operated a chlorine/bottling delivery company and later, sold coffee machines. Her stay-at-home mom worked outside the home when the children were older. Lita enjoyed helping take care of her brothers and sisters. She has fond memories of bringing her seven siblings to the large park a half block from their house. "It was special and so much fun! I had an assembly line of kids, and my brothers and sisters sat on all the swings and I pushed them one by one."

Lita attended Catholic grammar school and said she was overly religious then. "I never walked anywhere—I always ran, which helped me later when I joined the army." She played the guitar when younger and took up fishing as a child at her family's cottage on the lake—a sport she still enjoys.

"I made friends with some inner-city black kids who played in the park," Lita said. "At that time, there were no black people in our neighborhood. One day a black lady knocked on our door looking for me. My mother and aunt were surprised to find out she had a bracelet that the children made to thank me for spending lunchtimes with them. I learned when young to be okay with everyone. We're all one big family. I wasn't raised racist."

During high school, her family moved to the Chicago suburb of Oak Park. At her high school graduation, she wore a white dress. She wore the same dress for her wedding the next day. Later, she had three miscarriages before having two daughters, Jean and Kym. After getting a divorce, she was interested in a college education but unable to afford it, so she joined the army. Initially she wanted to be a nurse, and scored high on the test. However, she was told the army didn't need nurses, so she trained as a tank mechanic—rare for women then—and got an associate's degree in diesel mechanics. Reporting for her first assignment at Fort Riley, Kansas, she was told to go to the office to be a clerk. "I don't know how to type," she said. "I trained six months as a mechanic. Show me the toolbox."

She left the army after eighteen months, joined the Army Reserves and National Guard, and worked as a mechanic at a Chicago bus company. The buses had the same type of engine as the tanks. "As the only woman bus mechanic, I was harassed. The guys put pornographic stuff on my toolbox and threw nuts and bolts at me. 'Screw this,' I said. 'It's not worth it.'" She left for a smaller bus company in the suburbs, where she built diesel engines and was more accepted. She later worked maintaining a Mercedes diesel truck fleet for a postal delivery firm. Enjoying building cars, she said, "The first time I went over 120 miles per hour was in a 1965 Ford Galaxy 500, which I built in my bathtub."

Lita also owned Mercedes diesel cars and fixed them herself. "I don't anymore, but I also don't get ripped off when I need work done on my cars," she said.

When working on a truck engine assembly line at a manufacturing plant, she hurt her lower back—breaking a piece off her spine. Because truck starters weighed 60 pounds, she switched to cars with starters weighing 10 pounds. But bending over still put pressure on her lower back. In therapy for back pain, she found out about the recreational therapy field. Marrying again at age 36 to a guy she had met in the service, Lita then obtained an associate's degree, bachelor's degree, and master's degree in recreational therapy. Mobilized by her reserve unit, she was able to use her training and education for only a short while as a therapist in a hospital. While stationed at Scott Air Force Base in Illinois, she finished her military career living in a camper during the workweek and commuting home to Chicago on the weekends. Lita was in active duty with the army at the beginning, middle, and end of her career.

Following in her mother's footsteps, Lita's daughter Jean enlisted in the army out of high school. While doing the high jump, the last event of basic officer training, she fell, and her brain herniated into her spinal cord, resulting in serious brain damage. She got a gold medal anyway and was left with a permanent injury at age 26. Jean gets dizzy and passes out often, so she's able to walk only a few steps and uses a wheelchair. Lita retired as a major from the army after twenty-six years and became her caregiver.

When Jean was able to, she was a bone marrow donor and gave blood regularly. At Christmastime, Lita's family always helps others—giving scarves and hats to shelters, and food to food banks. Knowing her daughter missed being a donor, Lita, at age 55, gave Jean an empty box as one of her Christmas gifts. Inside was a note: "I am going to donate my kidney to a stranger in your honor."

Donating Her Kidney to a Stranger

Lita heard on the news that a young boy desperately needed a kidney, so she sent her blood test results to his hospital. She wasn't a match. Checking out MatchingDonors.com at her daughter Kym's recommendation, she read about a retired fire captain in downstate Illinois with her same A+ blood type. His daughter posted Rod's profile: "He spent most of his adult life saving other people and would never have given it up. With two grown children and four grandchildren, he wished to spend more time with them." Rod had Alport syndrome, a kidney disease, and his first kidney transplant from a cadaver had lasted ten years. He had been on the transplant list for six years and was spending ten hours every night on peritoneal dialysis. Lita wrote to him right away.

They were a match. Lita proceeded with all the required tests as a donor. She and Rod decided to meet at a restaurant after her blood tests. "I liked him and his family immediately," she said. "They are a super fantastic, loving family. I'm always open and person oriented, and his family are the same." Often potential donors and their intended recipients are not encouraged to meet before the transplant surgery because they might not like each other. Lita said, "It would seem weird to me not to meet the person my kidney was going to before the surgery. If you want to do this, you should be open to whoever will get your kidney. If you're prejudiced in any way, it won't work." Despite being in good shape, she hit the gym hard to prepare for the surgery. Because she was retired, she was able to devote the necessary time and resources to it. Other family members helped while she recovered. "It was a family affair," she said.

At age 56, Lita donated her kidney to Rod, age 58, at Barnes Jewish Hospital in St. Louis. Rod was discharged eight days later but returned for testing after eleven months when his body began rejecting the donation. Because he had Lita's kidney, he had the strength to have his aortic valve replaced, but he went back on dialysis to wait for another kidney. "I wish my kidney had given Rod more than eleven months,"

Lita said. "We never know the how or why of life's course—we just go for the ride and do our best. I will pray for smooth dialysis treatments and more donors for more need.

"I would definitely give another kidney and wish I had three. I constantly tell my friends and relatives to do this. Down and out for one week, donating a kidney was nothing. I do remember sneezing soon after the surgery and I didn't want to sneeze ever again! My hysterectomy years earlier was worse. When people hear about my kidney donation, most people say, 'That's nice,' and a few add, 'There's no way I would do that.'"

Taking a Proactive Stance with an Alzheimer's Diagnosis

For Mother's Day in 2013, Kym took her mom to see the play *Big Fish* and bought her a *Big Fish* T-shirt. While wearing the shirt that December, Lita commented that she liked her shirt but didn't know where it came from. Kym reminded her that she had bought it for her at the theater when they saw the *Big Fish* for Mother's Day. Lita had no recollection of going to the play. Concerned, her daughter suggested her mother see a specialist. A neurologist told Lita, age 59, that she had early-onset Alzheimer's. A PET scan showed plaque built up in her brain.

Later, Lita separated from her second husband after more than twenty years of marriage. Her doctor advised her to reduce the stress in her life. Not wanting to be a burden on her family, especially her daughter Jean, who lives with her, Lita is taking proactive measures to prepare for her changed condition. She moved into a one-story ranch-style house in Downers Grove, Illinois. "I had extra doors installed for when I may wander," she said. "Once I get worse, my mobility will go downhill. The doors have special locks in the wing where I sleep. My mother-in-law died of Alzheimer's. I took care of her for seven years. I watched her deteriorate. I know what it looks like. I worried about her when she lived with us. One night, she wandered off and was found a couple of miles away. I became a light sleeper—always concerned she would fall or wander away.

"After receiving my diagnosis, I was encouraged by a medical person to attend an Alzheimer's support group. Going to the meeting where each person was supposed to talk, some couldn't speak at all; others spoke garbled, nonsensical words, and some had no idea where they were. They didn't have us separated by severity—some like me could speak okay, others not at all. I was in tears. It was depressing. I told the nurse I was not coming back. Maybe it's good to have a support group for relatives, but not for those diagnosed."

She was unsure whether she wanted to see the movie *Still Alice*, starring Julianne Moore, whose character receives a diagnosis of early-onset Alzheimer's. She imagined it would be depressing, but she went and thought it was good. Kym and her three "grandboys," as she calls her grandsons, went with her. "I wanted them to know what it's like. As veterans, both Jean and I are eligible for home-nursing care with the Veterans Administration."

Lita and Jean share their home with Jean's three dogs—a terrier mix, a mixed breed, and a bullmastiff. None of them are therapy dogs; they're emotional stability dogs. Jean takes medications regularly. Though not trained, the little terrier mix knows the time of day she's supposed to take her pills and goes to the dresser at pill time to remind her. He also sits outside the bathroom door and waits for Jean to come out. She has fallen a few times, and her dog always barks to alert Lita when there's a problem.

Kym moved to a house two miles away from Lita and Jean. "Kym and my three grandboys will be there for me," Lita said. Her oldest grandboy, Sean, likes working with computers; middle grandboy Devin is a trained scuba diver and wants to be a buddy diver for people with disabilities; and the youngest, Trevor, is a dog lover and a vital link to their dogs.

Lita and her family are close. They travel together, and she enjoyed taking Devin, her fishing buddy, to San Francisco. They saw the sights, went fishing, caught halibut and stripers, and enjoyed eating them fresh at a restaurant.

Jean is a bright woman who spends much of her time online researching information for her family. Though it takes a lot of energy, she gets out when possible. When she and Lita attended a dollhouse convention together, Jean watched her mom make a piece of dollhouse furniture in a class. Lita is tenacious and resolved: when Jean's pain has increased, requiring a specialist, Lita has called the clinic every day—sometimes three times a day. Her persistence has paid off in getting Jean in for earlier appointments.

Lita's family continues to help others. She recalls her mother talking about her grandfather's kindness. "He brought home a homeless person to enjoy Thanksgiving with us each year. He would find a street person and invite him to join our family for a meal." Hearing such stories contributed to Lita being more considerate of the less fortunate.

When Lita lived with her parents a short time after active army duty, she let a homeless woman with a cat sleep in her van because the woman couldn't take her cat into a shelter. During the day, the woman used the shower in their house and joined them for meals. At night she slept in the van. Six months passed, and she disappeared after meticulously cleaning Lita's van. She left a thank-you note. "One year later, I saw her working as a cashier at one of the big chain stores in the area," Lita said. "I was glad I could help with a little boost."

Lita has delivered meals to the elderly with Meals on Wheels, Kym installed plastic sheeting on poor people's housing for better insulation in the cold, and at Christmas, Lita and her grandboys have driven around giving away McDonald's gift books to people on the street. "I want these people to know this is how people treat one another," she said.

Lita admits to having been in a funk for a bit and not feeling worthwhile after getting her Alzheimer's diagnosis. She is taking the memory-aid prescription drug galantamine and has noticed her memory has improved. She doesn't feel as "fuzzy," and is sleeping better. The medicine has given her a reprieve, she believes.

"At one time, I could juggle many things and multitask. I can't anymore. Those days are over. I'm not complaining—I just do one thing at a time now. I don't want to screw things up by spreading my mind too thin. The Energizer rabbit was me with lots of energy. I run out of energy now and get distracted. I always figured I'd live to be 120. Now that I have this problem, I'm setting things up ahead of time. Whatever happens happens. We'll deal with it when it comes. I don't want my daughter to have to take care of me. I hope something develops as a cure to help me."

Wanting to help veterans, Lita formed the Veterans Appreciation Network and brought concerts to hospitals to entertain veterans during summers and holidays. She would like to do more to honor veterans and ensure they receive proper burials. A believer in the Reserve Officers' Training Corps (ROTC), the college-based program for training commissioned officers for the US Armed Forces teaching youth to honor and respect our country, she would like to involve ROTC members in having a presence at veterans' funerals.

Thoughts and Advice About Risk

Lita defines risk as "doing something with no control over the outcome. It may jeopardize your life." She doesn't see donating her kidney to a stranger as risky. "I was physically ready for it, so didn't see it as a risk. I went to a good hospital and had a good doctor. Maybe it would have been risky if the hospital I went to didn't have a good reputation." Lita appeared as a town hero in a local newspaper article about her kidney donation, but she maintains that Rod, her kidney recipient, a retired firefighter who saved lives, is the hero.

"I had warmth in my heart and soul knowing I was giving someone else more life." Lita hopes that by telling her story, others will donate their kidneys and save more lives.

She won't put herself in risky situations. She doesn't drive fast, and won't go on any amusement park rides. "I'm skeptical of all of them—maybe the merry-go-round is safe." She does not go parachuting. All these things she views as risky.

A spunky, determined woman, Lita said, "I'm not dead yet!" She's excited to do new things. She likes to stay busy and is passionate about launching a podcast with her daughter Jean, and others, featuring people with various health issues describing their experiences. Jean affectionately calls her mom a "spitfire," as in a "spirited young woman."

Lita's personal motto is LLL, which stands for Live, Love, Laugh! "Without positive energy, I wouldn't have made it this far in life—through the bumps in the road."

Lita sporting her living donor T-shirt

Photo by Diana Coleman

ROSEMARIE NERVELLE

Published Memoir About Her Repressed, Abusive Childhood at 81

BIRTH YEAR: 1933

Surviving a hellacious childhood and young adulthood in Nova Scotia, Rosemarie was the target of her mother's abuse. After escaping, she married, had two children, and then divorced. Determined to get an education and be successful, she earned a bachelor's degree at 51. She acquired a real estate license and became an entrepreneur in her 50s. At 67, she learned who her father was. A coincidental cemetery encounter revealed more surprises. At 74, her first book was published. After ten years of writing, she self-published her riveting memoir, *Swamp Robin*, at 81.

Earlier Years

Rosemarie's story details her childhood and teenage years in Canada, with a short stay in New York City's Spanish Harlem. Fearing her mother, who was physically and verbally abusive, Rosemarie was subjected to a life in abject poverty—and was forced to take care of her mother's several illegitimate children. She grew up the subject of rumors, a child whose birth certificate proclaimed "father unknown." Rosemarie learned who her father was later in life. Although her grandparents were kind, they could offer no real protection from her mother. Her biracial mother loathed Rosemarie, the oldest of eight children. "My mother was very beautiful—she had wavy black hair and gorgeous brown eyes. Her good looks probably contributed to her downfall."

In *Swamp Robin*, Rosemarie writes about saying goodbye to her mother when she left at 18:

> I put my arms around her shoulders. Her reaction was explosive. She recoiled as if from a rattlesnake, her eyes blazing with hate. "Don't you touch me! Get away from me! If you're going, go and good riddance. I never want to see your face again."

Resolving to break away and educate herself, Rosemarie moved to the United States and diligently worked to earn a living. She married and had a son and daughter. Given her upbringing, she vowed, "I will never treat my children like my mother treated me."

Rosemarie's husband was physically and verbally abusive, and since she was abominably treated by both her husband and mother, Rosemarie felt it was her fault—that she deserved the abuse. After fourteen years of marriage, she filed for divorce and got professional help.

Using their Nantucket, Massachusetts, home from her divorce settlement as collateral for a bank loan, she bought a four-gabled Sears and Roebuck "fixer-upper" house in Hadley, Massachusetts, transforming it into a charming home. This led to her future entrepreneurial venture. While working two jobs, she attended the University of Massachusetts, Amherst, where she met an information technology specialist who became her second husband. Rosemarie earned a bachelor of fine arts degree in architectural design. She also took a helpful class called Assertiveness Training for Women.

After moving to New Jersey with her husband, she launched Nervelle Associates, renovating and selling homes. "My assertiveness training stood me in good stead when I was in this business." Upon retiring, Rosemarie and her husband moved to midcoast Maine.

Writing and Publishing

Although Rosemarie's English teacher at Yarmouth Academy in Nova Scotia encouraged her writing talent, it wasn't until she was in her 50s that she seriously put pen to paper. Down East Books published her engaging young adult adventure story, *The Witch of Beaver Creek Mine*, when she was 74. Her engrossing short stories are included in annual anthologies published by Goose River Press in Waldoboro, Maine. She confesses to being absorbed with her fictional characters. "They become real to me—they have their own personalities and thoughts. I can even hear their voices. I miss them when I've finished their story."

Rosemarie sought professional help after divorcing her first husband, and her therapist advised her to write down her hurtful memories and burn them. Instead, she stuffed her notes in a drawer. Those snippets helped her recall her experiences when she started writing *Swamp Robin*. Old photographs also triggered vivid memories of traumatic incidents from her childhood.

"It's been cathartic," she said of the memoir writing. "It is not a happy book, but it's my life and it's true. I didn't want to gloss over anything. It's out of my system now. I can talk about it like it happened to someone else. The guilt and unhappiness are gone. I feel just fine about myself.

"I thought my children should know what happened to me. I was getting old and didn't know how long it would take for me to write this book. My son called me in tears after reading it and said, 'You never told me.' I explained I didn't want him to know about my young life until he was mature enough to handle it.

"I could never be horrible and mean like my mother. She could cut you down with her words alone. I could never have written my book while she was still alive. I was afraid of her until she died."

Rosemarie was encouraged when her editor said, "This has to be published." After discouraging feedback from publishers not interested in memoirs, she self-published her book *Swamp Robin*, which reads like a novel.

Living in midcoast Maine and staying active, Rosemarie swims regularly. Downhill skiing is out for her now. She's afraid of any physical risk that could incapacitate her and would require regaining her independence. Experiencing health problems in her 80s, such as arthritis, Rosemarie and her husband sold their large home. She found a lot in the area and designed a small, one-story house to enjoy. "It is contemporary—lighter and brighter than the two-story country-style home we have lived in. I wanted all the accoutrements and wanted it to show my personality." Her talent and enthusiasm for making homes cozy is possibly a reaction to, and compensation for, the horrible places she lived in as a girl.

While waiting for her house to be built, a routine mammogram led to further tests and an unexpected double mastectomy. True to her positive nature, Rosemarie said, "It happens. You need to grasp it and deal with it." Reflecting on her life and admitting she has done most of the things she has wanted to do, she added, "Nobody owes me more time. I would like three or four more good years and am good with that."

At the top of her travel list is Greece. Living a year in Europe also appeals to her—it would be either southern France or Florence, Italy.

Every summer she returns to Nova Scotia—to Yarmouth, a port town on the Bay of Fundy, and Weymouth, a rural village on the Sissiboo River—places from her childhood. Since her book was published, she has reconnected with even more family members and friends, including the woman who saved her life. When Rosemarie was left on a neighbor's doorstep when she was three or four days old, the woman took her in and cared for her until she was 3. Even though she had many children of her own—eventually fourteen in all—she referred to Rosemarie as another one of her children.

Writing is a huge passion. Rosemarie is working on a collection of short stories and possibly a prequel and sequel to *The Witch of Beaver Creek Mine*. She also thinks about writing a book about the houses she's lived in. Pleased she wrote about her life, she would like a publisher to pick up *Swamp Robin* and distribute it widely. Appearing at book readings and connecting with people who know her and about her has been emotional and heartwarming. "'You're so brave,' people tell me when they meet me after reading my memoir." She has been applauded for rising above atrocious circumstances. One of her goals for her memoir is to show that abuse has many forms: verbal, psychological, and physical. She hopes abused women will read *Swamp Robin* and find the strength to change their lives.

Thoughts and Advice About Risk

Rosemarie sees herself as a risk taker. "Once a risk taker, always a risk taker. Starting out on your own without help from anyone is the greatest risk." Divorcing her husband with no place to go, no job, and a 7-year-old daughter was risky. (Her son was in the service at the time.) Fearing her vindictive ex-husband, she had to leave the home she had designed on Nantucket Island. Fortunately, a kind friend and neighbor took them into her home in western Massachusetts.

"Writing my memoir was a big risk for me," Rosemarie said. "I was afraid that some of my extended family wouldn't understand and would be ashamed that I exposed myself so honestly. I was also afraid that others, knowing my background, wouldn't want to be my friends any longer. But I was wrong to think that. My friends have been wonderful and even shared some of their own experiences."

To women who want to take risks but are afraid to, Rosemarie says, "The risk you're taking is for yourself. It almost always benefits you, though it may be difficult and you may have misgivings. I always took risks and felt, 'The devil take the hindmost.'" She thinks that many women can do better on their own today because they're able to make their own decisions.

"I've always been a very positive person. When I was young, I had no one to rely on except my grandparents, who were positive. Although they were far from well off, they always shared what they had. My grandmother, who raised six children, told me, 'Never put yourself down. Don't make light of your successes. They're yours. No one did it for you.'"

Remarkably resilient, Rosemarie has thrived with an optimistic perseverance despite tremendous odds. She is good-natured, with a soft voice and youthful face. "There's no point in worrying about what might happen," she says. She enjoys her family, friends, and life in Maine. "People can't believe I came from such a background. I am very proud of how far I've come."

Rosemarie and her memoir

Photo by Diana Coleman

TERESA ANN McLAUGHLIN

Transitioned to a Woman at 53

BIRTH YEAR: 1957

Teresa, formerly known as Doug, grew up poor in Mississippi and endured an abusive father who despised his pretty little feminine boy. Doug never fit in and felt like he lived on a different planet. Escaping home after high school, he became a gifted classical musician, pioneer gay country-and-western singer, skilled mathematician, and computer programmer. He found his way through Alabama, Missouri, New York City, and Europe. In San Francisco, he faced his long-term desire of wanting to become a woman.

Earlier Years

Living in the country near Tupelo, Mississippi, Teresa, then Doug, had parents with limited educations—his mother went to school through sixth grade, his dad through third grade. Doug's father was raised in a Pentecostal household. He flew into violent rages and physically abused his son and wife.

Doug and his younger sister were bosom buddies growing up. She was the tomboy; he was the girlie boy. His mother sewed at a garment factory, and his dad did masonry work. The family had very little. His mother once said they only had one potato to share. His dad often shot quail and squirrel for eating. Doug got squeamish watching his father and grandfather skin a squirrel for dinner one night. Sometimes there were raccoons and possums. Birds were his mother's favorite meat to roast or fry and serve at meals.

From an early age, Doug was an effeminate boy who wanted to try on his sister's and mother's clothes. He begged his parents to let him, and one day they relented. He happily twirled around in his sister's skirt until his father yelled, "That's enough! Take it off!" Doug said he understood that it was forbidden but didn't know why.

When his parents weren't around, he pranced about, wrapped in sheets like a gown, with a towel around his head and wearing his mother's jewelry. He played with his sister's dolls and put his "boy toys," such as small trucks, behind the tires of the family car so they would be destroyed.

Doug was surrounded by music during his childhood; his parents strummed guitars after supper, and friends and relatives joined in with out-of-tune pianos. They played hillbilly songs and white gospel—their music influenced Doug's future career.

White racist folks made Doug uncomfortable. "I hated the language my family and others used in the Deep South where I grew up. The adults talked badly about black people." Not understanding racism, Doug identified with black people because he too felt misunderstood for being different.

When Doug was young, his bricklayer father had him carry heavy bricks at his job sites to "make him a man." His dad also bought him a motorcycle and insisted he use it. While Doug was on his way to his dad's worksite on his motorcycle at 14, a car rammed into him, and his head crashed through the car's windshield. He wasn't wearing a helmet; they weren't mandatory then. The glass cut into his jugular vein, and he lost a lot of blood. A doctor at a nearby store rushed to his aid and helped stop the bleeding. Given a 50-50 chance of surviving at the time, he now wears a scar as a memory. After the accident, his father bought him a larger motorcycle and forced him to ride it. Doug wanted nothing to do with motorcycles. Carrying heavy mortar and bricks and riding motorcycles did not make Doug masculine.

His father's work led to building homes, and the family became better off. Doug thought his father sometimes felt guilty for beating him badly, and to try to make up for his abuse, occasionally gave him money. When Doug was in high school listening to a show about human rights on his car radio, he heard people say it was hilarious that gay people wanted rights. Someone else said, "If everyone came out of the closet, there would be no discrimination." Prompted by this at age 15, Doug told his friends he was gay. Formerly well liked, he was no longer popular or invited to the movies or to people's houses. "I was never called bad names, however."

Miserable, Doug wanted to leave home, but he thought he should graduate from high school. Doug did poorly in school and thought his father was right to call him "stupid." After graduating, he spent some time in Alabama and then went to St. Louis with a young woman friend.

Believing he was female, Doug contemplated gender transition, but realized that if he revealed his sexual identity, he wouldn't get a job or into college, so he didn't pursue it. He did well in a junior college, and entered Fontbonne University as one of a few male students in the formerly all-women's Catholic school. "Living in a female environment and put in the chorus alto section made it easier," he said. He excelled in mathematics and graduated with a math and computer science degree.

Always a singer, Doug joined a chorus and met Christopher Hogwood, a famous baroque music conductor from England. They performed Handel's *Messiah* in St. Louis.

Desperate to escape poverty and his conservative background, Doug got into therapy, moved to New York City, and became boyfriends with a dancer. He performed with the New York Ensemble for Early Music for many years, sometimes singing parts traditionally sung by women. He toured Europe, moved to Amsterdam, studied classical baroque music at the Royal Conservatory at The Hague, and sang medieval music. Returning to New York, Doug sang the role of Endymion in Cavalli's opera *Calisto* with the Bel Canto Opera, and received an outstanding review in the *New York Times.*

In a used-clothing store, Doug heard country singer Randy Travis over the sound system. "His voice was powerful and effective, and I began to cry right there in the shop. My partner told me that I really knew this style of singing and needed to sing it."

At 33, Doug tested HIV positive. His partner tested negative, and dropped him. He felt lonely and depressed. Writing country-style songs about innocent romantic love and the heartache of being gay helped him get out of his funk.

Two years later, he formed the Outband, a premier gay country-and-western band that produced three albums. They performed for primarily gay audiences all over the country, northern Europe, and Mexico. They also played at Gracie Mansion, Town Hall in New York City with Joan Rivers, and the Rainbow Room at Rockefeller Center. Doug got a positive mention in *The New Yorker*'s Talk of the Town column.

Wanting a more active gay country-dance scene, Doug moved to San Francisco and formed the Lesbian and Gay Country Music Association. The Outband changed its name to Pearl River to attract broader audiences.

Doug was a Web developer, got involved with a man who became his partner, and obtained a master's degree in information assurance. He and his partner bought a huge home near Tracy, California. When his partner's parents retired, they moved in with them. After several years, his in-laws grew critical of Doug's feminine style, as did his partner, which became evident when his partner called attention to it.

"I was peeing while sitting on the toilet seat, which I always did—I never felt comfortable peeing standing up—and my partner was in the bathroom too. He told me, 'You need to see a gender specialist. If you're diagnosed as transgender, you'll have to move out.' He thought I'd be cured with testosterone treatments and everything would be all right. I left and moved in with my former boyfriend from New York, who tried to help me look like a woman. But instead, he made me look like a drag queen, which wasn't what I wanted."

Transitioning to Female

At 51, Doug had his first gender therapist appointment in San Francisco. The woman specialist said, "If I didn't have to wait six months to confirm your transsexual diagnosis, I wouldn't. You need to dress like a woman in public and see what it's like living as a woman." Given a diagnosis as a transwoman six months later, Doug started taking estrogen. Because physicians and therapists are required to follow strict standards of care, he needed to wait two years for surgery and see two therapists for two years before receiving a letter authorizing "transsexual reassignment surgery."

At 53, Doug underwent sex reassignment surgery by the renowned Dr. Marci Bowers, the first transwoman to perform sex reassignment surgery and an expert in neovaginoplasty (vagina construction). A compassionate and skilled surgeon, Dr. Bowers has also performed clitoroplasty, or clitoral reconstruction surgery, to restore the clitoris damaged or removed by female genital cutting, and does not charge for these surgeries. She has appeared on an episode of *CSI: Crime Scene Investigation* and on the *Oprah Winfrey Show*.

Doug was not nervous about having the surgery. He felt he was doing what was meant to be. "When I had sex with men, I wouldn't allow men to touch my genitals. It never felt right, and I thought, on me, they were awful and ugly." Much of his male genitalia were reconfigured into female genitalia—the labia tissue was fashioned from his scrotum; the clitoris was formed from the glans, or penis head, with its nerve endings; and the vaginal lining was made from the penis shaft. Teresa experienced orgasms shortly after surgery. Though her new genitalia functioned well, two years later, she had revision surgery by another surgeon to enhance their aesthetics.

Teresa didn't need breast enhancement surgery. She began taking estrogen two years before surgery and continues to take it. "Having testosterone replaced with estrogen has been a big change," she said. "Testosterone makes you interested in a particular kind of sex—more wham, bam. I love orgasms, and estrogen changes everything. If a man came on strongly with his testosterone, I liked it. Not now, however. I like subdued flirtations—such as communicating with the eyes. On estrogen, I cry easily. It's cathartic, and I'm more sensitive."

When Teresa's mom was pregnant and thought she was going to have a girl, she wanted to name her Teresa. Then she had a son. After transitioning to a woman, Doug took the name Teresa. Her mother told her later that she had always thought of Doug as her daughter—she had even given him a makeup kit as a gift when he was 12. Teresa's father died one year before she began transitioning, shooting himself in the head after being in pain from skin cancer.

Teresa met a straight man on the Second Life website. At 58, she married him and they live near Portland, Oregon. "My husband and his family have embraced me." Her husband's family, Teresa's mother, and friends attended the wedding in their large home.

As a woman, Teresa stands five feet, seven inches, and has long, blondish-gray hair and blue eyes. She likes dresses, especially styles from the 1950s and '60s, and wears them almost all the time, with jewelry replicating ancient Greek, Roman, and Egyptian designs.

"Becoming friends with straight women and lesbians makes me really happy," she said. "I always thought that women were two-dimensional; men were multidimensional and more powerful. Now I notice that women are more interesting and fully dimensional."

An optimist who enjoys people, Teresa loves discovering new things and environments. "When I like something, I become passionate about it." She admits to getting depressed sometimes, and believes it stems from having been an abused child and dealing with rejection as a gay man. "It's been a challenge to deal with depression, but I spring back.

"I used to work out in a gym by pumping iron. But now, I am more into being fit overall and doing yoga." Her husband formerly hiked and camped, and they have talked about exploring the great outdoors together. Teresa may take up jogging again.

Teresa no longer cares for most country music. In the past, she used it for political reasons—to educate people about being gay. She enjoys medieval chants, has the same range as Ella Fitzgerald, and would like to perform again in the future, though not country music.

A *Star Trek* fan growing up, Teresa still likes science fiction. She loves to write and is working on publishing a sci-fi/fantasy book series. *The Love of the Tayamni* takes place in Sekhem 3800 BCE and at various times and places where she has lived in reality. Her primary characters are beings of energy who take on humanlike qualities. Working on it with her husband and their dear friend and housemate, the goal is to illuminate, honor, and promote the force of love.

Excited about these books and developing imaginative virtual-reality simulations, Teresa writes when she's not working as a cybersecurity specialist.

Thoughts and Advice About Risk

Familiar with risk, Teresa sees herself as a risk taker. "In the field of information security, we look at risk by (1) scanning the environment, (2) finding vulnerabilities and rating them, and (3) mitigating the vulnerabilities according to risk," she said.

"In my life, risk is when you have an established pattern that to the world might seem to be going swimmingly. Then you decide to try something else, throw it all away, and go on to another project. I left Tupelo and didn't know how to survive or what I was getting into. I think you need a degree of confidence. I look forward to discovering something new, and that gives me self-confidence.

"Every risk I've taken—going to St. Louis, New York, Holland, San Francisco, and Washington—has been wonderful.

"There are some risks I would have taken when I was younger. I always wanted to be an astronaut, where you risk the possibility of not returning to Earth. I thought it would be exciting to live on another planet. There are companies advertising to take people to outer space, and you may not come back. I would no longer consider doing this at my age. Going into another technical field no longer interests me.

"For anyone considering transitioning to female at age 50 or older, I recommend going to an online 3-D virtual-world simulation website like Second Life, and creating a female avatar. I tried this—you can create a female avatar with your appearance using no voice, to see what it feels like to be a woman. You can meet people on this site as well, and experience how the world interacts with you as a woman.

"I had lived life as a gay man so was already outside the norm. I had no wife or children. I had no one in my life who would be affected by my transitioning. Many do. I have friends who would be lost if they transitioned, and have known other men who transitioned and lost their families and friends. It's devastating. It's important to consider losing people in your life if you transition.

"Initially, I tried to be manly and felt like I was giving away my soul. Since becoming and living as a female, my identity didn't really change, nor has the way I see myself. What changed is having people accept me. People have a hard time with feminine men. I'm no longer dealing with being a gay man outside the norm, which has made things easier for me."

Fascinated by gods, goddesses, and spirituality, Teresa explores ancient human symbols to understand our place in humanity. "I would love to be able to help humanity and start a movement," she said. "I appreciate the value of love and the force of love, how essential love is to humanity's survival and evolution. The importance of love is minimized, misinterpreted, and not applied to all of humanity. I would like to do something to help love become more valued in our culture. I am not a Christian, but I try to live my life by Jesus' teachings. When I was struggling, a Jesuit priest friend gave me a rosary and advised going to a park or beautiful place, walk around in a circle saying 'Hail Mary' for each bead, and think of Mary as a feminine goddess. Though there was no specific intention, this helped me.

"Thinking about the feminine divine has made me most hopeful in my journey. I have a rich life now, and more to contribute."

Teresa

Photo by Teresa Ann McLaughlin

Part 2

GOING FOR IT!

10 KEYS TO TAKING FULFILLING RISKS

1. Decide what matters to you and be honest with yourself.
2. Commit to one risk at a time.
3. Avoid negative people.
4. Ask people you admire for advice. Learn about their backgrounds and successes.
5. Surround yourself with supportive reinforcements.
6. Find environments that provide time for you to think about *you*.
7. Listen to music you like and let your mind relax.
8. Indulge in activities you find fulfilling to enable your mind to wander and provide stimulating ideas.
9. Hire a coach or find a mentor to guide and support you.
10. Celebrate your achievements!

There are numerous resources—people, books, online sites, and more—for advice and help with your quest to pursue what matters to you. You may already know what you want and be able to achieve it on your own.

Have fun! You *can* do it!

GO FOR IT!

ACTION EXERCISE #1
GETTING STARTED

1. What risks did you take in your life before age 50 that were fulfilling?

2. What risks have you taken since turning 50 that you are proud of?

3. Determine what risks you want to take now. What matters to you now? What do you still want to do? List whatever comes to mind in any order.

4. Assign priorities to your risks. Review your risks list. If you have more than one item on your list, number them in priority order.

5. Code your risks. Next to your risks, write the letter R or O to describe each one:

   R=Ready

   Yes! I want to take this risk and am ready to make it happen.

   O=Obstacles

   There are obstacles with this risk—for example, lack of training or resources.

6. Review your #1 priority. If you coded it R, you're ready to start! If you coded it O, list your perceived obstacles. Review and analyze each one. Are your reasons valid? Your goal is to overcome your *perceived* obstacles. Keep this list to share with your support partner (see #7).

List the steps needed to make your #1 risk happen (whether coded with an R or an O). It may take a few steps or many steps to achieve. Put a date you are committed to by each step. Here's an example:

#1 Priority: Take a Trip by Myself

O = Obstacle

Would like to go now but lack the funds. Reduce expenses and save money over the next eight months to take the trip.

1. Research places (by January 1)
2. Decide where to go (by February 15)
3. Save funds to cover expenses (January 1–August 31)
4. Make reservations and plans (by March 1)
5. Take care of logistics and pack (September 1–14)
6. Go! (September 15)

7. Enlist a key supporter. Who do you know and trust to share your list with *and* who will hold you accountable for taking your risk? It is important to have someone to support you through the process, cheer you on, and celebrate your achievement with you.

8. Commit to your #1 priority risk.
    - Write what your risk is and post it in a visible place to look at every day.
    - Check in every week with your support person to see how you're doing. Your support person should check in with you if you don't.
    - If you coded your priority risk with an O, work through each obstacle and figure out with your support cheerleader how you'll overcome each one. Enlist other supporters as needed.
    - Input your dates on your calendars. Set reminders on your devices.
    - Look at your progress along the way.

9. Achieve your risk and celebrate!

10. Pursue another risk important to you.

ACTION EXERCISE #2
GETTING UNSTUCK

Are you stuck thinking about what risk you would like to take?

Perhaps you would like to take a risk or two—to do something that matters to you, but you can't think what.

Find a comfortable place where you can relax and be uninterrupted. Review and answer the following questions. Enlist a positive, supportive person who knows you to help you answer these questions if you get stuck.

1. Think back to a time in your life when you did fun things for *you*. What were they? Why were they fulfilling?

2. What have you become envious of, or excited about, that others are doing? When have you found yourself saying, "I wish I could do that"?

3. What subjects do you enjoy—from school or elsewhere?

4. What issues concern you?

5. What have others said you're good at?

6. When you were a child, how did you spend your spare time (assuming you had some)? Are any of those activities or related activities things you enjoy now? Wish to pursue?

7. What matters to you at this point in your life?

8. Is there anything you would like to change about yourself?

ACTION EXERCISE #3
"THIS I BELIEVE" VALUES

When you think about your life, what you enjoy, and what you would like to do, you may find it helpful to articulate your values and see how your values influence and affect what you do.

What are your values, or core beliefs? These can be expressed in terms of "I believe ..." statements.

Here are a couple of examples:

I believe in the gift of wisdom with age.

I believe in the joy of learning new things.

Write your "I believe ..." statements and review them. As you pursue risks and new experiences, see if your "beliefs" align with your goals.

My "This I Believe" Statements

ACTION EXERCISE #4
MILESTONES BY AGE

Think about your life and list your significant milestones by age category. They could be achievements, special events, pleasant experiences, or anything else that was important. Review your list. Do any of them prompt you to think about what matters to you in your future and what you want to do?

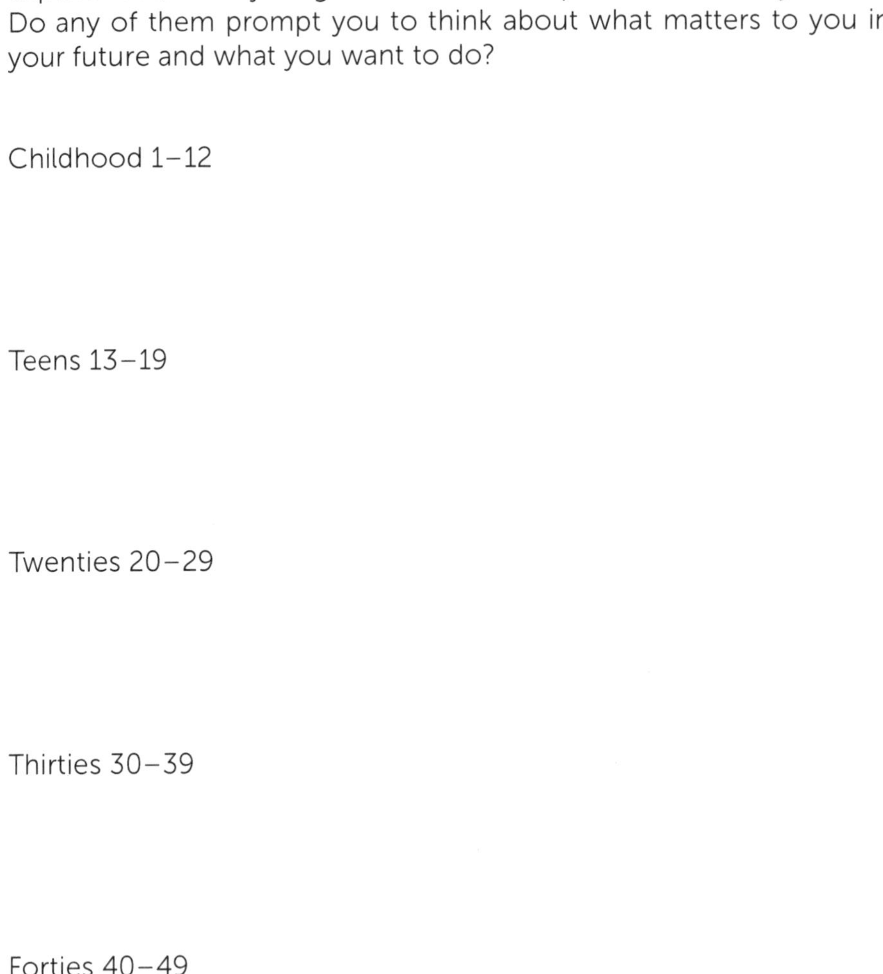

Childhood 1–12

Teens 13–19

Twenties 20–29

Thirties 30–39

Forties 40–49

Fifties 50–59

Sixties 60–69

Seventies 70–79

Eighties 80–89

Nineties 90–99

Hundreds 100+

ACTION EXERCISE #5
DINNER PARTY

To engage in a stimulating, risk-taking discussion, organize a lunch or dinner (or another type of gathering) for a group of women over age 50. Have the event in a setting where you can talk easily among yourselves.

Ideally, select a diverse group of women whom you admire and find intriguing but who don't all know each other. When seated, have each woman (including yourself) introduce herself and tell the group the most important risk she's ever taken and a risk she would like to take. You may wish to prepare other questions to ask the group about risk-taking. Why did they take a particular risk? How did they overcome their fear or any other obstacles to take their risk? How do other women feel about the risks shared? The conversation is apt to inspire and motivate you and others, and you'll get to learn about ways to overcome obstacles to particular types of risk-taking.

For comparison, you may wish to organize a group of females of different ages—younger and older—to see how risk-taking is similar or different. Add men and boys to a group and ask the same risk-taking questions. Do the risks people have taken, and those they are interested in taking, differ between the women's and men's groups? How? How do perceived obstacles compare?

My Dinner Party

1. Me
2. ______________________________
3. ______________________________
4. ______________________________
5. ______________________________
6. ______________________________

7. ______________________________

8. ______________________________

9. ______________________________

10. ______________________________

11. ______________________________

12. ______________________________

After your gathering(s), record your answers to these questions:

What do you admire about the participants?

What risks taken stand out for you and why?

Are there any new risks you wish to take after hearing about others' risks? If so, what are they?

ACTION EXERCISE #6
MEMORABLE PHOTOS

1. Look at photos of yourself at any age that bring you joy. How old were you? What were you doing? How did you feel then?

   Do you have any joyful photos of yourself that were taken within the past five years? What were you doing? Are you still doing it? How did you feel when these photos were taken?

2. Imagine a photo of yourself in the near future that you think would bring you pleasure. What are you doing? Where are you? Are you having fun? Are you excited? Finding fulfillment? Describe how you think you would feel and why.

3. How can you make this moment or experience happen?

4. Take a risk that interests you.

5. Get a photo of yourself while taking your new risk, or after you have taken your risk, and savor it. Let the photo be a reminder that you did it!

DISCUSSION QUESTIONS FOR GROUPS

1. Whose story or stories inspired you and why?

2. What are the fears and challenges women had to overcome to take the risks they did?

3. What helped these women be successful at risk-taking?

4. Each woman offers risk-taking advice. What advice did you find helpful?

5. What is a risk for you?

6. Has this book inspired you to take a new risk? If so, what risk do you want to take at this stage of your life?

7. What risks are you glad you took after 50? Why? How did each one benefit you? What challenges did you have to overcome?

8. Guidelines and exercises for taking fulfilling risks are provided in Part 2. Which did you find helpful and why?

AFTERWORD

I hope you have been inspired by these women's stories and want to share your own risk-taking stories. Everyone has stories. This book represents a small sampling of women over 50 who have taken diverse risks that were important to them.

Sometimes we have the chance to take serendipitous risks. We may be challenged by someone to take a risk, which is what happened to me when I was in Costa Rica. Each of us defines risks differently. This was one of my risks, which I happily share with you.

A Personal Risk at 64

While I was studying Spanish at Maximo Nivel language school in the beautiful, seaside resort of Manuel Antonio, Costa Rica, Karen, one of the school's staff members, recommended zip lining. "No, that's not for me," I told her. "I'll sign up for the sailing and national park walking tours." Zip lining sounded scary. The idea of hanging on to a rope high up and flying fast through the air frightened me.

"It's not a big deal," Karen said. "You can do it. My 5-year-old daughter, Kayla, goes zip lining with me and loves it! We'll go with you!" Before I could respond, Karen picked up the phone and booked our trip.

Riding in the tour van to the site, my stomach churned as I talked with friendly little Kayla and tried to snuff out my fear. We arrived at Titi Canopy Tours. Greeted by muscular male Costa Rican guides Caterpillar and Dragonfly, I told them I was nervous. "You'll be fine. We take safety seriously, and you won't get hurt," Dragonfly said in excellent English. Good thing, because I had had only six days of Spanish lessons by then.

We walked down a path into the rain forest, over a suspension bridge, and up a hill. There in a clearing I was outfitted with a large, padded helmet, a belt with heavy clamps, thick gloves, and a harness that fit under my crotch. We were told there were eleven separate steel cables with walks between each one and stairs leading to platforms. My stomach lurched. It was 98 degrees Fahrenheit midday. The sun was blinding. I wore a T-shirt, long pants, and running shoes. Sweat dripped off my face. Perspiration soaked my shirt. I felt panicky. "Karen, why don't you and Kayla go ahead and I'll watch. It's okay. I don't need to do this," I said.

Caterpillar turned to me. "No worries! We need to get going!"

My heart beat fast. I wiped my face with my rough, enormous suede gloves as we walked farther into the woods. Caterpillar led the way; Dragonfly brought up the rear. Stopping, I looked up and saw green metal stairs to the sky alongside a humongously tall tree. We climbed up the steep staircase to the platform. My breathing was labored. Caterpillar harnessed up, put Kayla in his lap, and secured her tightly. Off they flew, her joyful screams piercing the quiet. Karen jumped up and got clamped on to the cable. Last-minute commands were given, and she soared down the cable and disappeared into the trees.

"Your turn. Jump up so I can clamp you to the cable," said Dragonfly. Up I jumped. "Higher," he said.

I jumped as high as I could. "OUCH!" I said. The strap around my crotch rubbed tightly across my upper thighs.

"Put your legs straight out in front of you and cross your ankles. Remember—don't grab the cable! Keep your arm away from the wheel or you will have a BIG OUCH!" I stepped off the platform and away I flew. My body swiveled sideways. "Keep your body straight ahead!" he yelled. I tried. I kept turning to the right. I jerked my body to the left and hit the platform below, feet-first, within seconds. Caterpillar grabbed the cable and harness and unhooked me. "You did great!" he said.

My first flight was over in a flash. Kayla shouted, "More! Let's go!" Off we walked. We climbed stairs to the next platforms and zoomed down four more separate cables. The sixth cable was longer. I started to relax as I stepped off the platform. I looked for monkeys and sloths.

It was impossible to see anything. The dense trees flew past in a blur. Midway, high up, I jerked to a stop. I leaned forward. I couldn't move. Ahead, far down below, stood Caterpillar on the platform. "I'm stuck! I can't move!" I yelled.

"It's okay. I'll come get you. Hang on!" he shouted back. I talked to myself. *It will be fine. You're clamped on to the cable. They're strong. Enjoy the tops of the trees. How many times do you get to see trees from this vantage point? Pretend you're a monkey.* Caterpillar turned upside down and pulled himself along the rope with his arms and legs. When he reached me, he attached his clamp to my rope and pulled me to the next platform.

"What happened?" I asked. "I didn't touch the cable, so I didn't brake."

"If you don't weigh enough ... and with this heat, the cables are slower," he replied. I'm sure he added the weight comment to flatter me. Hot and sweaty, my arms and legs shook and my upper thighs were sore from jumping up to get hooked on to the cable on each platform. The next long ride, it happened again—I got stuck midway. Repeat save. And then again I was stuck. I spent the second and third times stopped midway, dangling. I began enjoying the view high up over the thick green forest though my stomach still fluttered. After three stops and rescues, we rested on the ground and drank refreshing ice-cold water conveniently stashed in a cooler by a tree.

The last cable rides were shorter. I didn't get stuck anymore. Two hours later, standing on a platform high up by a tree for the last ride, my arms ached. Dragonfly said, "You have a choice. You can grab the rope that goes straight down and jump to the ground, or you can take one last cable ride." I surprised myself and said, "I'll hang on to the rope and go down"—the scarier option for me. I didn't dare look down. He pulled the long rope toward the platform, I grabbed it with both hands, and whoooooooooooosh! I plummeted, let go, and dropped to the ground.

I was thrilled and happy that I had done it! Ravenous, I eyed the *casado*—a typical combo lunch platter—served afterward. I devoured the rice, black beans, fried plantains, chicken, and salad on my plate and gulped down a cherry drink.

"I told you you could do it," Karen said, smiling.

Kayla said to me, "Wasn't it cool?"

"Yes, very," I agreed.

I'm glad Karen talked me into zip lining. Watching her brave, laughing daughter convinced me I had to do it. Granted, Kayla sat on the guide's lap, but she loved the thrill of speeding over treetops. I can still hear her happy screams. The memory of hanging from the cable mid-ride still makes me laugh.

Thank you for reading my book. May you find the courage to take risks that are important to you, enjoy the experience, and support others in their quest to take fulfilling risks.

All the best to you,
Diana Coleman
WomenGoingForIt.com

ACKNOWLEDGMENTS

My sincere thanks and enormous gratitude to the many women over age 50 whom I interviewed about their risk-taking experiences, and especially, to the twenty-six admirable women in this book—for your time in telling, and help in editing, your stories, and granting permission to share them. Thank you for your courage, candor, humor, perseverance, and optimism. You are impressive, inspirational role models.

Special thanks for your enduring encouragement and guidance: Carole Mazzarino, my smart, creative sister, who patiently listened and graciously offered advice; Dr. Vickie Driver, "bestest" friend, extraordinary physician and medical leader, and talented Michael Ann French, for their unwavering support, wisdom, and generous hospitality; Gin Mackey, successful author and loyal writing partner, for keeping me on track with superb mentoring; Fran Hodgkins, award-winning author and writers group facilitator, Rockport Library in Maine, who said, "You must publish this book!" (and members Ros, Jon, and Kate); Eileen Wilkinson, for editing and writing savvy; and Jackie Ogega, eloquent women's rights leader, for support, and for introducing me to your mother, Marcella, and the Mpanzi women and children in Kenya.

Loving appreciation to other family members who fortified me with advice, delicious homemade wine and meals, and rejuvenating visits: Gary Mazzarino, Linda Storm and John Mazzarino, Pam Storm, Seana and Mike Oskandy, Maria Mazzarino and John Carrick, and Olga and Tony Mazzarino.

Thank you for your inspiration, referrals, and support during my book writing and publishing journey: Lee Sevey and Tim Hatfield; Susan Taylor; Ann Jennings; Annie Mahoney; Sherry Gagne; Joann Hooper; Vicki Harner; Karen Meunier; Jennie Watson; Carol Prince; Tom Nolan and Larry Friesen; Dave Landis and Sean Dowdall; Bob Brenneman; Deborah and Phil McKean; Monique and Bob Downey;

Mary Lou Carolan; Rosemarie Hyatt; Beverly Stone; Monzi Figueres; John Kazzi; Sarah Cummings; Tim Rogers; Paola Gianturco; Ida Boatright; Dr. Julie A. Nelson; Jodi Paloni; Pam Maus; Monica Chau; Jill Lang; Mike Pierce; Sarah Ruef-Lindquist; Maura Melley; Dorothy Havey; Courtney Sylvester; Chelsea Maude Avirett; Bobby Schneider; Cindy Eastman; Colleen Haggerty; Kay Rock; Janann Sherman; Sarah Kate Ellis; Carole Fleming's daughter, Sue, and Carole's widower, Myles; Mimi O'Hagan's nephew, J. Byrne Murphy; Karen Campos Mora and her daughter, Kayla; the Roller Derby Over 50 group; Harvey Mysel of the Living Kidney Donors Network; and the Maine Women's Network members. Thank you to everyone who approved the use of their photos.

For your appreciated professional expertise: Laurel Robinson, copy editor; Cindy Huggins, developmental editor; Jeannine Owens, creative designer; and Nina Pierce, formatter and adviser; my sincere thanks.

My heartfelt gratitude to Sara Montgomery, my much loved, short-lived, courageous partner, who enthusiastically endorsed this book when it was in its conceptual stage and humbly asked to be remembered in it. You are greatly missed, and your optimistic spirit lives on.

To my mom, Ruth Coleman, a good-natured and artistic woman, and my dad, James A. Coleman, science professor, community leader, and author of five books—I miss you both and am sorry you are no longer around to read this book. Thank you for your belief in me.

As a work in progress for five years, this book has been supported by many other people too numerous to recognize individually—thanks to each of you beyond those named here.

ABOUT THE AUTHOR

Risk taker and women's advocate Diana Coleman conducts engaging presentations and shares inspirational stories to motivate women over 50 to take life-changing risks. She has lectured about women and girls overcoming daunting challenges for the Camden Conference's Community Lectures, Rotary Clubs, universities, and women's groups. A former administrator and fundraiser, she led teams in raising more than $200 million for education, health, the environment, and women's economic empowerment, for organizations including Save the Children; the University of California, Berkeley; Project Open Hand; the California Academy of Sciences; the International Museum of Women; and the Pen Bay Healthcare Foundation. She serves on the board of Mpanzi, supporting women and girls in Kenya. Diana's work and studies have taken her to Costa Rica, England, Egypt, Ethiopia, Jordan, Kenya, the Philippines, Indonesia, and Guatemala. Her essays about Kenya and a cross-country road trip are published in the *Goose River Anthology*.

Diana has received multiple awards, including a Women of Influence award for Russell Sage College's 2017 Centennial, an Outstanding Service award from the San Francisco Commission on the Status of Women, and a service award from the University of California, Berkeley. She earned a bachelor of arts degree from Russell Sage College, Troy, New York, and a master's degree from American University, Washington, DC. Originally from Massachusetts, Diana lived thirty years in San Francisco and, when not traveling, resides in Maine. She has fun taking simple photos of people, shapes, and shadows wherever she goes. Her website is WomenGoingForIt.com.

Made in the USA
Columbia, SC
26 August 2018